The Glory Days

The Glory Days

Michael Twist

Farming
BOOKS AND VIDEOS

First published 2001
Farming Press

Reprinted 2004
Farming Books and Videos Ltd.

Copyright © Michael Twist

ISBN 1-904871-01-1

A catalogue record for this book
is available from the British Library.

Published by Farming Books and Videos Ltd.
PO Box 536, Preston, Lancs PR2 9ZY

www.farmingbooksandvideos.com

We would like to thank the Rural History Centre, University Reading
for the use of their photographs.

Cover design by Pigsty Studio

Printed and bound in UK by
The Lavenham Press, Lavenham, Suffolk

Contents

To Marguerite and Ann

1. Rejected and Dejected

'Whatever are you doing down there?'

I opened my eyes and, momentarily, couldn't think where I was. Then I realised I was home, stretched out on my bedroom floor, snuggled under an eiderdown, with a pillow under my head. I smiled up at mother, 'Sorry, the bed was too soft. I couldn't sleep.'

My dear mother gave an almost imperceptible snort as she put a cup of tea on the bedside table. As she did so she said, 'Breakfast time hasn't changed whilst you've been away. Don't be late, or your breakfast will spoil.' With that she left the room.

I had been in the army. At the time of the Munich crisis in 1938, several friends and I had joined the Territorial Army – the Royal Artillery. It had been one of those spur-of-the-moment things. It hadn't seriously crossed our minds that we might ever be called upon to fulfil our role as soldiers; we thought that Hitler would never be so stupid as to take on the might of Great Britain, the Empire and France. In any case, hadn't Neville Chamberlain returned from his meeting with Hitler and, waving a piece of paper, declaimed, 'I believe it is peace in our time.' How wrong can one person be?

To join the Territorials one had a most cursory medical examination. Further, the doctor, who was not necessarily one's own GP, received seven shillings and sixpence ($37^1/_2$p) if he passed a volunteer A1, but only five shillings if he failed a potential recruit.

When war was declared on 3 September 1939, we were already mobilised, having been called up two days earlier. The amusing frolic was over, now soldiering was suddenly serious business. One or two of the more sensational daily papers assured readers that most of the German tanks were only cars, camouflaged with a plywood superstructure to give the impression that the vast and much vaunted Panzer divisions really did exist. Further, they assured readers that our brave boys would easily have the job done by Christmas.

Along with several others in our battery, I applied to go on an Officers' Training Course, which the CO unhesitatingly supported, but in the meantime we knuckled down to the job in hand. When called up we were temporarily stationed at Taplow Grammar School, only a mile or so from Cliveden, the stately home of the Astors, which overlooked a beautiful and then unspoilt reach of the Thames. Following church parade on 3 September, Lady Astor appeared to review the troops and give us a little pep talk. She ended by saying, 'Many of you will know that we opened Cliveden as a military hospital for the wounded during the last war. We intend to do so again. So I shall look forward to seeing some of you in the near future.' From somewhere in the rank behind me a voice called out, 'Not if I can bloody well help it!' This led to a roar from the RSM, a somewhat hasty retreat by her ladyship, accompanied by an apologetic CO and a confused subaltern giving the order 'left turn, quick march' to the troop under his command instead of 'right turn'. It did, however, help ease the tension which had been apparent just before Lady Astor's address, after the CO had announced that as from 11.00am that Sunday morning we were at war with Germany. A few days later, in the middle of the night, we moved to a farm just outside Newbury. Our sleeping quarters were lofts over open-fronted cart and machinery sheds. When windy, the draught whistled up through the cracks between the floorboards. We had neither mattresses nor palliasses. The latter we could have stuffed with straw but one quickly becomes used to hard boards – the reason I now found my bed too soft.

The morning before mother found me happily asleep on the floor, several of my chums and I had been summoned to the battery office. The Adjutant had informed us that we were to proceed immediately to Catterick to be enrolled on an Officers' Training Course – that was, as soon as we had been before the Army Medical Board. The Army Medical Board consisted of a major and three other commissioned doctors. When my turn came, I was called before a lieutenant. The examination could well be described as efficient, but lacking sensitivity. When the doctor got around to listening to my heart, he looked up sharply and asked, 'Have you ever had rheumatic fever?'

'Yes sir, when I was fourteen.'

'Stay here, I'll get the chief medical officer to take a look at you.' Some ten minutes later, by which time I was nearly blue with cold, for it was late October and there had been a sharp frost the night before, the chief medical officer, a major, appeared. He was short to medium in height, had a pursed up little mouth, a mean expression and he was a bustler – all quick and exaggerated movements. He snapped at me, 'What the hell are you doing?'

'Nothing.'

'Nothing? Nothing, SIR, you moron. Straighten up there and come to attention when I'm talking to you.'

Stripped to the buff and standing on the wet concrete floor of a cowshed, it seemed a bit idiotic standing to attention, yet alone straightening up. He listened to my heart, made me step up and down on to a chair about fifty times and listened again. He then proceeded to give me a right bollocking for being so stupid as to volunteer with my past medical history. I had the temerity to interrupt him, whilst in full flow, to point out that I had been passed A1 by a doctor. However, this only led to a tirade on the subject of civilian doctors. Finally he stopped and, smirking, told me I was not wanted in the army and, in his opinion, my future was limited. Two hours later I and three other gunners, who, like me, had volunteered to do their bit for King and Country, were on our way back to Civvy Street. On one thing we were in complete unanimity, we all thought the major was a really nasty little man, but I must admit we didn't put it quite as delicately as that.

I got to my feet and, as I drank my tea, crossed to the window and looked down across the garden to the spinney beyond, with its neatly clipped blackthorn hedge, with horse chestnuts, ash and spruce beyond. At regular intervals, towering above all these, were the tallest poplars I had ever seen. Directly opposite my window was the biggest. It had grown in such a way that it looked like some vast trident. The spinney, which bounded the full length of the arable field adjacent to my home, had poplars for its entire length, but the further they were from the house the more normal their height. A footpath led past our garden and on across the fields. A map dated 1790 shows that this was known as Piggy Lane. Undoubtedly regular livestock fairs were held around the area where the lane joined the road, which is still known as Hog Fair Lane. This resulted in the soil being enriched with manure over many decades, which almost certainly accounts for the abnormal growth of the poplars.

As I gazed out of the big sash window a green woodpecker alighted on the lawn; whilst another, from a nearby tree, pierced the morning quiet with its almost laughter-like call. However, that morning late in October 1939 my mind was not really focused on the local wildlife. I was thinking of my friends, who by now would be at Catterick, of others left behind at Newbury and my brother, Ralph, who had gone to India two years previously to become an assistant manager on a tea plantation in Assam. Around the time that I enlisted in the Territorials, he had joined the equivalent in his area of India, the Assam Valley Light Horse and, now a lieutenant, had recently been posted to Poona.

As I went down to breakfast I was not a happy man, for apart from the resentment I felt at being so unceremoniously chucked out of the army, there was a major question lurking at the back of my mind – what was I going to do now? When I entered the dining room my parents, largely obscured by their newspapers, had already started. Mother lowered hers long enough to say, 'Your breakfast is in the oven' before resuming her immersion in the *Daily Telegraph*. Father greeted me, but he too, it seemed, was not in the mood to make conversation. That suited me fine, I was in no mood to chat either. I collected my breakfast, a vast fry. I felt mother was under the impression that her youngest must have been starved in the army, which certainly was not the case. After retrieving my breakfast from the oven, I picked up the most recent copy of *Farmers Weekly*, which I scanned to see what jobs might be going.

Mother put down her paper and asked if I would like another cup of tea. At the same time father folded his paper, cleared his throat and addressed me. 'Right, Michael, you mustn't take this too much to heart. You volunteered, you tried to do your bit and you still can by doing the job you're trained for – farming and estate management. Take it from me, food is going to be very, very scarce before this is all over. However, the first thing you must do is go up to London and see Dr McGowan.'

Dr McGowan was a brilliant homeopathic doctor who Edward Clifton-Brown, whose Burnham Grove estate father managed, had urgently called down from London when I had been so ill with rheumatic fever, after the two doctors from the practice which cared for us said there was little more they could do. Edward Clifton-Brown, always referred to as ECB, was a governor of the Homeopathic Hospital in London, where Dr McGowan was a consultant. He also had a thriving practice based in Harley Street. I readily agreed to father's suggestion. I had great faith in Doctor Mac and the prognosis of the wretched major the day before had added considerably to my overall anxiety.

Some six weeks later, after several visits to Harley Street, Dr McGowan gave me the all clear, and said he did not need to see me again and, providing I was sensible, there was no reason why I should not lead a perfectly normal life. Further, that the prediction that I wouldn't make fifty – according to my friend the major – was totally unfounded.

Now I could seriously set about looking for a job. My ambition, from a very early age, was for one similar to my father's, namely land agent-cum-farm manager on an estate with herds of pedigree livestock and, to really make it Utopia, horses. I was a reasonably accomplished horseman and for several seasons had schooled difficult horses to hounds with the Old Berkeley Hunt, for my friend Billy Oliver. Billy had a large livery and riding stable adjoining the Burnham Grove estate and an even bigger one at Wendover, on the edge of the Vale of Aylesbury, as well as two other livery stables and riding schools establishments.

I had talked over my ambition with my parents. They were encouraging, but father said I was aiming far too high. I was hoping to run before I could walk and, once Dr McGowan had said all was well, he would start to contact some of his many friends to see what jobs might be available. In the meantime I could earn myself some money, for Edward Clifton-Brown had said I might help out on the estate if and when required and be paid. Further, when not wanted in this connection, I could assist in the never-ending war that had to be waged against the hordes of rabbits and woodpigeons that did so much damage to crops. What made this even more inviting was that ECB said I could keep half the proceeds from the sale of whatever I accounted for. The latter was great news. The price of everything was creeping up, that is everything barring petrol, the cost of which had rocketed to the unbelievable figure of 1/9$\frac{1}{2}$ per gallon, (about 9p).

One could still buy petrol for domestic purposes, for there was a basic ration of five or seven gallons a month, according to the size of one's car. In addition one could get a supplementary allowance for business purposes. By comparison with petrol other increases were small. A penny here, a ha'penny there, sometimes as little as a farthing, but it all added up. Nowadays a penny would be looked upon as being valueless, but in those days it was still real money. A sizeable bar of milk chocolate could be bought for 2d and a packet of 20 cigarettes cost 10$\frac{1}{2}$d at the time war was declared. Ha'pennies and farthings regularly appeared on price tags, for a large range of goods, particularly in haberdasheries and shops dealing in ladies' clothing, where, for example, a blouse might be priced at four shillings and eleven pence three farthings. If one handed over 5/- in payment for such an article, it was common in these shops to be given a packet of pins in lieu of a farthing's change, a custom which infuriated father when he went to buy something for mother. He always insisted on receiving the appropriate coin, claiming pins were not legal tender. Ten farthings he would point out to a harassed shop assistant added up to 2$\frac{1}{2}$d, for which one could buy a packet of five Woodbine cigarettes, not that he would ever have smoked them – it was just the principle.

The day I returned from London and the all clear from the doctor I was so elated I decided to pay a visit to The Crown at East Burnham for a pint and a game of darts. Driving at night was a somewhat hazardous business, for headlights were virtually blacked out by spherical fittings that screwed into place over the lamps. There were four slits, each of approximately half an inch in depth and around two-thirds of the width of the attachment. Over each slit was a baffle-plate which directed what little light there was on to the ground, allowing visibility of no more than twenty-five yards at the most. These masks were as compulsory as the rest of the blackout rules. However, they had two great plusses going for them, they were a wonderful deterrent to speeding and they helped to conserve petrol, for at the speed one could travel with safety at night the minimum amount was used. Of course, in addition, one always hoped they would make one's car less conspicuous to marauding enemy aircraft.

Just as I was leaving The Crown, around 9.30pm, I could hear the wail of air-raid sirens. Again I paid little attention for we were going through the period often referred to by the media as the phoney war. Nevertheless, automatically I glanced skywards. There was a full moon, with not a cloud in the sky, nor, as far as I could see, a plane, either German or British, anywhere in sight. As I put my car in the garage some fifteen minutes later, the all clear sounded – yet another false alarm. I headed straight upstairs to bed and, after reading for a while, prepared to settle down for the night.

Just as I switched off the bedside light the air-raid siren started its piercing wail yet again. I paid little attention, but just as I was dozing off I heard what was to become the well-known and distinctive throb of a German Junker's engines. I listened carefully. It sounded as though there might be two. That it was the enemy was confirmed when every ack-ack gun within the area started to fire. I jumped out of bed, switched off the light, pulled back the blackout curtain and opened the window to lean out and watch. Searchlights sweeping the sky for one brief moment illuminated two Junker bombers – the first I'd seen. It seemed as though every anti-aircraft gun for miles around was in action; it was as though the crews were at last able to unleash after weeks of frustrating and boring inaction. The flashes, puffs of smoke and bangs as the shells burst made a spectacular show, but sadly they were short of their target. I leaned further out to get a better look. Suddenly there was a swishing eerie whistling sound, as a large lump of shrapnel came hurtling over the house. It seemed it was only inches over my head, whereas, in reality, it probably passed some thirty to forty feet over the house. Whether it was inches or yards it was scary, but before I could duck back inside there was a deafening crack, coupled with the sound of splintering wood. The centre branch of the poplar trident crashed to the ground, severed from the trunk so neatly it was as though it had been cut through with a crosscut saw. Somewhat shaken and bewildered at the suddenness of all that had happened, I stood gazing at the vast gap in the top of what had been a magnificent specimen tree. Little did I realise how fortuitous this unwanted pruning of the poplar would much later prove to be.

I was up early the following morning, as I was to act as stand-in for Tom Rose, the foreman, who had a bad bout of 'flu. He lived at Biddles Farm, about two miles away on the far side of the estate so I took my bike – it wasn't worth getting the car out and using up petrol for so few miles. I checked all was well at Biddles Farm and then returned to Lynch Hill, where once there had been a big dairy herd, but now the cow byre and yards housed bullocks for fattening. After a quick word with the staff I was on my way again, this time to Britwell Farm, the hub of the estate, where the carpenter's, blacksmith, granary and spares' store were situated. As I rode into the yard I saw Jummy Young, who was in charge of outside maintenance, busy shovelling something up and putting it into a barrow. I walked over to see what he was doing. He was clearing up bits of shrapnel, the debris from the previous night's barrage by the surrounding ack-ack guns at the Junkers. He told me in the most explicit terms that he wished it had been bits of the bombers. Jummy, who I'd known for as long as I could remember, was always cheerful and a great worker, but was no lover of Germans. He had served all through the Great War and been wounded four times. Amazingly he was shot, all on different occasions, through both hands and both feet, and the fifth time he was sent up to the front he was gassed. Very lucky to have survived, he eventually returned to Burnham, to find that his wife had run off with another man, leaving the children to fend for themselves. There was no counselling in those days, but Jummy once said to me, when I asked him how he'd managed, 'Well, I rolled me sleeves up and bloody well got on with life o' course.'

2. Rabbits, Pigeons and an Exciting Prospect

Christmas 1939, for me and my parents, was a quiet affair, with my brother away in India and various cousins who usually joined us for the day caught up in the war. However, my mother's foresight and good housekeeping meant that we lacked for nothing on the festive table. By tradition there was a serious pheasant shoot on Boxing Day on the estate and this went ahead as usual. All the farm and estate workers, except those responsible for the livestock, turned out as beaters, pleased to have the opportunity to earn a little extra in overtime and a free bottle of beer at lunchtime. However, this was not their only reason for being present, it was a good day out, they enjoyed the sport and many were forthright and discerning critics of the standard of marksmanship displayed by visiting guns. They took pride in the fact that their 'guvnor', Edward Clifton-Brown, was recognised as one of the finest pheasant shots in the country.

Boxing Day 1939 turned out to be a very memorable one for me. Around 7.30pm on Christmas evening, we were in the drawing room, heads buried in books – gifts we had received from each other – when the phone rang. Father looked up and asked me to answer it. It was Edward Clifton-Brown. One of his guns for the morrow was suffering from a bad bout of 'flu. He was a gun short and none of his friends were available. Would I like to shoot? I most certainly would. I was probably almost inarticulate in my thanks – I'd never shot on a big pheasant shoot before. ECB went on to say I would be the walking gun all day – that meant walking in the line with the beaters to try and bag any birds going back. That certainly was no problem, in fact nothing would have been such was my excitement, especially as I was aware that if windy the walking gun often had excellent shooting.

The next morning, together with father, I proudly joined the rest of the guns at Burnham Grove, all of whom I knew well. It was a glorious crisp sunny morning with frost still sparkling on the ground as we walked down through the gardens and out across the two fields to the main coverts. Bill Yeoman, the head gamekeeper, greeted us at the gate leading into the wood. Just inside, on the main ride, was the gamecart. This was a heavyweight four-wheeled type of wagonette, built on the estate, drawn by a massive Suffolk Punch mare, Sprey, her mane and tail carefully plaited and braided with ribbons, her chestnut coat gleaming in the winter sunlight, but there was little or no heat in the latter. A strong south westerly was growing ever stronger, which would certainly make the birds fly high and boded well for me as walking gun. With luck I'd get some real screamers coming my way, high above the towering oaks. I was not disappointed and, for a few hours, we all forgot the problems and worries of the war, which was still in its infancy. Our euphoria might not have been quite so great, as we bid each other goodnight, a happy New Year, and a speedy end to the war, had we realised it would be the last major shoot on the estate, now long since buried beneath a multitude of houses, even after being designated green belt land!

January, however, saw things start to change rapidly. Over two million young men were to be called up and the German U-boats were becoming increasingly active. Butter and bacon were already rationed, and soon sugar and meat, but living on a farm the rationing, as yet, had little effect on us.

I applied for several jobs and in all cases was interviewed, but they weren't really what I was looking for. Father had started to contact his friends, but without any success. However, financially I was doing very well – particularly from rabbits, the price of which had doubled since the beginning of the war and which were much in demand. Then, suddenly, towards the end of the second week in January, I found myself with time on my hands. It started to freeze hard and kept on freezing – night after night, and frequently all through the day. The ground became like well-set concrete and it would have been madness to have worked ferrets, for if they got 'laid up', that is killed their quarry underground, short of using a pneumatic drill there would have been no hope of digging them out. The frost continued for days and became so severe that, for the first time for over fifty years, the Thames froze over. If this wasn't enough, at the end of the month, just as it was beginning to thaw, we had what was said at the time to be the worst storm of the century. Fortunately, February saw an improvement in the weather and I was able to get back to earning some money.

On the last day of the month, just as dawn was breaking, I pulled my car on to the stubble adjoining the lane that ran from Lynch Hill Farm to Biddles. It was bitterly cold, a stiff north wind bringing flurries of snow to add to the light carpeting that already whitened the surrounding fields. Shivering, I got out of the car. It was the sort of morning that had old Charlie Davis, the head carpenter on the estate, been working outside he would undoubtedly have wrapped his torso in two layers of the heaviest brown paper, with a very liberal application of goose grease between them. He was a Welshman who would tell his workmates, 'You'll never get cold boyo in brown paper and goosy grease. Like a cocoon it is – see.' As far as I knew no one on the staff had ever tried Charlie's method of insulation; but neither did they try some of his other remedies – such as four drops of turpentine on a lump of sugar, every few hours for a cold. But the one that fascinated me most, as a child, was his cure for a sore throat. He would take a lump of bacon fat, about an inch cube, cleverly attach a piece of string to it, swallow it, pull it up and repeat the procedure three or four times every hour. 'Greases the throat – see.' Bizarre though his panaceas may sound, he was never treated by a doctor until shortly before his death.

I turned up the collar of my jacket – there were no lined waterproof shooting coats in those days. A good, heavy Harris Tweed was about the best protection one could get from the elements. I'd also thrown an old riding mac into the car, in case the weather became too foul. The forecast wasn't good, but then trying to shoot in a heavy mackintosh wasn't either, and I was after woodpigeons. I was heading for a hedge between Winding Shot, the field in which I'd parked the car and Big Field which was just on 100 acres, although father had planted a belt of trees right across it, splitting it into two. This was both to make a windbreak and to provide nesting sites, along the edge, for partridges. Just beyond the hedge, in

Big Field, was some twenty acres of thousand-head kale and swedes, sown in alternate widths of the drill for late winter folding by the Hampshire Down flock. Two days previously, following a light fall of snow, pigeons had homed in on this in their thousands and I really do mean thousands. In two days they had stripped the leaf off the kale and guzzled the tops of the swedes for some thirty yards out from the hedge – leaving it so bare that it looked almost as though the sheep had already been penned over it. I certainly had never seen pigeon damage like it before and nor had Bob Hedges, one of the gamekeepers, who had come along the previous evening as I was building a hide between two massive English elms.

I gathered up my decoys and cartridges and after several moments' hesitation I added the riding mac to my load. Gun under arm, I headed off across the stubble towards the hedge. Quickly I set up my six decoy pigeons on the edge of the kale. Having placed these to my satisfaction I walked across and entered my hide, filled my right-hand pocket with cartridges for quick and easy loading and settled down to wait on a very nice shooting stick that I'd recently bought at a farm sale for two shillings.

Financially I'd had what could only be described as a fantastic week thus far. On Monday I'd bagged nineteen rabbits. I used purse-nets and, of course, ferrets. The latter were part of the country scene, a number of people kept them, but few, if any, looked upon them as pets. They were for 'ferreting' – bolting rabbits from their burrows. Normally one worked the bitches, or if you prefer jills, loose and the dogs as 'liners'. Frequently a bitch would kill a rabbit underground, or drive one, or more, up a dead end and remain there. When this happened a light line was attached to an equally lightweight collar around a dog ferret's neck. He would then be tried down various holes; if when one pulled on the line it remained tight and the ferret would not come back it was an indication that he had caught up with a rabbit and, hopefully, that was where the missing bitch was located. When this happened it was a case of off with one's jacket, pick up a rabbiting-graft (a specially curved and strengthened type of spade) and get stuck in following the line. This was not just a case of digging a trench; most people used a tapping-bar to drive down into the ground, find the hole, break through at this point and, hopefully find the line, thus saving an immense amount of digging. Of course, compared to modern-day electronic equipment it all sounds very archaic, but the good and accurate use of a bar could save an awful lot of sweat!

Whilst Monday had been a very good day's work, Tuesday was even better, resulting in a record bag for me when on my own – thirty-one. It was quite late in the afternoon when I put two bitches to ground in a big open burrow. Within minutes several rabbits had come flying out into the nets, bringing my catch for the day up to twenty. One of the bitches appeared and remained above ground long enough for me to pick her up. I popped her back into the specially constructed ferret-box, used for carrying them around, which already held a polecat-coloured bitch. A real little tigress, I purposely hadn't used her due to the lateness of the hour, as she was a devil at killing rabbits underground, which always necessitated digging. In the box with her was Jumper, a big white dog who I used as a liner and very reliable he was too, for when I pulled on the line and he didn't come back immediately I knew I was in business. I waited five minutes, but there was no sign of the second bitch, so, quietly cursing, I took Jumper out of the box, put his collar on and started trying him down holes. He kept coming back. I was beginning to get worried, for the light was going by the time I tried the last hole. I could see that a couple of feet inside there was a T junction – Jumper turned left. The line kept disappearing and I hadn't much left when it stopped. From the marks I had on the line I judged him to be between seven and eight yards away. I picked up the graft and quickly opened to the junction. I lay on the ground and put my arm up the hole, it seemed to be straight. I tried with the tapping-iron: success. I tried a yard further on, once more I was into a hole. I dug down, thankfully it wasn't very deep, cleared out the loose soil and there, much to my relief, was the line. I pulled it through from the start, checked which way the hole went, drove in the bar, dug down and again I was lucky.

Quickly I was at the three-foot marker, from then on I followed the line which fortunately wasn't deep. Minutes later I lifted Jumper out and, thankfully, the jill followed him. I popped them both into the box, lay down and reached in and pulled out a rabbit. I tried my arm up the hole again: yes, there was another one. Over the next five to ten minutes I kept digging out a little more and pulling out rabbits. To my amazement, when I'd finished, I'd added eleven more to the bag. By the time I had gutted and hocked my catch, filled in the holes I'd dug and gathered up my gear it was dark. I slung the rabbits back to back across the bar and got them up on to my shoulder. Then, with some difficulty I managed to get the ferret box strap over the other shoulder, gathered up my bag of nets and the graft and started the mile trudge home, tired but elated. Eleven proved to be the most I was ever to get from a dead end in many years of ferreting.

The next day I accounted for a further fourteen, for a total of sixty-four. I sold sixty of them at a record price of 3/6 each, keeping four back as ferret food. This meant I had, even on my fifty-fifty arrangement, earned in three days more than any of the farm or estate staff did in a week. From my point of view this was great, for the phoney war, as many had been calling it, had ended and everything was going up in price.

My thoughts were suddenly interrupted by the clatter of wings, as three woodpigeons landed in the big elm to my right. Cautiously I brought my gun up, aiming at the nearest one. The fact that it was sitting in a tree was immaterial. I wasn't there looking for sporting shots; my main purpose was to keep the pigeons off the kale and swedes and at the same time bag as many as I could to help increase my bank balance. I pulled the trigger and saw my sitting target crumple as I swung on to one of the others as they flew from the tree. That, too, was in the bag. By now it was light, well as light as it was going to get with a blanket of lowering cloud as far as the eye could see in any direction, which suggested that heavy snow could be imminent.

The cold was intense. I scanned the skyline anxiously; there was not a sign of a pigeon. Fervently I hoped they hadn't changed their feeding ground. I sat and shivered, constantly looking at my watch. I had just decided that if nothing had happened by 9.30am I'd pack up as there was no point in getting pneumonia. Suddenly there was a swish of wings as a bird came hurtling downwards from high above the elm to my left, but it certainly wasn't a pigeon. I jumped to my feet just in time to see its powerful claws grab at one of my decoys, before realising its mistake and departing as quickly as it had appeared.

Momentarily, I thought it was an overly large sparrowhawk, but realised this was somewhat improbable. Could it have been a goshawk? They resemble each other in many ways, but the latter is considerably larger and whilst a sparrowhawk would not be averse to taking a woodpigeon, it seemed unlikely with the wealth of smaller birds readily available. Whatever it was it had hit my decoy, which incidentally was solid wood, so hard that it had knocked it over. I left my hide to set it up again. It was one of my new ones, not a scratch on it when I first put it out, but there were now talon marks clearly visible. It must have been a goshawk to strike with such force. On reflection I was convinced it was and was thrilled that I had seen such a magnificent bird of prey in the wild for only the second time. As I returned to the hide I couldn't help laughing, for, whatever it was, it surely suffered both a surprising and jarring experience! Regrettably, my identification was proved right, for later that day one of the gamekeepers arrived at the estate office with a hawk he could not identify for certain, having shot it as it swooped through the trees on its intended prey.

For the next ten minutes I continued to shiver and was about to pick up when suddenly pigeons started flying in from every direction. It seemed that no amount of shooting deterred them for more than a few minutes. For just over two hours they flew into the decoys, as though guided by kamikaze pilots, a term at that time as yet unknown to the world as a whole. Then, almost like turning off a tap the attack stopped; this was probably just as well as I was down to just a handful of cartridges in my pocket. I had brought five boxes of twenty-five each with me to the hide, leaving another three boxes in the car. I waited ten to fifteen minutes, during which time there wasn't a pigeon to be seen anywhere and so I started to pick up. The final count was ninety-two – not a bad morning's work. I tied them up in fours and carried them across to the car. Having done this, as there still wasn't a pigeon in sight, I decided to deliver my morning's bag to a buyer in Maidenhead, who had agreed to take up to 100 at 2/6 each. Only a few months earlier the most one could hope to get was 6d apiece. Having done this I arrived back home just as lunch was going on the table, one of mother's specialities for really cold days – piping hot Irish stew, made from the best end of neck (mutton), pearl barley and a host of root vegetables. This was followed by baked apples, Bramleys, of which variety there were several trees in the garden, with home-produced clotted cream and brown sugar.

Feeling replete and distinctly warmer, I returned to my hide, together with another load of cartridges, confident there would be a further onslaught by the woodies before they departed to their respective roosts. The cold was not quite as severe, but cold enough. However as is so often the case when the temperature rises a degree or two and snow is imminent, big white flakes slowly started to descend. Quickly my decoys were turning from grey to white, but still there was no sign of any pigeons. It seemed I had done my job well, but I stuck it out until 3.00pm when I decided to call it a day. I was just about to leave the hide to pick up the decoys when I heard a strange snuffling, grunting sort of sound away to my left. I peered out and, for a moment, couldn't believe my eyes. Lumbering along, about a yard out from the hedge was a badger. In all the years I had lived on the estate I'd only ever seen one before. I couldn't think where it had come from; there wasn't a sett anywhere in the neighbourhood that I knew of and certainly not one on the estate. Further, it was strange to see a badger on the move in the middle of the afternoon, for it is essentially a nocturnal animal. I remained motionless as 'brock' passed within three yards of my hide, but I was downwind and so he had no idea I was watching him. It was indeed a 'he', a big old boar and, poor chap, he looked pretty moth-eaten. He stopped where I had made a heap of the pigeons, prior to tying them up, before lunch. He spent several minutes sniffing around where they'd been, before urinating and going on his way. Where he came from, or where he was going I had no idea, but he greatly added to the pleasure of my day.

After a really hot bath, afternoon tea. This wasn't just a mug made with a teabag and a biscuit, but a real sit-down meal with hot, buttered toast, muffins or home-made scones with strawberry jam and Devonshire-style clotted cream, which mother used to make two or three times a week, followed by an assortment of home-made cakes. Looking back at those far off days it seemed extraordinary how we remained slim, but we did. Breakfast, sharp on 8.00am, was always a fry, in winter preceded by porridge, well covered with demerara sugar and rich creamy milk, that less than two hours before had still been in the cow. Summer or winter we finished off with a slice or two of toast, with plenty of home-made butter and, equally, home-made marmalade, or honey from our own bees. Lunch was at noon, to fit in with the time the farm and estate staff took their midday break. This was the main meal of the day. Supper, usually around 8.00pm, would be a large omelette, Welsh rarebit, a heaped plate of scrambled eggs or something else hot to sustain us throughout the night, but whatever it might have been we finished with fresh fruit. These days such a daily intake sounds almost gluttonous, but in those days we needed it, at least in the country, for we used up so much energy. People often walked several miles to work as, indeed, did school children. Men working on farms, if ploughing with a pair of horses, would do anything from $10\frac{1}{2}$ to $11\frac{1}{2}$ miles a day, according to the width of the furrow being cut. Much the same would apply to horse-hoeing root crops, harrowing and dozens of other jobs. From the age of about fifteen, at the height of summer, I thought nothing of getting up around 4.00am, cycling the $2\frac{1}{2}$ miles up to my friend Billy Oliver's stables adjoining the northern boundary of the estate and setting off to ride a horse from there to his main stables at Wendover, exactly twenty-one miles away. I would breakfast with him, spend the day riding out, helping school young horses and if required, as was the case on several occasions, ride another one back in the cool of the evening to Burnham.

In spite of this we did sit down and relax, read one or two books a week and, if there was something of interest, listen to the wireless and that is exactly what I was doing, after my day pigeon shooting, in the company of my parents, around 7.00pm, when the phone rang. Father put down his copy of the *Fishing Gazette* and went to answer it. He was back in seconds. Mother looked up from her book and asked, 'Who was that?' Father looked over the top of his half-glasses he used for reading, 'Clive Haselden, wanting to know if Michael would be interested in taking over the management of Colonel Devereux's estate in the Vale of Aylesbury. I told him not to be so ridiculous and that Michael was far too young and inexperienced even to be considered for the job.'

I leapt to my feet. 'You did what? Don't you realise who he is? He's one of the country's leading industrialists. It's just the sort of job I've been praying for, never mind looking for and you bloody well said no.' I glared at father, before rushing from the room to put a call through to Clive, an exceptionally talented young vet and a great friend of mine. It seemed like eternity before I heard Clive's phone ringing, but in those days one didn't just dial the number. First I had to ring the Burnham exchange, then give the number. They in turn had to contact the major exchange for the area one was calling, in this case Aylesbury. It was not unusual to be told the lines were engaged. Thankfully that evening they weren't. Aylesbury then rang Stoke Mandeville, Clive's local exchange, who in turn rang the number which was required. I was on tenterhooks until I heard the operator say 'I'm putting you through caller', but seconds later I heard Clive's voice.

When Clive realised who it was he sounded a bit piqued and was somewhat caustic in his comments when I declared I was very interested in the job. Apparently father, on hearing what Clive was calling about, had simply said, 'Don't be so damned stupid' and hung up. However, I calmed Clive down and then he told me that about three weeks previously he had been contacted by Devereux himself, who had just fired the vet that had been doing his work and asked Clive, to take over. He went on to tell me that things were in a terrible mess, particularly in the case of the pigs. A fortune had been spent on buildings, including vast Danish-type piggeries to accommodate up to 1500 pigs at any one time. It was in connection with the pigs that Clive had been called in. He told me that when he first visited Marsh Hill Farm, where the piggery was situated, he just couldn't believe the state of things – dead pigs in all directions and, in Clive's opinion, a totally useless pigman in charge, who greeted Clive, 'I'm Mr Prouse, manager of the pig unit.'

Clive went on to say that there was a bad outbreak of swine fever and in addition he had diagnosed erysipelas and paratyphoid. He continued that the overall standard of management was pretty poor. On the plus side there appeared to be a very good foreman if he was given a chance and an equally good head herdsman in charge of the pedigree Dairy Shorthorn herd, in which the Colonel took a great interest as he was anxious to build it up to one of the foremost in the country. However, things weren't going as well as they might even in this section. The Colonel had retained the services of a neighbouring farmer to advise and oversee the management of the estate but he had received his marching orders at the same time as the vet. Both had been quickly followed by the lady who had been in charge of the stables. It sounded as though management was non-existent and that Clive's opening remarks, namely that things were in a terrible mess, was a vast understatement. Clive ended his discourse on the Colonel's Roundhill estate with, 'Well, there you are, I can assure you that if you take it on it will be no sinecure. Still interested?' With the enthusiasm of youth and, looking back, an obvious over-sized helping of egotism, my reply was immediate. 'Yes, very much so. Just the sort of job I've been looking for.'

'Right, I'll phone Colonel Devereux and call you back. I suppose you'd be available any time for an interview?' My reply was in the affirmative. I hurried back to the drawing room to give my parents the stupendous news and relate all Clive had told me. Father gave me a rather pitying look, folded his *Fishing Gazette* and shook his head. 'You've just confirmed all that I've been hearing about that place. You're stark staring bonkers even to contemplate taking it on. What you should do is find a job as an assistant farm/estate manager and thoroughly learn all aspects before taking a place on your own.' At that moment the phone rang. I made a dash for it, not giving father a chance to spike my guns, should it be Clive. It was. The Colonel, he told me, was most interested, thought perhaps I was a bit young, but would give the matter careful consideration if father would agree to come to my rescue should I need help during the first six months. If this was acceptable the Colonel would meet us at his house at Round Hill, a little over twenty miles from my home, at 2.00pm next day, Saturday. I assured Clive we'd be there and went back to my parents to tell them of my news. Father, as I knew he would, readily agreed to the Colonel's request, but still maintained I was mad. That night I slept soundly, confident that I could pull off what had to be a chance of a lifetime to fulfil all my greatest hopes and dreams.

3. Decision Time

It was exactly 2.00pm as we turned into the driveway leading to the house at Round Hill. Father was a stickler for punctuality and so we had waited half a mile up the road to ensure we arrived at the agreed time. To the right, as we turned on to the drive, I noticed a stand of tall trees, where rooks were already refurbishing their nests. The drive widened out into a parking area, from which a gateway, flanked by two borders planted with small flowering shrubs, led to the stable yard. The main drive went on past the house, terminating at a gate leading into a grass field.

A magnificent grey-green Bentley, the latest model, produced just before the outbreak of war, was parked opposite the front door. Tense at the prospect of being interviewed by one of the leading industrialists in the country my nerves were made worse by the fact that Col Devereux was also Joint Master of Foxhounds for the Old Berkeley Hunt and that status demanded maximum respect. Even so, for a few seconds I relaxed as I visualised the thrill of driving such a car. But when Father brought his car to a halt and I got out, suddenly, but fortunately only momentarily, all the self-assurance and egotism I had felt the previous evening deserted me. What the hell was I doing here? Why had they chucked me out of the army? Why wasn't I at home, earning all the money I needed catching rabbits, shooting woodpigeons and filling in where required on the estate?

The apprehension that was churning through my mind was thankfully halted by father saying, 'What are you standing there for? Come on. Wake up, or are you now sorry you came?' That did it. I wasn't sorry, I wanted this job. As I looked across at the stable yard, I realised just how much I wanted it. All the irresolution left me and I quickly joined father as he walked towards the house. I had just reached him when the front door opened and the Colonel appeared. I recognised him at once, for I had seen him in the hunting field on a number of occasions when I'd been schooling horses for Billy Oliver. Dev, as he was known to all his friends, was about five feet eight inches in height, slightly rotund, with greying hair and a neatly clipped moustache, his well-chiselled features slightly marred by more than a hint of a double chin, but, to me, his most striking feature were his steely grey-green eyes. As he approached he positively oozed energy and charm. One realised within minutes of being in his company that he had a dynamic personality. His greeting was warm and he immediately made it clear to father that he appreciated his coming. He quickly admitted he knew little about agriculture and estate management, but even so he knew enough to realise that, as he put it – 'things were in a hell of a mess'.

We started with a tour of the stables. These, the Colonel informed us, had been the original farm buildings, which he'd had converted into an impressive range of loose boxes. The old tithe barn had been transformed into a ballroom-cum-lecture hall, with a stage at one end and a massive open brick fireplace at the other. It was all most impressive, but even more so for me was what was in the loose boxes that formed three sides of a square. There was no doubt that the Master had some truly magnificent horses, but, sadly, we did not dally, except with one – Ratcatcher, a superb bay heavyweight which the owner claimed was the greatest hunter that any man ever threw a leg over. He told me, although I had already heard from Clive Haselden, that up to a week ago there had been a manageress in charge of the stables. However, according to the Colonel, she had forgotten who owned them and blatantly ignored his instructions on a number of occasions, leading to her sudden and immediate dismissal the previous weekend. On the positive side, with the number of horses already reduced because of the war, there was at present adequate and experienced staff and the head groom, Bob Hitchcock, seemed to be coping well.

We then climbed into the Bentley and crossed the road to a set of new farm buildings – described by the owner as a model farmyard. To the right of the concrete road leading to these was a pair of equally new cottages, which, for those days, could be described as having all mod cons, at least as far as a farmworker's cottage was concerned, for they had an inside loo, bathroom, hot water system and electricity. The Colonel informed us that the foreman, Tom Burrows, lived in the nearest one with his family, whilst Bob Hitchcock and his wife occupied the other.

Model farm it may well have been named, but, within minutes I began wondering about the knowledge of the designer. Whilst it had a loo, plus a wash-hand basin – a very great rarity on a farm in the late 1930s and 1940s – there was abysmally poor storage space for hay, straw and other feeding stuffs. We learned that the development of a really outstanding herd of Dairy Shorthorns was high on the agenda. To this end a considerable sum had already been spent on foundation stock, but the Colonel said he was prepared to invest a great deal more to achieve his ambition. He took us into a cowshed through double sliding doors at the side of the building. To my horror I saw that approximately one-third of the standings had been ripped out, to be replaced by a six-unit milking parlour. The Colonel warmly greeted a man, who I was later to learn was Ron Chamberlain, the head herdsman. The reply he received, whilst polite, was not what could have been described as particularly cordial, leaving me with the feeling that all was not well in this area.

The cows were already in from the field for afternoon milking. I noted that those housed in the standings that remained were really top representatives of the breed. Almost immediately I recognised Greattew Barrington 2nd, who had won first at the London Dairy Show in 1938. We went out through a door at the end of the byre into a large concreted yard, with open-fronted shedding on two sides. Some twenty-five to thirty cows stood around waiting to pass through the parlour and be machine milked. In those days milking machines were a long way from achieving perfection and were felt by many to be a major cause of mastitis, frequently causing the loss of one or more quarters and so a considerably lower milk yield. While the Colonel was discussing something with father I took a quick walk through the herd. They were a pretty motley non-pedigree lot which, I had already learned, were to be replaced by further top-quality pure-bred cows and heifers. I noted that nearly half were light of a quarter and in some cases only three-quartered. This appeared to support the opinion, also held by my father, that milking parlours were the source of much mastitis and could not compete with good hand milking.

We continued our tour around the building at a brisk pace. As we were leaving through the main entrance the Colonel pointed to a door to our right. 'That's the farm office in there. I have a young man, Harrison, in charge of that, but he's likely to be called up any time now. No, that's not quite correct, because Jackson, assistant company secretary with my major company, High Duty Alloys at Slough, oversees Harrison, but when I appoint an agent to run the whole estate Jackson will cease to have anything to do with it.'

We climbed back into the Bentley and sped off down the road heading, we were told, for Marsh Hill and the piggery. As we did so we passed another pair of new cottages, similar to those at the farm. When we arrived at our destination, I could see some old farm buildings away to our right, much the same as they had been when built a century or more before. Ahead was another stretch of concrete road and yet another pair of new cottages to the right of this. The road led to an impressive layout of buildings, that looked as though they would have been more at home in Slough Trading Estate, adjacent to one of the Colonel's factories, than out in the wilds of the Buckinghamshire countryside. We drove into the spacious yard, to the left was a long building, which I was to learn was the feed store. At right angles to this were four buildings, each about 250 feet long. Furthest away was the farrowing house. Next came the weaner shed with extensive concreted outside yards, then two fattening houses. The first thing that struck me was their height. Pigs thrive if warm and will generate much heat for themselves in correctly constructed buildings, but they would have little or no hope of doing so, unless packed to the maximum capacity, in the recently erected housing at Marsh Hill.

As we got out of the car I spotted a scruffy looking individual, aged about thirty-five, lolling up against the wall of one of the fattening houses, hands in his trouser pockets, a cigarette hanging out of the corner of his mouth. 'That,' said the Colonel, 'is Prouse, supposedly the head pigman. He doesn't impress me one iota. He was engaged by a farmer who has been advising me over the pigs. He's bought in a lot of expensive pedigree Wessex Saddlebacks, plus hundreds of weaners from nearby markets for fattening. He also has a feeding stuffs business from where, so I understand, we buy all our requirements. His brother is a builder and has done all the work on the estate for me. There is a third brother, who has a bacon factory and buys all our finished pigs.' Father looked at me, Devereux caught his look. 'I know what you're thinking, Mr Twist, and you're probably right, which is why I need an agent to watch my interests.' He turned and walked towards Prouse and called out, 'How are things?' His pigman did not move but, I thought quite miraculously, managed to spit without taking the cigarette from his mouth, or, indeed, his hands from deep within his pockets. He remained lounging against the wall, as he spat again and then deigned to answer, 'Bad! Down to 1302 when I had a count yesterday evening, but there'll have been a lot more die since then. I haven't looked.' His employer grimaced. 'We'll take a look round.' His herdsman made no attempt to move, but spat again before replying, 'Go ahead, they're your pigs – what's left of them.' The Colonel turned almost scarlet, it was obvious that he was furious, but much to my surprise he said nothing.

It would be pointless to dwell on the devastation and mess we were to view in the course of the next ten to fifteen minutes. I felt sure that some of the very young piglets which lay dead with their mothers in the farrowing house had died from cold rather than disease. Clive Haselden had certainly not exaggerated. As we returned to the Bentley, two things were very apparent. Firstly, Prouse was still propping up the wall and, I noticed for the first time, immediately above him was a large notice which read 'Strictly No Smoking'. Secondly, the Colonel was virtually speechless with anger, but, quite out of character I was to learn later, never said a word. I think father, a strict disciplinarian, was equally furious. We got back into the car and sat there in utter silence for several minutes which seemed like eternity. The Colonel looked at his watch and quietly said, 'Just time for a quick talk and a cup of tea, then I must rush off back to Slough. I've a very important meeting at 5.00pm. That means we haven't time to go to Little Marsh Farm, but there's nothing there except a barn and a few old sheds.'

On the way back to Round Hill we passed a house, actually a pair of cottages, plus a few small buildings. Devereux indicated towards it with his hand, 'I'd like to buy that place, it's not very big, about eighty-five acres. It cuts right into my land. The farmer, who was advising with regard to the dairy herd and the farming in general has made enquiries, but says the owner doesn't want to sell.' 'Is that the same farmer who has been advising you over the pigs?' I asked. The Colonel gave a rather sardonic laugh. 'No, that's another one. What with him, the one overseeing the pigs, a manageress for the stables and Jackson in charge of the office I've probably had too many chiefs and not enough Indians and, what I have of the latter, it wouldn't surprise me if half of them didn't earn their wages, if that fellow Prouse is anything to go by. However, what with being so involved in the aircraft industry and having been preparing in my business for this war, since I visited Germany and met Hitler in 1937, I just haven't had the time to keep an eye on what has been going on here.' We drove on in silence for a moment, then I enquired, 'What is the actual acreage sir?' 'I'm not absolutely certain,' came the reply, 'something over 500 in hand, plus Manor Farm, adjoining Round Hill, that's about another 240 acres. At the moment it is let, but I'm anxious to take it over as soon as possible – at least as soon as the current problems are straightened out. Once that happens I'd like to double, even treble the acreage in years to come.

We drew up in front of the house. It was the old farmhouse that had been renovated and made into a small but comfortable home. The Colonel ushered us into a long room that acted as both sitting room one end and dining room the other. He left us for a moment, but was back before father and I could exchange even a few words on what we'd seen. He waved towards armchairs and a comfortable-looking sofa. 'Sit down, make yourselves comfortable. Tea is on its way.' He looked at his watch. 'Right, I've about twenty minutes to tell you what I want and, most importantly what the job will involve and what I'll expect.' He then elaborated clearly on his plans for the future of the estate and what was entailed, which I was delighted to hear would include hunting at least one day a week. He paused for some seconds before going on. 'There's one rotten job that has to be done. Neither I, nor anyone else can carry surplus horses, for, before this war is over and I can assure you that will be several years hence, every possible acre will be required to produce food. There are at least five horses here surplus to requirements, which, sadly but inevitably, will have to be put down. These include a very useful point-to-point winner and two promising young steeplechasers which I had in training. The trainer was in the Territorials and, of course, had to join his unit when war was declared and so his yard closed down. I offered them to the army as Remounts, but they weren't interested. Said they were too light boned to make troopers, or pull a gun, but commandeered four of my best heavyweight hunters. Poor buggers, they'd have been better off left here and, if necessary, shot for hound meat. These bloody Whitehall halfwits make me sick. Their brains, that is if they have any, are still geared to 1914. Forcibly taking much loved friends, indeed pets in some instances, for the cavalry. Cavalry indeed! If they'd seen some of Hitler's Panzer divisions, as I have, they'd realise how totally ineffectual mounted troops would be. Anyway, be that as it may, these horses have to be put down. Actually, that was one of the reasons I fired the stable manageress, for I must have told her half-a-dozen times to get the job done. This doesn't mean I, in conjunction with all members of the MFH (Masters of Foxhounds) Association, am not going to keep hunting going, even if it has to be on a much, much smaller scale. After all what would be the point of fighting this wretched war, if part of it isn't to maintain our way of life, heritage and traditions? That bastard Hitler had already stopped hunting in Germany when I was over there. We'll have to keep things going with the minimum of staff and a lot of sweat, but we'll do it. That's about it. Oh yes, one thing more, my daughter from my previous marriage, Ethne, lives here. She's twenty-one and, at present, helps in the stables. My two younger daughters from my current marriage – Ethne's mother was killed in a car accident – Marguerite and Ann, plus nanny, together with Rose McKellar, wife of one of my co-directors and their two children are evacuated here for the duration, making quite a house full. Any questions?' The Colonel looked straight at me. He had insisted I sat opposite him whilst he was talking and never took his eyes off me the whole time he was doing so.

Father started to say something, but was quickly stopped. 'Sorry to seem rude Mr Twist, but it's your son I'm interviewing.' I hesitated for a few seconds and then replied, 'Yes sir, masses, but, as you have to go in a few minutes, I obviously can't. Therefore, it seems to me that there is little point, that is unless you are going to offer me the job.' Those steely eyes seemed to bore into me, but, with great difficulty, I held his gaze. It seemed like forever before he spoke. 'Yes, I am, on the condition your father will come to your aid, should you need it, for the first six months. After that you're on your own. Now any questions?'

'Yes, sir, you haven't mentioned salary, accommodation, or transport.' He looked thoughtful for a moment, before replying. 'Right, £250 per annum, to be reviewed after twelve months. You can have all your meals here at the house, but where you sleep is up to you. There is an empty cottage just down the road, where the stable manageress lived, but you can decide. I'm putting you in charge of my estate; having done that I don't expect to be worried by such detail. As far as transport is concerned, there's a Hillman that used to be Ethne's, but I gave her a 1.5 litre MG as a twenty-first birthday present, so you can look upon the Hillman as being the estate's car. Now, when can you start?'

'Any time, Monday if you like. My chief problem will be getting here.'

'No problem over that. I'll send a car and chauffeur to pick you up from your home at 1.00pm.' He paused for a moment, then went on, 'I've only one reservation about engaging you. Namely, will you be strong enough to sack men twice, even three times your age? Frequently, in industry, I find promising young executives who fall down over this.' I replied, 'Well if it's a case of their job or mine, then it really isn't an issue.' The Colonel smiled, got to his feet and said, 'We'll see. I must go. I'll notify Burrows that you'll be arriving on Monday and will be in charge of all sections. There's no doubt there's been too much fragmentation of authority up to now. I'll send you a letter, via the chauffeur, confirming your appointment and clearly stating that you have full authority to act as you see fit on my behalf. I will also enclose a letter to the manager of the bank in Aylesbury, authorising you to sign cheques up to £100 per day.' He looked me straight in the eye, smiled and held out his hand. 'Good luck. Make a success of things and your efforts won't go unrewarded. Cock things up and I'll fire you in much less time than I've taken to hire you.' At that moment the door opened and an attractive young girl walked in. The Colonel embraced her, 'Glad you're back, Ethne my dear, this is Michael Twist, who I've just appointed as agent-cum-farm manager. He will be in complete charge of everything on and to do with the estate. He starts on Monday and I'd appreciate it if you would give him all the support you can.' After a few quick pleasantries with Ethne, father and I left with the Colonel.

4. Realisation and Apprehension

We followed the Colonel up the road to Kimble village, the parish in which the estate was situated, where we turned right on to the main road for Princes Risborough. It was then that we realised how big a hurry my future boss must have been in, for in seconds he was out of sight. We continued in silence until father said 'Michael'. He never addressed me as such unless I'd done something that caused him annoyance, or worry, normally it was 'Mick'. In this case I think it was both! 'Michael, I'll give you all the support I can, but, quite honestly, I think by agreeing to go to Roundhill you've taken on more than you can chew. It might be different if it was a place running smoothly, but I would still think you would be too young even then. But the mess that place is in – well may God help you and believe me you'll need his help. What worries me is, that up to now, there have been about half-a-dozen people supposedly running the place, so they could all blame each other. But, as from Monday, there's going to be one person only – you, and that's where the buck will stop.'

I quietly thought over what father had said. There was no doubt that the euphoria which had overwhelmed me when the Colonel offered me the job was wearing off. In fact, the more I thought about what I was about to take on the more it diminished. After several minutes I turned to father and said, 'Yes, you are absolutely right and had I been given a few days to think about it the chances are I'd have chickened out. However, I wasn't. So if I can survive the initial first few weeks I think I've a good even-money chance of making a success of it. The actual farming, building up the herd etc doesn't worry me. It's all the clearing up that has to be done first, before getting down to serious business, which is the major concern. At least it seems I will be able to get on with the job without constantly having to refer things to the boss.'

The further I got away from Kimble, the more my confidence returned and by the time we reached home I was sure I'd made the right decision, but somewhat to my surprise I felt suddenly exhausted. But, exhausted or not, mother had to hear all the detail, during which she dispensed tea and home-made cake. Her main concern was my accommodation. She couldn't believe that the Colonel had simply said that, having given me the job and full responsibility for the running of the estate, the problem was mine, not his. I assured her that there was nothing to worry about and that I was going to phone Billy Oliver at Wendover to ask him to give me a bed for a few nights. His home could not be more than five miles from the estate. Then I told my parents I would phone Clive Haselden, following which I intended to have a very hot bath and relax.

I got hold of Billy, who was just in from a day's hunting with the Bicester, where he'd been trying a horse for one of his wealthier clients. He was in good form, delighted at my news and assured me that a bed would be no problem. He was a good friend and I told him of some of my worries. These he pooh-poohed, assured me that I was a born manager and had he not been so certain of this he would never have asked me to come to his rescue in mid-July 1938 when he had had major staff problems at two of his stables. The girl who he normally left in charge at a riding school had gone off with one of the male clients and whilst there were two or three stable staff, there was no one to organise rides, look after the money and various other matters involved in running a successful stable. I'd just started my summer break from Reading University and jumped at the chance. It had been a hectic four weeks, averaging over sixty rides a day and a laugh a minute, but very hard work. I protested that running a riding stable was very different to taking over the management of an MFH's estate and stables. Billy laughed at me, told me to stop being stupid and that he'd expect me in time for a meal on Monday evening. I then rang Clive, his congratulations were warm, but somewhat spoilt by him saying that he wondered if he'd acted hastily in putting me forward for the job. I replied that only time would tell, but then added, laughing, he'd better watch what he said in future, otherwise I might find another vet. Before he could reply I hung up and departed to soak in a really hot bath – something I have always found most relaxing.

Just before 7.00pm I joined my parents, declaring as I entered the room I'd go through to the larder and get a glass of perry. Father had a good friend in the pedigree livestock world, Stafford Western, who farmed in Herefordshire and made the most beautiful perry, a case of which he frequently sent to father. I was surprised when father said, 'No. Come with me.' We went through to the dining room, where he crossed to the sideboard, took a bottle of Dimple Haigue, his favourite tipple when he drank (which was seldom), out of the cupboard and picked up a 'fun' whisky glass mother had once given him. It had three gold coloured rings around it. The first one would have been a little in excess of a generous double and, at this point has a crowing cockerel painted on it. The next ring is about a third of the way up the glass and there, well portrayed, is a picture of a pig and finally, two-thirds of the way up from the bottom, a third ring and an excellent likeness of an ass. Father carefully filled the glass with whisky to the cockerel and then topped it up precisely to the ass with soda water and handed it to me. 'If you're going to do a man's job you may as well have a man's drink.' Smiling, he put his arm round my shoulder. He then said, 'But it doesn't change my opinion. The glass tells you that, but I'll do all I can to help you make a go of it.' I looked at the glass, as I had many times before, but it took a second for the penny to prop. Dad thought me cocky and an ass. I laughed, raised my glass. 'Cheers and thanks for your support.' I seldom drank whisky and didn't care for it greatly, but by the time I got just below the pig I began to feel mellow and definitely pleased with the outcome of the day's events.

After one of mother's excellent Welsh rarebits and fruit, we settled in front of the drawing-room fire. Just before the 9.00pm news on the wireless, father left the room. He returned minutes later bearing two glasses. He handed me one, saying, 'Get that down you before you go to bed. You'll sleep better for it.' He was right, for I was away in the land of Nod before 10.00pm and didn't stir until nearly 8.00am the next morning.

Sunday I spent packing what I thought I would need, which in actual fact was most of my clothes and a few of my favourite books, including several of the works of Kipling, with whom my maternal grandfather had been at school and in whose writings I could always find solace. The rest of my belongings could remain at Pound Cottage until I had settled into my new surroundings. Just before lunch I phoned Eric Guy, a well-known photographer of pedigree livestock, whom I had known for as long as I could remember. I told him of my new job and hoped that in the years to come I'd be in the position to ask him to photograph winners from the Roundhill herds as he had done for so many years with the winners at Burnham. However, before that day came could he visit the Roundhill estate later in the week to photograph some horses? He could and suggested Thursday which was fine by me. Father asked what my call was all about. My reply was that I wanted a record of the lovely horses which that bastard Hitler was responsible for sending to their death. It was going to be the toughest assignment of my new job.

5. The Moment of Truth

I arrived at Round Hill Farm early on the afternoon of Monday 3 March 1940. I had already been to Wendover to drop off my cases and various other belongings at Billy's house. Having thanked the chauffeur who had driven me over from Burnham, I walked slowly down the concrete road leading to the farm buildings, a thousand different thoughts racing around my brain. I had a plan, but before I could implement it there were several hurdles to get over and I was about to face the moment of truth when I would discover whether I was man enough for the job. If I was going to grapple successfully with the many problems that lay ahead I would have to assert my authority right from the start. I knew father had his doubts and mother's parting words – 'I'll keep your bed made up' – were not exactly encouraging.

I opened the wicket gate in the double doors and stepped through. I stopped and almost laughed out loud as I momentarily likened myself to a gladiator entering an arena in ancient Rome. In retrospect it wasn't a bad analogy, for I was about to start and fight for my job. I squared my shoulders, took a deep breath, turned left and entered the farm office. A young man looked round from where he was seated at a desk. 'Yes?' He looked inquiringly at me. 'I'm Mr Twist, your new boss and you must be Harrison.' The latter looked bewildered. Before he could speak I realised what had happened. 'Obviously you haven't heard from the Colonel, although he assured me that he would telephone you this morning.' I held up a hand as Harrison was about to speak, 'Hang on.' I delved into the folder delivered by the chauffeur and extracted a copy of my letter of authority from Colonel Devereux. Fortunately his secretary, Miss Moon, had done a number of carbon copies – all signed. I handed the letter to Harrison, 'You'd better keep that in case anyone queries my authority with you.' He read it, his face was a study, then he looked up, smiled broadly, stood up and held out his hand. 'Welcome, am I glad to see you. If it wasn't inevitable that I would be called up in the near future, I would have left. This place is and has been for months, utter chaos. Have you heard of Mr Jackson?' I nodded. 'Well he's my main bugbear. He seems to spend his days thinking up totally meaningless forms to be filled in weekly. There's over thirty of them. I've just …' He never finished whatever it was he was going to say, for the door opened and in walked a thickset man of medium height. He gave me a shrewd, but slightly quizzical look, 'Mr Twist?' 'Yes.' 'Well I'm Tom Burrows, supposedly the foreman, but I've had so many people overruling me of late that, frankly, I don't really know any longer what I'm supposed to be. The Colonel came down yesterday and called in to see me, in the afternoon, to tell me that, as from today, you'll be in charge of everything, for which I truly thank God. Welcome, sir, and the best of luck.' He grinned and held out his hand. As I took it he gave a chuckle, 'At least, from now on, we'll only have one boss, instead of half a dozen to cock things up.' I withdrew my hand. His grasp was akin to putting one's hand into a vice. His eyes never left mine. 'Thank you Burrows, but from now on cock-ups are going to be a rarity, not the norm as they certainly seem to have been.'

'That's the best news I've had for months and Tom if you don't mind sir. I was going to give my notice in this weekend, but when the Colonel told me you were coming I decided to wait and see what happened.'

'Well, Tom, I'll tell you what is going to happen. Between us we'll make this one of the leading agricultural estates in the county, hopefully in the country.' Harrison joined in the conversation, 'I was just telling Mr Twist about all the forms we have to fill in for Mr Jackson.' Tom Burrows gave a snort of derision, 'The man's mad. About the only thing we haven't got a form for is to record how many times a day an ole ewe farts when on turnips and that's only because we haven't any sheep. None of the advisers, I suppose I should say ex-advisers, were sheep men. I, on the other hand, as a Cumbrian hill farmer's son, am.' I looked at my watch. 'Right Tom, let's go.'

'Where?'

'Good question.' I hesitated for a moment. Then I

remembered a favourite saying of my old nanny, when I complained about having cabbage on my plate, but knew I would eventually have to face up to the horrible stuff and consume it – 'eat what you don't want first'. In other words get the worst part behind you. High on my agenda was to sack Prouse – the lazy, useless so-called pigman. I'd never sacked anyone in my life and I was not looking forward to it, but I was damned if I was going to have the Colonel say to me, 'I told you so.' The answer to Tom's question was clear – in nanny's phraseology I'd eat what I didn't want first. I smiled, 'Let's go and see Mr Prouse.' Tom grinned from ear to ear. 'You mean Pockets? That's what we call him, because his hands are never out of his and, when they are, it certainly isn't to do any work.'

I stopped as I reached the door and turned to Harrison, 'Have you any petty cash?'

'Yes, between £10 and £15.'

'Fine, that should be more than enough to make up a couple of weeks' wages for Prouse.' I turned to Tom, 'Do you know on what basis he's employed?'

'Yes, weekly, like the rest of us.'

'Good.' Both men looked at me obviously puzzled by my enquiry, though neither said a word. Just as I was going out through the door, Harrison stopped me. 'By the way, Tom usually takes me down to Kimble station to catch the 5.10pm to Aylesbury – that's where I live. If I miss that there's not another train until 7.20pm. Is that all right?'

'Of course, no problem. Come on Tom, let's go and see how many pigs have died since Saturday. I saw the Hillman parked outside when I arrived.' Minutes later we pulled up at the entrance to the food store, there wasn't a sound – not a grunt, not a squeal. The piggery was like a morgue. Perhaps it was. Perhaps all the poor wretched pigs were dead. Tom slid back the door leading into the store. There, just inside, was a man seated at a high old-fashioned desk, on an equally high stool, busily writing.

'Jack, this is Mr Twist, our new governor.' Tom turned to me, 'This is Jack Bonner. He looks after the grinding and making up of the rations for the pigs, but most of his time is spent filling in forms for Mr Jackson.'

I said hullo and then enquired, 'How long does that take?' Bonner looked thoughtful, then replied, 'Normally, several hours a day. I have to keep a record, to the nearest pound if you please, of how much meal goes out each day to sows with litters. How much to sows and gilts in-pig. How much to weaners and finally how much to fatteners. If there's more than a 2$^{1}/_{2}$% variance from day to day, his nibs wants to know why and he kicks up hell if he doesn't receive an immediate answer in detail.' He gave a wry smile. 'But thankfully it can't be for much longer the rate the poor brutes are dying.' I looked at him for a minute, trying to size him up. He didn't look like a farmworker. I leaned forward, took the sheet with its neatly filled columns of figures off the old desk, glanced at it and tore it in half. Bonner jumped down off his stool, 'Hey, what the hell …', but I stopped him before he could say more. 'It's all right. As from today Mr Jackson has ceased to have anything to do with the estate. Do you know where the head pigman is?' Bonner looked slightly puzzled. Tom cut in, 'Mr Twist means Pockets.'

'Oh him. Last I saw he was going into No. 1 fattening house. No doubt he'll be sitting on his backside, doing nothing as usual.'

He was right. Tom and I entered the section of the piggery that Bonner had named and there, halfway down the long building was Mr Prouse, happily sitting on the front edge of the feeding trough, hands in pockets, legs stretched out across the centre passage, leaning comfortably back against the tubular bars, which were set so they sloped inwards, with a bag of hay or straw making a comfortable back rest. A cigarette hung from the corner of his mouth. Tom, who was leading, turned and winked at me. 'Hullo Pockets, busy as usual I see. This is Mr Twist, our new boss.' Prouse gave me an insolent look, but made no attempt to move. I passed Tom and stood in front of the reclining pigman. He ignored me and addressed Tom, 'He bloody well ain't mine.' He spat with great deliberation, just missing the toe of my shoe. Quietly I said, 'Stand up, take your hands out of your pockets and put that cigarette out. You know smoking is not allowed in the buildings. Now, on your feet and you address me as sir.' I could feel my heart racing. Prouse neither moved nor looked at me, but spat again, hitting me squarely on the ankle. I could feel his disgusting spittle soaking through my sock. That did it, for with a roar, of which I'm sure my old RSM would have been envious, I leaned forward and yanked him to his feet and before he knew it he was outside the building. I pointed at the gate, 'Out. You're fired, as from this minute, now go.' He started to say something about my not being able to fire him. I moved towards him, 'Out. Burrows will bring you this week's wages and a week in lieu of notice later this afternoon.' As I took a further step towards him, he fled. Tom was doubled up laughing but eventually he gasped, 'That was great, the best thing that's happened around here for months. I've been longing to do that ever since the lazy bugger got put in here six months ago. I tell you what, sir, that's the fastest I've ever seen him move.'

Suddenly I realised my heart had stopped racing and the butterflies had miraculously left my stomach. I felt good. I was over the first obstacle. Further, in under an hour of taking over the reins I was fairly confident I had a valued ally in Tom Burrows. Still chuckling he said 'I think we should go and find Jerry – Jerry Whelan, Pockets' helper. He's as thick as two planks. Well, he'd have to be to put up with what he has for the last five or six months, but he's a real hard-working chap when he knows what he should be doing.'

'Right, but firstly is there a tap around here? Tom looked slightly surprised, 'Yes, just inside the door, but why?'

'So I can rinse my sock. I'd sooner it was damp from clean water than Prouse's disgusting spit.'

Ten minutes later Tom and I set off across the fields towards Little Marsh, having first had a chat with Jerry. From him I learned that since Saturday just over 300 more pigs of various sizes had died. Most were piglets and weaners, but a score or more of baconers and two in-pig sows had succumbed as well. I told Jerry that I had sacked Prouse and he had finished. I went on to tell him he would have to manage the best he could until I got things sorted. He shrugged his shoulders, almost smiled and said that as far as

Pockets was concerned he had never started, so it really wouldn't make any difference to him.

Tom told me when we moved from land which was part of Marsh Hill Farm and on to that which went with Little Marsh. In several places I picked some up and rubbed it between my fingers. It seemed good friable soil which, I thought should be easy to work. He took me to what had once been a farmyard, now overgrown with weeds. There was a big barn that looked reasonably sound and a few ramshackle sheds, which certainly weren't, plus a big pile of rubble which had once been the farmhouse. We headed on through a small paddock towards an old meadow. Tom told me it was sixteen acres and he had instructions to get it ploughed and ready for spring wheat. I looked at Tom, 'That's leaving it pretty late isn't it?' Tom nodded, 'I know – but, until now, it's been a case of mine not to reason why and do what I was told. I sent the tractor driver down with the plough about an hour before lunch.' By this time we had entered the field. I took one look. Tractor driver the man might well be, but ploughman he most certainly wasn't! I had seldom, if ever, seen a worse job. I turned to Tom. 'That's the most amateurish bit of ploughing I've ever seen. He's not even turning the sod over and has obviously made no attempt to set the plough. Wherever have all these morons come from? I could have done a better job by the time I was ten. What's his name?'

'Swaine. His dad works here. A real good old-fashioned farm labourer, can turn his hand to anything, but has no time for his son. A sentiment I fully subscribe to. He doesn't know his job, is a bad timekeeper and nearly as lazy as Pockets. He wasn't engaged by me, but by the farmer who has been advising the Colonel and who won't hear a word against his protégé. He's useless.' The tractor reached the headland, the driver tripping the plough as it did so. Tom signalled him to stop, then introduced me, as Swaine climbed down off the hard iron seat. I noticed he hadn't even bothered to stuff a sack with hay, or straw, to make it more comfortable.

'Done much ploughing?' I enquired. I received a surly look before he replied, 'Fair bit, but I don't see it's any business of yours.'

'Ah, but that's where you're wrong. What Tom hasn't told you is that I'm your new boss and, so there is no misunderstanding, when you address me you say sir.'

'Will I hell. I'm not taking orders from the likes of you.'

'Please yourself. You've two options, do as I say, or if you won't then you're fired.' Swaine glared at me. 'You can stuff yer job.'

'Fine. Take the tractor back up to Marsh Hill and Burrows will bring you your money and cards.'

'Take it back yerself, I'm off.' With that he turned and set off across the field. I looked at Tom, who was grinning like the proverbial Cheshire cat. 'Where's he off to?'

'He lives only a few fields away at Bishopstone. If you don't mind my saying so, you're doing well.' He pulled a watch out of the breast pocket of his jacket and glanced at it. 'You haven't been here two hours yet, but you've already got rid of the two laziest so-and-sos it's ever been my misfortune to meet. I tell you what, there won't half be some chat at The Prince of Wales tonight.' As he talked Tom unhitched the plough. 'Jump aboard and I'll drive us up to Marsh Hill.' On the way Tom explained that The Prince of Wales was the local pub and the centre point, well really the only point, for socialising in and around Marsh. It was the only place to buy fags, baccy, beer and, until recently, chocolate, other than at Kimble, which was about two-and-a-half miles away.

6. The Last Straw

I slumped into Harrison's chair – whilst physically very fit, I felt utterly and completely drained. Had this not been the case, I would have been overjoyed by the progress I had made in such a short time, but, it seemed, problems did not come singly at Roundhill. On the way back to Marsh Hill Tom had told me there was no one left on the staff who could drive a tractor other than himself. Several of the old hands could plough with horses – the snag was there was only one horse, an old Shire mare, Smiler, but, even had there been another horse, there was no horse plough. This was an additional and unexpected problem that I didn't really want on top of the many others. As soon as Tom dropped me off at the office, I put a call through to *Farmers Weekly*. The editor was a good friend of my father and, although, officially, it was too late to get an advertisement into the forthcoming issue, after I had told him of my predicament he agreed to bend the rules and have one put in for me for a tractor driver. Having done this I went off around the yard to find Ron Chamberlain, the head herdsman.

He had obviously heard of my arrival from Tom Burrows, but I could hardly describe his greeting as cordial. It quickly came to light that he too was considering leaving. In fact it was the first thing he told me – he'd had enough of the flaming milking machine. There had been nothing but trouble from the moment it was installed. Three times he'd insisted that an 'expert' from the manufacturer should be present during milking to point out what they were doing wrong. He could find no fault with the way it was being used, but, Chamberlain assured me, they kept getting case after case of mastitis. He perked up considerably when I told him that the sale of the milking machine was high on my list of priorities. It was then that he dropped a real bombshell. The farmer who had been overseeing the herd and farming in general had, three weeks previously, bought twelve in-calf non-pedigree Shorthorn heifers, due to calve around the end of

April, at what, Ron said, appeared to be a knock-down price. The previous Friday, the day before I met the Colonel, one had aborted her calf, another followed suit on Sunday and another one that morning. He'd called in the new vet, Clive Haselden, who had taken samples to send away for testing, but had said that, short of a miracle, it had to be Contagious Abortion, in those days something feared by all dairy farmers. Fortunately, it seemed the heifers had been kept totally isolated from the main herd and except for what had been sent away for testing, the three aborted foetuses had been buried in the field and well covered in quicklime. Further, a tub of strong disinfectant had been placed at the entrance to the field for Ron, who was the only person going near the heifers, to dip his rubber boots in every time he left the field. I knew that all had been done that could be done until we heard from Clive but I had no doubt what the answer would be. We had been standing in the food store at the end of the cowshed. As we talked I started to walk down past the milking machine to where the pedigree cows, well bedded, stood, or lay, in their standings, contentedly munching hay. I stopped opposite a well-made roan cow, turned to Ron and said, 'Now that's my idea of a Dairy Shorthorn, Greattew Barrington 2nd isn't it? How's she doing?' I recognised the animal as I had admired her greatly when she won her class as a heifer at the London Dairy Show a couple of years earlier. Ron visibly relaxed. 'You know her?' I smiled, 'Oh yes and I know her breeder, Ralph Tustan from Great Tew in Oxfordshire. My father has known him for years and I was born on the neighbouring farm to his.' I looked at my watch. I didn't particularly want to know the time, but now Chamberlain had somewhat mellowed I thought it best to leave him to think things over. 'Right, I must get on. I've a lot of phoning to do and, Ron, don't worry. Between us we'll get everything straightened out.' His 'goodnight' was considerably friendlier than his greeting half-an-hour earlier had been. He was obviously an above-average herdsman, I only had to look at the animals in his care to appreciate that and such men were hard to come by.

Before he left for the station Harrison had told me that

Miss Ethne had called at the office and left a message – would I please call at the house before I went. However, before that I had much thinking and phoning to do. I was relaxing for a few moments, quietly mulling things over in my mind and slowly filling my pipe when there was a knock on the door and Bob Hitchcock entered. I hadn't actually met him, but he had been pointed out to me on Saturday by the Colonel. 'Sorry to disturb you sir, but will you be riding out tomorrow morning?' I laughed, 'Not a hope I'm afraid, but, subject to there being no major crisis, I hope to spend an hour or so with you on Wednesday. However, if there are any problems in the stables let me know at once. Actually I'm glad you called in. I've arranged for a very good photographer to come on Thursday to take photos of the poor unfortunate horses that have to die, thanks to Hitler. It's a horrible gruesome business, but, as the Master rightly said, this war isn't going to end quickly and, much as we love them, the horses will have to make way for fields of corn. It may be a bit bizarre but I felt there should be some small reminder of them, they didn't start this war poor devils.' Hitchcock looked grim, then said, 'I think it's a nice gesture, sir, for it is surely the slaughter of the innocent. But I'd sooner they were shot here, than taken off for the army, possibly to be blown to bits, or wounded as four of them have been. I'll have them looking their best. Goodnight, sir.' He stopped at the door, 'May I wish you well. I'm afraid you've a big job ahead of you.' With that he left.

Twice I reached out towards the phone, preparatory to twiddling the handle to call the Stoke Mandeville exchange, the same one that Clive Haselden was on, to put a call through to father. Twice I thought better of it. He'd agreed to come to my rescue if I needed help, but to me that meant a situation arising to which I didn't know the answer. I knew the answers to my immediate problems. The question was: did I have the courage to implement them? If I was to succeed the answer had to be 'yes'. Finally I picked up the phone, gave a good brisk turn to the handle that rang the exchange and picked up the receiver. A girl's voice answered, 'Number please.' I gave Clive's. The telephonist replied, 'You're in luck, he's just got home. You must be Mr Twist,

welcome to Kimble. I'm Renee Allen ...' She got no further as
I heard Clive answer his phone. I immediately started to tell
him what I had in mind, but he cut me short, 'Hang on a
minute. Renee get off the line.' There was a giggle and a click.
'Right, now fire ahead.' After a short chat about what I had
achieved so far, I learnt that if anything was of a private
nature, then one should always make sure Renee wasn't
listening. I then arranged to meet Clive at the piggery at
10.30am the following morning, together, if he could fix it at
such short notice, with the local Ministry of Agriculture's vet.
It was, I told Clive, my intention to send what pigs were fit for
human consumption for immediate slaughter and get rid of
the remainder to any knackermen who would take them.

I then called a good friend of my father's, Arthur Saunders,
with whose sons I had been at school. Amongst his several
interests he owned a number of butcher's shops. I told him
of my problem over the non-pedigree heifers. Having listened
to me, he laughed and said he had no doubt he could solve
my problem, providing I was not as hard to do a deal with as
my father. He arranged to meet me at Round Hill Farm at
9.00am on Wednesday, to take a look at the heifers.

Having taken these decisions, it was though a vast weight
had been lifted from my shoulders. It had just turned six
when I groped my way out of the office, for it was pitch dark.
With the aid of a couple of matches I found the car where
Tom had left it and drove across to the house. Again with the
aid of matches, I found the front door and rang the bell.
Within seconds the door opened and, thanks to a chink of
light escaping through the curtains across the double swing
doors leading into the main hall, I was just able to see it was
Ethne Devereux. 'Good evening Miss Devereux. You wanted
to see me?'

'For goodness sake, what's this Miss Devereux business?
I'm Ethne and I hope you're Michael.'

'Yes, of course.'

'Right, now that's settled come and meet the family.' I
followed her through into the room where the Colonel had
interviewed me only just over forty-eight hours before. It
seemed like light years ago! Sitting on the settee were two

little girls and a small boy, whilst in the armchair, where I had sat on Saturday, was an attractive blonde, at a guess in her late thirties, busily knitting. It was to her that Ethne first spoke. 'Rose, this is Michael Twist. Michael this is Rose McKellar.' Then with a grin she added, 'Our evacuees from Richmond and, sitting with my two young sisters, is her son Ramsay. Come on you two, move yourselves and come and shake hands with Michael.' Ethne formally introduced them. Marguerite, the elder of the two, had large sensitive and beautiful brown eyes, whilst Ann was from every aspect her father's daughter. She came forward immediately, hand outstretched and looking me straight in the eye, said, 'Daddy's going to buy me a pony and he says you're going to teach me to ride.' I smiled as I bent down and solemnly shook hands. 'Of course I will, just as soon as you get your pony.' At that moment the door opened and Nanny Hurst entered. Ethne introduced us, then Nanny called, 'Come along children, your supper's ready in the nursery.' Smiling at me she shepherded her flock from the room. Meanwhile Ethne had moved across the room to a drinks cabinet; turning she enquired, 'Whisky? I think you must be in need of one from what I've heard. Amongst other things, I gather you have already fired that awful man Pockets.' I must have looked surprised, for she laughed and added, 'News travels fast around here. Sit down, you must be exhausted. I'll bring it over to you. Same for you Rose?'

It was about a quarter to seven when I left, still feeling drained, but much more relaxed and much more knowledgeable about the estate than I had been an hour before. It was just before 7.00pm when I pulled up in front of The Red Lion hotel in Wendover and almost ran into the nearest bar to buy a packet of cigarettes as I knew Billy Oliver would be waiting to have his evening meal, which he normally liked to have at 7.00pm. I couldn't have been gone three minutes, but it was long enough for someone to have stolen the car! I couldn't believe it and ran up and down the road to make sure I hadn't parked it somewhere else, but, no, it was gone. I couldn't have locked it, even had I wanted to, for, like many pre-war cars, it wasn't fitted with a door lock.

There was an ignition key of a sort, but any small flattened piece of metal would suffice to switch on the engine. I was both mortified and furious as I walked down the street and round the corner to the police station. My mood was not improved when I reported the theft. The sergeant just laughed. 'Don't worry, sir, it'll turn up in the morning. It's almost a 100 per cent certainty that some of the lads from Horton RAF Camp will have borrowed it for the evening. On the whole they're a grand lot of boys, they've probably gone into Aylesbury – it often happens. I'll phone you at Mr Oliver's as soon as I have any news for you. I'd bet any money it'll turn up in the morning, parked somewhere up by the camp.'

Soon after 6.00am Billy woke me from a deep sleep, he was already dressed. The sergeant had phoned, the Hillman had been found, as he predicted, close to the camp and, when I'd collected it, would I please call at the station and let him know if all was well. I dressed hastily and Billy drove me up to the camp. There was my car, windows closed, parked on the grass verge. When I opened the door I found a note on the driver's seat. It read, 'Thanks for the loan. We had a great evening. Have siphoned some petrol out of one of His Majesty's lorries and filled up your tank. Hope this makes up for any inconvenience caused.' A grand lot of boys they may well have been, indeed, even thoughtful boys, but the evening before, after the day I'd had, their nicking the Hillman had been the last straw to a day I will never forget.

7. Unparalleled Inspiration

It was Saturday morning, the week had flown by and it had certainly been a momentous time. In fact it had been a week I would never forget. All the pigs had gone by Thursday afternoon, those passed by the Ministry vet for human consumption, the remainder collected by a series of knackermen from around the county and one even from Oxfordshire.

The twelve heifers affected with Contagious Abortion, confirmed on Tuesday by the laboratory where Clive had sent a sample for testing, had been sold, at a profit to the butcher, Arthur Saunders. Apart from Pockets and Swaine, the so-called tractor driver, the staff had been reduced by a further four. I had found them, around 11.00am on Thursday morning, playing cards around a fire which they had lit in the centre of the barn at Little Marsh, only two or three yards away from tons of straw.

On the plus side, as far as labour was concerned, luck had been with me. A very experienced tractor driver, Smith, who fortunately was single, had arrived at the farm office that morning, soon after 9.00am, complete with luggage and excellent references. Having interviewed him, I asked him to wait outside. I rang Renee at the telephone exchange, gave her the names and addresses of Smith's two most recent employers and asked her to see if she could get them on the phone for me. This she did, fortunately both were in and spoke highly of Smith, saying how sorry they had been to lose his services. Further, that there didn't seem to be any reason for his leaving. One suggested that it was because he had spent a number of years in Australia and had worked with Aborigines on various sheep stations, the latter having a habit of suddenly going 'walkabout' and possibly Smith had caught the habit off them. Whatever the reason he had left his previous jobs I decided to take him on and called him back into the office. Accommodation was no problem, for he could live at the Bonners', who occupied the cottage adjoining the one Prouse had had at Marsh Hill. They had a spare room and had been told by the local authority that if it was not needed for a farmhand they would have to take a couple of evacuees. I explained to Smith about his lodgings and also about the ploughing that urgently had to be done. When could he start? The reply was as soon as he could change into working clothes and he didn't mind doing overtime on Sunday. At that moment Tom Burrows appeared. I introduced Smith and Tom took over. I saw Tom later in the morning and asked how Smith was getting on. His reply was great, then he laughed, 'The clutch on that International tractor of ours is a bit sharp and when he let it in it jumped forward. Old Joe Swaine was there and said 'Him's sudden.' From that day on Smith was known as Sudden. It was as well that I took him on, for he was the only applicant I had from the advertisement – an indication of the rapidly dwindling pool of skilled agricultural workers.

I looked at my watch, it was just coming up to 10.00am. Reluctantly I got up from the desk in the farm office, where I'd been signing letters Harrison had typed the previous evening. Wishing him a pleasant weekend, I left the office. With a heavy heart, I made my way across the road to the stables where I was about to implement the Colonel's instructions, as repulsive to him as they were to me – namely putting down five beautiful, healthy horses, all in the prime of life. Sickening as it was it was unavoidable, for food for humans took precedence over sentimentality. Sadly it was a tragic and regular happening, at that time, throughout the country. It is impossible for the millions of Britons born after the war to appreciate even vaguely the situation as it was in 1940, and the even worse years that were to follow.

The five condemned horses were either in the field just behind the stables, or actually stabled. I had arranged that one should go to the hunt kennels as hound meat every fifth day. There was no alternative. I gathered from Bob that the girl who had been in charge of the stables had even advertised them as being free to a good and approved home, but everyone was in a similar situation. It was a ghastly nightmare that had to be faced by many hundreds of horse lovers. Bob Hitchcock was waiting for me in the yard. He looked grey and drawn. I had told him earlier what was going to happen and, like so many good stockmen, whatever they cared for, their charges were akin to children. I saw that the truck used for collecting carcasses had arrived from the kennels and was parked in the back driveway to the stables. Johnson, the only young groom remaining who had not been called up, stood quietly by, ashen and looking physically sick. Bob cleared his throat. 'Which one sir?' I reached into the pocket of my jacket and took out five pieces of folded paper.

'Take off your cap Bob and lend it to me for a minute.' Obviously puzzled by my request he did as I asked. I took it, dropping the five bits of paper into it. Turning to Johnson I said, 'Right, draw each piece out singly and call out the name.' After a moment's hesitation he did as I bid. He unfolded the first one and gave a gasp. Tears started to roll down his cheeks. I looked at him, 'Well?' His reply was a little more that a whisper, 'Prince – Stormont Prince. Oh God, not him. I've cared for him ever since he came into the yard. He's such a character and there isn't an ounce of vice in him. Why should he die because of those bloody Nazis?' Stormont Prince was a lovely thoroughbred gelding, brought over from Ireland some eighteen months previously. He had won point-to-points and had great potential as a steeplechaser.

In silence we finished the draw, a draw for a longer life, be it only measured in days. Feeling as sick as the proverbial parrot, I said, 'I'm as sorry as you both are, but it's got to be done. Which of you is going to fetch him?' Johnson, without saying a word, went into the feedroom, collected a bowl of oats, a headcollar from the tackroom and, tears streaming down his face, led Prince across the yard. Clive Haselden drove up and minutes later the whole gruesome business was over – at least for a further five days. Johnson, sobbing like a child, turned to me and, with difficulty, said 'I'd like to take Tuesday morning off sir. I want to go into the recruiting office in Aylesbury and join up. I'm not waiting for call-up papers. I want a chance to avenge poor old Prince's death and God help any German I get in my sights.' Within days he was gone and, after initial training, quickly transferred to the paratroops. He saw a great deal of action, but came through the war unscathed. He visited us once when on leave, proudly wearing his red beret. I asked him how he was getting on. He gave a low and somewhat grim laugh, before replying. 'OK. At least I've avenged poor old Prince's death a fair few times. I told him that his job would be there for him when the war was over, but he shook his head. 'No thanks. After Prince I'll never work with horses again.'

As the kennel truck drove away, Clive and I walked towards the house. At the end of the stable yard, a path led to the drive and straight across to the house. Clive stopped as we neared this and pointed to where there was a recess in the wall, forming a porch, to the left of which was a toilet and ahead a room about twelve feet square, that was used for keeping riding boots and valeting hunting clothes. To the right of the opening was a loose box. Two men were busy knocking a hole from the porch through into this. 'What's happening?' Clive looked inquiringly at me.

'I'm turning the valeting room into an office. I must have somewhere to work, interview people, somewhere that is a bit private. The office over at the farm is too small, there's hardly room for a second chair. The loose box I'm having converted into a bedroom. It's only a few yards across the drive to the house and there are all toilet facilities in the downstairs loo – shower, everything. It's essential I live on the estate and, as I'm having all my meals in the house, virtually living there, except for sleeping, this seemed the obvious answer. I'm certainly not going to use the empty cottage down the road, where the stable manageress lived, just to accommodate my bed – I'll need that for staff. The small loose box round the back, by the hay store, I'm converting into a boot room.' Clive raised an eyebrow.

'Have you discussed this with the Colonel?'

'No. He's given me written authority to get on and straighten out the place and when he engaged me he told me where I lived was my problem.' I laughed, 'He, also, said most forcibly, that if I mess things up he'll kick my backside out through the gate.' It was Clive's turn to laugh. 'He probably would too, quite likely literally if you really upset him.' He told me last hunting season that he'd twice been the runner up for the light heavyweight ABA championship. Did you ever hear about the fight he had with the farmer, who used to be at Meadacre Farm, a few years ago?' I had. It was widely known and, indeed, acclaimed. It appeared that before the Colonel became Joint Master with Captain Stanley Barratt, hounds were in full cry and ran straight across Meadacre.The field was blocked by the farmer who owned it and his son, at the main entrance, brandishing a four-pronged dung fork. It was impossible to jump into the adjoining field, as the roadside hedge had a barbed wire guard fence on the inside. Everyone went galloping off up the road to find a way round, except Dev. He stopped behind and told the farmer he'd become a right miserable bugger. What was wrong, for he'd always been very pro the hunt? Things had become very heated. Finally the farmer told the Colonel that if he'd get down off his horse, instead of skulking on its back like a bloody coward, he'd soon straighten him out. Dev quickly obliged, throwing the reins of his horse to the boy, telling him to hold it as the two men began to exchange blows – although it was a very one-sided exchange. Devereux's skill was far too great for the farmer to cope with, for in seconds he had a bloody nose and a cut over one eye. The latter, realising he was outclassed, is said to have let out a roar like an enraged bull and charged his adversary, bringing him crashing to the ground.

The farmer's wife had seen the fracas from the house and came running down the drive, shouting at the two men to stop. Once she arrived on the spot she quickly ended the rough and tumble, ordering them to stop behaving like a couple of overgrown schoolboys. She insisted that the Colonel came back to the house to get cleaned up and, at the same time, told her husband she would deal with him later. Over what appears to have been an almost mandatory cup of tea, well laced with whisky, Dev discovered what was the trouble. Apparently the farmer had grazed two horses the previous summer for a man who claimed to be a member of the hunt. However, when he collected his horses he did not pay for their keep, some £60, claiming he'd forgotten his cheque book but promised to post a cheque as soon as he got home. In spite of numerous letters the farmer had not received any money. Dev took the offender's name and address, who it turned out was a member of an adjoining hunt, not the Old Berkeley, but in the meantime paid the farmer in full. From that stage on the account of the event seemed to vary, but broadly, Dev having put his horse in a loose box and thrown a rug over it, the two men did considerable damage, in the course of the next half to three-quarters of an hour, to what remained in the whisky bottle. It almost goes without saying that the farmer became as strong a supporter of the hunt, as he had been before the problem of the grazing fee.

When we reached the front door I asked Clive, 'Are you coming in for a minute? I don't know about you, but I could do with a dram. I know it's very early, but I truly feel sick over what we've just had to do – the ghastly thing is that we've got to face a similar ordeal four more times. A small one for medicinal purposes?' Clive hesitated for a moment, looked at his watch and then said, 'Why not? I must say, as I pulled the trigger, I wished that it had been Hitler's forehead the barrel had been pressed against, instead of that poor ruddy horse.' As we entered the house I remarked, 'I'm going home soon after lunch and will stay the night. After this last week I could do with a little quiet relaxation and a bit of a lie-in tomorrow morning.' As we were crossing the hall, the door opened from the living room and Ethne appeared. She greeted Clive warmly, then turned to me. 'I'm glad you've come in. I was just about to go looking for you. My old man's just been on the phone. He'll be down for lunch and, unbelievably for these days, he's staying over the weekend and hunting on Monday. He told me to tell you the main point of his coming down today is because he wants a full report on your first week in charge and there is much he wants to discuss with you. Further, I am to tell you that, had you made any plans for the rest of today and tomorrow, you had better cancel them.' Inwardly I cursed, but there was nothing I could do about it and, if I was honest, I wouldn't have dared to go against his wishes anyway.

Just before 12.30pm the Bentley drew up at the front door. The Colonel was accompanied by his wife Dorothy, a delightful lady, who greeted me warmly. Sherry was dispensed liberally before lunch by my boss and there was much general chat. When I started to say something about the estate, he raised a hand and said, 'Later.' Over lunch the talk was mostly about hunting, from which emerged the fact that I was to hunt on Monday and ride a quality 17hh heavyweight, The Priest, bought for the Colonel by the girl who had been running the stables. He was jet black, hence his name. He had a deep-seated predisposition to buck at the most unlikely moment and, when he had a go he meant business. I had ridden him twice during the week and, the second time, he'd nearly caught me napping as we were entering the stable yard after nearly two hours exercise, when he decided it was time I dismounted. He wasn't successful, but it was a close thing. Ethne told me he was not averse to kicking a hound if it came within range. Hardly a suitable mount for an MFH!

Lunch over, the Colonel announced to one and all that he had much to discuss with me and wished us to be left alone in the sitting room as he had no study at the farm. This gave me a great opening to tell him what I was doing with the valeting room and the adjoining loose box. He nodded, 'That makes sense, now tell me what you've been up to. Sit over there.' He waved me to the chair on the opposite side of the hearth to where he was already seated. With difficulty I started as from the moment of my arrival, becoming more fluent and positive as I warmed to my account of the week's happenings. He listened without interruption, but those steely grey-green eyes held my gaze the entire time I was talking. I finished by telling him we were abysmally short of machinery to work the land as it should be.

When I stopped my boss sat eyeing me silently. It must have been nearly two minutes before he spoke. They were the longest two minutes of my life – it seemed like eternity. By the time Dev did speak I was panicking, certain I was going to get my backside kicked out through the gate. Then he gave a deep chuckle and smiled broadly. 'Well done. You've achieved a hell of a lot more in a week than I had ever hoped for in several months. Now, before I tell you my ideas and what I want in the future, I've a few questions for you. You've quite rightly got rid of Prouse and the pigs. What are you going to do about replacing him? Experienced workers, in all fields, are becoming increasingly difficult to come by. So, whilst I accept Prouse was worse than useless, where do you think you'll find a really knowledgeable pigman. What do you propose doing?'

'I've already done it. No, correction, that's not 100 per cent true. I have Fred Goodchild, who was head pigman for father for many years at Burnham, coming for an interview on Tuesday. Really it's only a formality to let his wife see the cottage, which I know is vastly superior to anything they've had before. I've offered Fred more money than he's getting at the moment and I know he's not happy where he is at present. So, as I have said, I think an interview is purely a formality.' 'Good. What about restocking?'

'Oh, I've that all in hand, subject to your approval ...' Laughing, the Colonel interrupted, 'I'm glad I'm going to be consulted. Carry on, tell me your plans.' I felt a bit embarrassed, almost blushing. 'As I said, subject to your agreeing, I propose starting a herd of Large Whites and one of Berkshires. My idea, once Goodchild is installed, is to buy top-quality in-pig gilts and, of course, suitable boars, one of each breed to start with. I intend to pen them over some of the rougher grassland before ploughing it, as we undoubtedly will have to, housing them in portable pig arks and leaving the piggeries empty, having thoroughly scoured them out with a strong solution of washing-soda, for six months. By so doing there will be no fear of reinfection. The vet from the Ministry said two to three months would be enough, but, if you're agreeable, it's better to be safe than sorry.'

The Colonel nodded. 'Sounds fine to me. Now what about staff?'

'Land Girls ...' I got no further, for the door opened and Dorothy Devereux entered. Smiling, she said, 'Time's up, you two can stop nattering. It's nearly a quarter to five and Rose and I want our afternoon tea and Verna (the cook/general) has made some of her delicious scones you enjoy so much.' Her husband stood up and smiled at her, 'So do I and I dare say Michael could do with a cup too.' He turned to me, 'While the girls are bringing in the tea, slip out to the stable and tell Hitchcock I will be riding tomorrow morning at 7.30am and I'll want you to come with me. It should be light enough by then.' With that he turned his attention to Ann, who'd come rushing into the room, showering him with questions as to when he was going to keep his promise and buy her a pony. Inwardly I cursed, I had been looking forward to a least a Sunday morning lie-in, for with the exception of Tuesday, when I'd slept through my alarm, I'd been up every morning at 5.00am, but this was not to be.

Fortunately the morning was fine and not too cold. Not that the latter would have made much difference, as the Colonel set a cracking pace, with much cantering and a fair amount of jumping. Where we went I had no idea, but certainly our ride wasn't confined to the estate. However, we circled round coming back on to the estate at the far end of Marsh Hill Farm. As we rode through the old farmyard Dev reined his horse to a halt. Turning he enquired, 'What do you know about grass drying?'

'You mean haymaking?'

'No, I do not mean haymaking. I mean drying young, high-protein grass, when still very green, with hot air, up around 420°F, or even a bit higher.' I must have looked completely mystified before replying. 'Frankly, nothing. It was never mentioned or even referred to at university. I think I did see something about it in *Farmers Weekly*, but didn't pay much attention to it.'

'Well you should have. It may surprise you to learn that you will shortly have the opportunity to become one of the country's leading experts on the subject. Before you ask how, I'll tell you. I bought a company, some months ago, Templewood Engineering. They produced a rotary drier about a year ago, undoubtedly the best in the country. Actually, there is only one other available, which is a tray drier made by ICI. However, it can't compare with the Templewood, which is vastly superior. Proof of this is that

Colonel Pollitt, who farms in Shropshire and is head of ICI's agricultural division, installed one in time to have it fully operational at the beginning of last July. I've already asked him if I could send someone up to study his methods, when he starts up at the beginning of May. You now will be that someone. Incidentally, I didn't buy the factory for the purpose of producing driers, it will have a far more important role to play in the war effort, but we will still produce driers for specific orders. I'm confident there will be a great demand for high-quality dried grass, at least throughout the war years and a good number after it is over. The carotene content together with the protein is what determines the price, particularly the former, which Bertelli, the managing director of Templewood, tells me is and will be even more so in the future, extracted for medical purposes, the remainder being utilised in animal feeding stuffs. The biggest problem will be a building to house the drier. What is needed is something akin to an oversized Dutch barn, a bit higher, but at least double the width. The actual drying area needs to be roofed, but must be open on three sides. The fourth has to be closed forming one wall of the milling and storage area. A vast amount of steam is generated through the drying process and, of course, has to be able to escape. Steel, as no doubt you know, is unobtainable except for arms, shipping and projects absolutely essential to the war effort. The roof will want to be of corrugated iron sheeting. which is equally in short supply and virtually impossible to come by. Largely because it has been and still is being used for constructing Anderson air-raid shelters. So, Michael, that's something for you to think and, indeed, worry about.'

'Me?'

'Yes, you. I told you that anyone who works in a managerial position for me does just that. I don't do it for them and if they don't they are out. I have a drier reserved at the factory and want it installed and working, at the latest, by the end of the summer. All things are possible, but I admit on this occasion I've given you a tough nut to crack.'

The horse I was riding was a real fidget and, while the Colonel had been talking, had turned round, resulting in my facing not only my boss, but, also, back along the way we'd come, past the old farm buildings. The Colonel's words had really shaken me, for it seemed as though he was asking the impossible, which I thought, frankly, was bloody unfair. If he, one of the top industrialists in the country, didn't know where to obtain the required material, how the hell did he expect me to? Suddenly, I had the answer, truly, at least from my point of view, a moment of unparalleled inspiration. 'That shouldn't be a major problem, sir.' The Colonel looked at me as though he couldn't believe his ears. 'Oh yes, have you a hidden reserves of material vital to the war effort that no one knows about?

'No, but you have.' The look I received was positively withering. 'What the hell are you talking about? If I had what was needed I wouldn't be talking to you about it.' I pointed back the way we'd come. 'The cattle yard. It's huge and at least twice the width of a Dutch barn. I had a good look at it only a couple of days ago. It's all in excellent condition, including the corrugated iron roof. I had considered dividing it into three sections. One to accommodate dry cows during the winter months, another for heifers and a third for either more heifers or, possibly bullocks if we steer any bull calves which we don't want to run on as potential breeding stock. However, it seems that a major part of it could have a different use. The building for the drier is already here. It just needs moving to the chosen site, heightening with concrete piers and a section bricked up to make the store. As I say it's huge. I imagine five sections would be ample for the grass-drying unit, leaving two to provide a spacious yard for wintering young stock.'

The Colonel eyed me for a moment, then started to laugh. It was most infectious and I found myself laughing too. I've no idea what my boss was laughing at, but I know, as far as I was concerned, it was from sheer relief.

After breakfast the remainder of the day was spent going around the estate which included a visit to Manor Farm. The owner told the tenants that he would want to take it over before long, but would give them the appropriate notice. They were quite unconcerned, said they had been expecting it and were already negotiating about renting a farm in Northamptonshire.

When we returned to the house we sat in the car for a considerable time discussing many, many aspects of the estate. We discussed machinery at some length, which ended up with my being given carte blanche to buy what was necessary for the smooth and economic running of the estate. I received similar freedom in buying more pedigree Dairy Shorthorns. I stayed for what was in those days called high tea, at 5.30pm, because this was easier with the children to be cared for. I thought I'd be off after that, but oh no, it was 8.45pm by the time the Colonel said, 'Well, I think that covers everything. Let's hope we get a good run tomorrow, because I doubt I will get out again this season – I'm off to America on Wednesday for nearly a month in connection with the war effort.' He was exuberant and still oozing as much energy when I left as he had when I had joined him thirteen-and-a-half hours earlier, whilst I felt drained, exhausted, elated at solving the problem over the building for the grass drier and much, much wiser.

8. Beginning a New Era

It was around 3.00pm that the Master, Ethne and I rode down the lane from Marsh Hill, heading for home after a successful day's hunting. Two foxes had been accounted for, both found in areas where there had been a lot of chicken killing and some substantial poultry claims had been paid out over recent weeks. In those days it was customary for the hunts to pay for poultry losses due to foxes, providing such claims could be reasonably substantiated. The Kennel-huntsman, David Griffiths, hunted hounds, as Dev's Joint Master; Captain Stanley Barratt, managing director and main shareholder of Barratt's Sweets, who normally hunted them, was away doing his bit for King and Country.

At the meet Ethne had introduced me to John and Joan Robarts, who owned Kimblewick Farm adjoining both Round Hill and Manor Farm, who became lifelong friends. I also met Ruth, Joan's sister and her husband, Frank Roads. Frank farmed a few miles away across the vale and was a leading point-to-point rider. Joan and Ruth's mother, Mrs Terry, who lived in the adjoining Whaddon Chase hunt country, was a legend in her own lifetime in the world of horses. She was a fearless horsewoman, rode sidesaddle and it was generally accepted that when hounds were running, few, if any of the field, ever headed her. In addition I was introduced to Ted Clarke, another farmer, and his wife Molly. Only a few fields separated the start of Ted's considerable acreage and Marsh Hill; they too became good friends. Ted was held in high regard in the local farming community and, I was soon to discover, was never slow to say what he thought. As we hacked on to the first draw, Ted rode up beside me and said, 'Well, I'll give you this, you've a heap of nerve to take on Roundhill; the question is have you the knowledge to straighten it out? I told the Master, not so long ago, he was being fleeced left, right and centre, but he took no notice. Time will tell, but I wish you luck and if I can be of any help don't be afraid to ask.' Another member of the field that day was Phil Oliver, the current occupier of Meadacre Farm. I already knew Phil, having met him several times at various shows, gymkhanas and hunter trials where I had ridden horses for Billy Oliver. The two men were not related. Phil was primarily a horse dealer and seldom beaten showjumping at local shows. His eldest son, Allen, was to follow in father's footsteps in this sphere and became one of England's most successful riders. Up to the war Phil had dealt only in horses, but once this reasonably lucrative means of making a living ended, Phil turned his dealing ability to virtually anything to do with agriculture.

It had undoubtedly been a good day. Although I'd seen the Master out hunting a number of times prior to this, I'd never paid much attention to his ability as a horseman. He rode with the same verve and determination as he tackled life in general, but, whilst it was obvious he did not know the meaning of the word fear, he was no great horseman. I'd had an interesting day on The Priest. It seemed he could jump anything, he pulled like a train and was not averse to trying to drop whoever was riding him when the mood took him. After what I had seen and experienced it was obvious he was not suitable for the Master. What puzzled me was why the men from the Remount Depot had not taken him.

As we came abreast of Long Hill Farm, the one which the Colonel had said he wanted to buy the day he had shown father and I around the estate, I turned to him and said, 'By the way I was talking to Perry (the owner) a couple of days ago and walked the land. It's all grass – about eighty-four acres. Like so much land throughout the country, it hasn't been cared for and is obviously low in nutrients. I shouldn't think it's had a good top dressing of dung, or fertiliser for that matter, for years. He's very keen to sell. However, if he does it would be on the condition he could remain in one half of what he calls the house, it's two cottages really, up to a maximum of six months until he obtains alternative accommodation.' The Colonel reined in his horse and rather briskly said, 'Why the hell didn't you tell me about this yesterday? You know, or should know, that I'm very anxious to buy the place.' I nodded, 'Yes, but after a thirteen-and-a-half hour day I'd about had it and, frankly, forgot about it. Don't worry. I have an agreement with Perry that you have first refusal. I think he's very hard pressed for cash and certainly doesn't want to pay fees to an estate agent.' My boss looked a little appeased. 'Did he say what he'd take for it?'

'Yes, £60 an acre.'

'That sounds cheap. Why didn't you close the deal?' The Colonel was beginning to get hot under the collar again. 'Simply because I thought I was supposed to be looking after your interests and I know I can buy it for less. I bid him £45 an acre, but he wouldn't accept it. The fact that you are off to America for the best part of a month complicates things a bit, because, when we do agree a price, he'll want his money as of yesterday. I'm pretty sure I can buy it for you at around £50 an acre.'

'That's no problem. I'll leave an open cheque for an amount up to £5000 with the solicitor who deals with everything to do with the estate. That should be more than adequate. But don't you dare lose it.' I smiled, 'Don't worry, I won't.' At that moment The Priest, just as I was relaxed and had him on a comparatively light rein, decided it was time for a rodeo. This time he was successful but, fortunately, I landed on my feet and was able to hang on to the reins. When I remounted I turned to the Master and enquired, 'Do you think this fellow has the right temperament for the type of horse you want, sir? I know you could ride him all right, but Ethne tells me he's not averse to kicking a hound or two if he gets the chance.' If I was truthful, from what I had seen I was quite certain that The Priest would not only take off with the Master, but would quickly deposit him on the ground. The Colonel was silent for a moment then replied, 'No, he hasn't. That damned girl should never have bought him, but I'll need another horse. The Remount people took two of the best heavyweight horses I've ever owned. Anyway, you're managing the stables now, so deal with it as you think best. What I can't understand is why they left a great strong seven-year-old gelding like him?'

The following morning I reduced the staff further. There was one man who had been consistently late every morning since I'd taken over the estate. Work started at 7.00am for the general farmhands, 5.00am with those working with the dairy herd, although I was to learn that Ron Chamberlain was always in the yard by 4.30am, and in the stables by 6.00am. The man I got rid of was quite a good worker, when he eventually arrived, which was usually after 8.00am and he had a tendency to do a vanishing act, if he could, shortly after 4.00pm. I had given him several warnings. It was 8.20am, that Tuesday morning, when I was heading back to the house for breakfast, that I spotted him cycling along the road in the most leisurely fashion, from the direction of The Prince of Wales. I waited for him and told him he could finish at the end of the week. His reply was quite polite – but, no, he didn't think he'd bother. He'd pick up what was due to him when Mr Harrison arrived. If that was what he wanted, who was I to argue?

I had made an arrangement whereby Tom and I met at 9.00am every morning to have a general chat about what was happening, having planned the day's work the evening before. That morning he greeted me cheerfully and said, 'I gather you sifted out the last of the chaff this morning. What's left now is good grain, if you follow my meaning, but there's not enough.' I followed him perfectly and explained that from now on we were going to start building things up. It was a long session that morning, for I had much to tell Tom and, indeed, ask him. High on my list was did he know if any fertiliser had been ordered? As far as he knew the answer was no. In those times one didn't have a large choice of ready mixed fertilisers. It was a case of buying superphosphate, potash and sulphate of ammonia, mixing the three laboriously by hand on a barn floor to one's own requirements, bagging it all up again and carting it out to wherever it was required. Certainly the field 'Sudden' had finished ploughing the previous evening at Little Marsh was badly in need of something to get any sort of a yield off it. I would have put it into spring barley, but the wheat seed, Squarehead Master, had already been bought and was in the feed store at the piggery. It was too late to get any great result from superphosphate for the coming harvest and similar remarks, but perhaps to a lesser extent, applied to potash. One had to be careful when mixing all three together, because if not applied quickly the sulphate of ammonia had the effect of turning the whole mix into a gunge that clogged up the spreader. However, we had to do something to help the impoverished soil, even if to a small degree.

There were several vast heaps of pig dung on Marsh Hill that should have been spread, but instead remained heaped, slowly losing their goodness. Similarly there were heaps of cattle dung on Round Hill and a large amount to clear out of the open-fronted yards. I asked Tom who was the best supplier for fertiliser in the area. He named a firm in Aylesbury, but said he'd not been allowed to organise anything like that, so we might get a better deal elsewhere. I suggested I might phone Ted Clarke – Tom thought this an excellent idea and Ted, who fortunately was at home, was true to his word and contacted the firm whom he considered to be the best in the area. Their managing director phoned me within minutes and arranged to meet me at the farm office at 11.00am. The next day two loads of fertiliser arrived – the first of many over a number of years. Whilst on this subject I asked Tom why there was so much dung lying around in heaps. His answer was straight and to the point, 'Because we haven't got a bloody muckspreader. Just poor old Smiler, a dung cart, a muck rake and when available our one and only tractor and trailer. We've had to put it out in heaps and hand spread what little's been used with forks, as has been done for centuries.'

I had one ever-present worry, there just weren't enough hours in the day to cope with everything that needed attention, but I arranged to meet Tom, later in the day, as soon as I'd swallowed my lunch, to walk as many of the fields as we could. I took an auger with me to examine the soil and a notebook to record what needed doing in each field. To some readers it may appear that I was in an unnecessary rush, almost to a degree of being on the verge of panic stations. Believe me that wasn't the case, but if it had been I can assure sceptics that the desire to survive is a most compelling spur! German U-boats were becoming more and more of a hazard to our shipping and the tonnage being lost, together with their cargoes, was pretty horrific. This meant that British agriculture, so wickedly neglected by every government between the wars and grossly undercapitalised, was being asked, no told, it had to make good the resulting shortfall, which of course was impossible, but we had to do the best we could and as quickly as we could. Suddenly to the urban dweller farmers and farmworkers were jolly good chaps – no longer country bumpkins with straw sticking out of their ears!

We started in a grass field at the back of the piggeries. I suggested to Tom that we plough it for spring barley, but he said no, the amount of slurry that had gone on to it would positively blow the crop out of the ground. On hearing this I decided to sow marrow stem kale to cut and cart for the dairy herd in the coming winter. We covered a number of fields, planning their future as we went. We moved on into an arable field, previously old grassland, that Tom told me had been ploughed early the previous autumn and which he was not at all happy about. It had been sown with winter wheat, a good old variety – Yeoman. As we walked across it I realised there was more than wheat coming through, for charlock was very apparent and if it was apparent in March it was nothing to what would manifest itself in the spring. Charlock, now easily controlled by spraying, was back in 1940 a persistent and difficult weed to control, with a quite prodigious output of seed from just one plant if allowed to reach that stage. It could destroy a cereal crop by choking it. Before spraying was possible it was not unusual to see fields as yellow from flowering charlock as one can see today where rape is the crop. Botanists claim that the seed can remain dormant in the ground for half a century, then germinate when land is tilled and it is brought close to the surface. I zigzagged across the field as we walked, the damned stuff was everywhere. Tom looked at me, 'I had a feeling you wouldn't be pleased with this.'

'How right you are, but we've got to make what little use we can of it and the wheat, that is if it doesn't smother the latter. As I told you, we're going to leave the piggery empty for six months, or thereabouts, and set about building up new herds. The Colonel has agreed that I should either buy, or employ someone here on the estate to build, pig arks and pen the nucleus for the two herds over poor grassland that we're going to have to plough. Every morsel of food will be important.'

I had no idea how nutritious charlock was, but it was a member of the brassica family – cabbages. I remembered hearing, during the course of a lecture at Reading University, that whilst an infestation of this dogged weed was the bane of any farmer's life, it is recorded as being regularly sold in Dublin as a vegetable back in the 1700s and was in great demand as such. Further, well into the nineteenth century, it was used for the same purpose in the Hebrides. If it was all right for humans, then why not for pigs? I explained to Tom what I had in mind and that once it had been eaten off by the pigs we would give the field a bastard fallow. Up to the war years fallowing a field, namely cultivating it throughout a year but not sowing it, was a regular practice and part of fixed four- or five-year crop rotations. A bastard fallow was to plough and cultivate throughout the summer to germinate and kill weeds, before sowing with a winter cereal crop. I commented to Tom that I most sincerely hoped, when we came to plough other old pastures, that we did not turn up trouble of a similar nature. Fortunately, my hopes were fulfilled.

When we got back to Marsh Hill we went and sat in the feed store and discussed the findings from our walk. The soil was good, neither heavy nor gravelly, should be easily worked and with the proper care, be productive. There was one note common to each field – hedges and ditches. The condition of the former was bad. The vast majority needed laying, but in many cases the ditches were non-existent. Tom said that both old Joe Swaine and his counterpart, Harry Montague, both of whom I estimated were well into their sixties, were good hedgers and could lay them as well as most. He laughed and added, 'But not as well as me. It's a job I love and before I moved down south used to compete in and won quite a few competitions. But you know we've only a few weeks left this winter to tackle them. Nevertheless, I could send old Harry

North, Left-legged Harry he's known as, I'll tell you why in a minute, with one of the old lads. Harry's a bit queer, but he's a good honest worker. There's a man, Dick Spittles, lives between Marsh and Stoke Mandeville, who's a good grafter and is looking for a job. I could get him to come and see you. If you liked him, he could go with Harry or Joe.'

'That sounds good to me, but we won't get much hedging or ditching done now, it's too late. Whilst on the subject of labour, it's my intention to take on probably six Land Girls. Some can live where the stable manageress lived and others can be found billets by the Land Army. They'll have to be trained of course. My father has four on the Burnham estate; he took them on within weeks of the war starting. I can tell you, Tom, they're damned good workers.' I looked at my watch, 'We must get on, otherwise Harrison will miss his train.'

As we drove back to Round Hill, Tom told me how Harry North came to have the nickname Left-Legged Harry. 'If you look at him he seems to have two left feet. I'm not kidding, it looks as though he is wearing two left boots, in fact I know he is. Poor old Harry, he lives alone and it's rumoured that under his stairs there is a cupboard full of boots for the right foot. Rumour has it that his ambition in life is to meet a man who has two right feet the same size as his and then he thinks he'll be in the money.'

I laughed, 'You're not serious?'

'I am, absolutely. You take a look tomorrow, or whenever you're next talking to him, but for heaven's sake don't pass any comment. He goes real bonkers if anyone does.' Actually I hadn't had a chance to talk to him, or the other two older hands, other than to introduce myself – I had been too busy getting rid of the 'chaff'. Tom dropped me off at the house and I headed for the yard to see how my bedroom was progressing. I was just in time to catch the two men, from the builders in Wendover, who had been doing the job. The one in charge, who I'd told there would be a quid in it for him and his mate if they got finished by Tuesday evening, greeted me with a grin. 'Come and have a look boss, we've finished. I reckon we've made a damned good job of it.' He was right. I pulled out a pound note, thanked them and then weighed up what was required next so that I had a 'home'. By Thursday afternoon, both office and bedroom were completed and the Post Office had promised faithfully to install a telephone extension from the farm office to mine – a promise they fulfilled.

On Thursday evening, around 8.00pm, Ethne suggested we go down to The Prince of Wales. This we did and I met for the first time Mrs Leversuch, a motherly old character who had a quite remarkable hair style. She had long grey hair, plaited and then coiled round over each ear, making her look as though she had oversized grey earphones. She was not the licensee, that was her husband, but he never did a stroke of work. It was the smallest pub I have ever been in. There was a passage, barely four feet wide, at the end of which to the left was a room, at the best fifteen feet square, with an old open brick fireplace, where, in winter time, old man Leversuch would have a fire so hot that it would have roasted an ox. It seemed he sat in the corner by this, fire or no fire, throughout the year. He had served about thirty years with the army, much of the time in India.

Halfway along the passage on the right there was an opening in the boarded partition, about three foot square, with a shelf, into what served as a bar, which was only half as wide again as the passageway. On the far wall there was a strong wooden rack, about two feet off the ground, which accommodated four barrels of beer. Looking to the right of this would be two, sometimes three, bottle crates stood on end, where minerals, tonic water etc, were kept. A small cupboard, two shelves and a wooden bar stool made up the rest of the fittings. The till was an open wooden structure with four sections for coin, copper, then sixpenny and threepenny bits together with shillings, one section for two shilling pieces and one for half-crowns. Beside these was a space wide enough to take notes, which were always safely anchored by a one pound weight from the kitchen scales. I received a great welcome from Mrs Leversuch who, saying she had heard so much about me, delved into the cupboard and produced a bottle of whisky, poured what must have been about a treble and passed it to me saying 'On the house dear.' Turning to Ethne, she enquired 'Your usual dear' and without waiting for an answer, again reached into the cupboard and produced a bottle of gin, saying 'I keep it safe for you dear, hard to get now you know.' I tried to pay for Ethne's drink, but I wasn't allowed.

I quickly learned the local etiquette, namely the passage did service for a saloon bar and one didn't normally venture beyond the portal to the one and only room – the public bar. Ethne looked through the opening and greeted the inmates, there were only three. Old Leversuch sat in his corner and next to him was Renee from the telephone exchange who greeted me by name, although I was certain she had never seen me before. When I asked her how she knew who I was she replied that she had heard me talking in the passage and quite simply recognised my voice, adding that she had heard it enough over the last ten days. The third member of the trio was black, nothing to do with his pigmentation – just soot. He was the local sweep and known as Gilbert. Whether that was his surname or Christian name I never discovered. He lived in an old horse-drawn caravan, probably long past its days of mobility, parked on a little patch of ground about thirty yards by twenty, about half a mile, or less, up the road towards Kimble from Round Hill. He had an old trap drawn by an equally old pony, also black, in which he went around the countryside plying his trade. His water supply was undoubtedly from a cattle watering trough, some twenty yards away in one of John Robarts' fields. Toilet facilities were probably of a similarly basic nature to those of the ancient Britons, but he harmed no one, was a good sweep and providing one put down plenty of paper on the floor when he was paying a visit, made little mess. I bought all three a drink, another gin for Ethne and a beer for myself. Mrs Leversuch wouldn't have one, she said she only drank two things, tea or water.

We made our way back to the house, where there was a message for me to phone a retired cavalry captain who I knew slightly. I had heard he had been involved in the selection of the horses that were taken from Round Hill as

Remounts. Fearing that he might still want more for this outdated purpose, I put a call in to him. I knew he had done a little dealing in top-quality hunters – apparently he still did. The reason for his call was that a client in Leicestershire had just lost his last remaining hunter, after a visit from the Remount people, from a terrible bout of colic and was anxious to buy a good heavyweight, would the Colonel consider selling The Priest? I said I didn't think so, but would phone and ask him. After waiting twenty minutes I rang the Captain back, saying my boss wasn't keen, but would sell at a price. Eventually, a deal was struck at £25 more than the original purchase price, providing The Priest would pass the vet, which I knew he would. I went off to bed in my loose box, now a comfortable and warm bedroom, pleased that I was freed of what I thought was going to be quite a problem and that fate had, on this occasion, been kind to me.

9. A Diamond and Playing a Hunch

During the war and for many decades before, the most popular and indeed commonest milk cows throughout the country were Dairy Shorthorns. Friesians were few and far between and had the reputation of producing milk low in butterfat and not suitable for a system of mixed farming – how things change! Consequently the sale of young bulls for breeding was a very important factor in the viability of a pedigree herd. Producing top-quality ones, apart from pedigree, required both skill and time in order to present them for sale with the bloom and condition which would ensure getting the best possible price. There were numerous collective auctions, during the year, throughout the country, but the main event was the Shorthorn Society's Show and Sale held at Reading in November and second to this was the Society's March Show and Sale at the same venue.

I had only been at Round Hill about three weeks when I was approached one evening, as I was finishing up in my office, by Tom and Ron Chamberlain. It transpired that prior to my arrival they had been to look at a young bull, not quite a year old, at a small, but very select herd a few miles the other side of Aylesbury – the Diamond herd, owned by a charming, but very frail elderly lady, Miss Heap. That and her small farm were managed by Archie Andrews. He was single and no doubt in these days of a classless society, it is politically incorrect to describe him as very much a gentleman, but that is how he was looked upon then, even if thought slightly eccentric by some because of his way of life. Quite simply, he loved the country, he loved Dairy Shorthorns and the Diamond herd was his major interest and hobby, along with bridge, at which he excelled.

Certainly the youngster the two were keen on sounded excellent, for the dam had for five consecutive lactations produced over 1000 gallons of milk in 315 days, twice over 1200 and with excellent butterfat content. Further, she had won numerous top honours at major shows including second, in a very large class, at the 1939 Royal Show. I telephoned to make an appointment and Ron and I went over the next day. There was no doubt that this young fellow, Diamond Wild Duke, was something a bit out of the ordinary. I enquired of Archie what he was asking for him. His reply was 100 guineas (all pedigree stock were sold in guineas), and 100 guineas was a lot of money in those days for a yearling bull. He took me to one side and whispered, 'Of course the shillings on the guineas will be yours if you buy.' I looked at him for a minute, then replied, 'Thanks, but no thanks. Would you do Miss Heap out of £5?' He went very red in the face and said, 'Of course I wouldn't. What do you take me for?' I laughed, 'Exactly. You don't swindle your employer out of money, nor do I, but I'll knock £5 off the cheque.' Poor Archie was most apologetic, saying that normally most people asked for a handback. I did not, for once, attempt to bargain, but pulled out the chequebook and paid him immediately. It was the best investment I was to make for the Roundhill herd, for Duke turned out to be one of the top sires in the breed throughout the main of the 1940s. Having finished our business, we took an in-depth look at the herd; there was no doubt they oozed quality. As we left I complimented Archie on them. He gave a big sigh, thanked me and said Miss Heap was far from well and when she went the herd would be dispersed. He continued that her nephew, her sole heir, had no interest in the herd, nor the country in general and had made it quite clear to Archie that, when his aunt died, everything would be sold as soon as possible.

About a week after Diamond Wild Duke took up residence at Round Hill, Harrison received his call-up papers, leaving me only two weeks to find his replacement. I advertised and phoned the Labour Exchange, but no joy. However, two days before he finished Mrs Snookes, a lady in advanced middle age, applied and came for an interview. After a quick chat, I left Harrison to take her through the general office routine and wise her up on what went on. He wasn't impressed, nor was I, but it was a case of Hobson's choice and she agreed to start the next day. Harrison had told her she could be ferried to and from the station if required, but she assured him that would not be necessary. She was delivered by car each morning about two minutes before 9.00am and left, whatever was happening exactly at 5.00pm. I assumed the driver was her husband. She was far from efficient and I don't think she typed one letter that didn't have to be redone. At the end of her second week she presented me with a bill. It was for £7, the hire of a taxi to bring her to and from work. I pointed out that nothing had been said or agreed about this and I was not prepared to pay it. She flew into a rage, which included telling me that I shouldn't be skulking on a farm, I should be fighting for my king and country – exit Mrs Snookes!

Rose McKellar volunteered to help out as much as she could, but she already had numerous commitments. We muddled on for a couple of weeks and then out of the blue, one morning, I received a phonecall from a girl with a very nice sounding voice. 'Was I by any chance requiring a secretary/bookkeeper?' I asked her how she knew there was a vacancy. She replied that she didn't, she was currently unemployed, but had always thought she would like to work in the office on a large agricultural estate and so had rung on the off chance there might be a job going. I asked where she was calling from and she told me she lived in Aylesbury. I made a few enquiries as to her experience. It sounded as though my prayers were about to be answered. Could she come for an interview? Of course, as soon as I liked. Trying to keep the sound of both the delight and, relief that I was experiencing from my voice, I said, 'If you could check the time your train will be arriving at Kimble, I'll send a car to pick you up.' There was a happy, cheery laugh, 'Thank you Mr Twist, but I'll cycle out, it's only eight miles. Would 3.00pm be convenient?'

'Certainly, come to my office, not the one at the farm. Mine's opposite the house, at the end of the stable yard.' There was a pause and I was about to say see you then, when she added, 'Would you be very offended if I appear for an interview wearing slacks? It's so much more comfortable when biking.' I was so elated at the thought of getting a secretary who sounded as though she might be efficient that

I only just stopped myself from saying come in your birthday suit if you like, just as long as you come. Instead I replied, laughing, 'Of course not. I never wear a skirt when I ride my bike.' There was a friendly chuckle and she hung up.

When I went into the house for lunch, both Ethne and Rose, the latter having spent the morning making butter, remarked on how cheerful I seemed. I told them why and Ethne said, 'This calls for a drink.' She crossed to the cabinet and poured the equal of at least three schooners of sherry, passing one to Rose and I. Normally we didn't drink at midday unless the Colonel was present when it was the normal practice. Ethne raised her glass, 'Cheers, here's to … what did you say her name was?' It suddenly dawned on me that I had been so euphoric at the thought of getting some help in the office that I had totally forgotten to ask her name. I had to admit my failing, much to the amusement of the two ladies.

At 3.00pm precisely there was a knock on my office door and I called 'Come in.' An attractive brunette with bobbed hair and a pleasant smile entered. She stepped forward as I stood up, hand outstretched, 'Good afternoon. I'm Kay Browne, I forgot to give you my name when we were talking on the phone this morning. I do apologise.' I waved her to the comfortable leather armchair that I'd added to the furnishing of my office to accommodate the Colonel when we had talks about the estate. She smiled, seated herself demurely, and at the same time once again apologised for attending an interview in slacks. I assured her that it was no problem and suggested we get down to business. She seemed to have all the necessary answers and finally I asked if had she any references. She had, they were in the carrier bag of her bike. She collected a folder which she handed to me and resumed her seat. The references were excellent. Two were from businesses in Birmingham and one at High Wycombe, none of which I'd heard of, but all were typed on good-quality paper, all had phone numbers and, most importantly, all extolled the virtues and ability of Kay Browne as a secretary/bookkeeper. I jotted down the names of the companies and the phone numbers and handed the references back to Kay. 'They seem excellent. Why did you leave the firms concerned?' She did not hesitate, 'Well, the first one was because, after two years, I was still getting the same money as when I started and, although I asked they wouldn't pay more. So I left to better myself and earn an extra £1-10-0 a week. That was a great job until ...' She stopped and looked down at her feet, then continued, 'one of the bosses wanted ... er, well he wanted more than work, if you follow my meaning?' I nodded understandingly, 'And the job at High Wycombe?' She smiled, 'The war. As you will see from the paper heading, they manufactured high-quality ladies' handbags – that sort of thing. Materials and demand were dramatically reduced and, regrettably, so was the staff. I was one of the ones to lose my job.' It all seemed very plausible. 'Right, I'll check your references and come back to you.' She looked a little crestfallen. 'Er ... couldn't you do that now? You see if you don't take me on, I have a provisional appointment tomorrow for another job, but would much sooner come here.' I thought for a minute then, smiling at Kay, said, 'Why not.' The last thing I wanted was to lose this girl, who it seemed could almost certainly solve my office problems. I rang Renee and gave her the names and phone numbers of the companies concerned. She had a problem getting through to Birmingham, but after three quarters of an hour I was able to turn to Kay Browne and say, 'Fine. Now, if you still want to come here, all we have to do is to agree terms. It is of course a five-and-a-half-day week, finishing at twelve on Saturdays, the other days it's nine to five.' I offered her the same wages as Harrison had been getting and she seemed delighted. I walked her across to the farm office and as we were about to enter I pointed out there was a washroom next door. I also explained how the switch worked to put phonecalls through to me. 'Does it include the house?' she queried. 'No that's a separate line. Just as well as Mrs Devereux is often on for a half-hour or more chatting to nanny about the girls.' She nodded understandingly. 'Tell me, is the Colonel often here over weekends?'

'No. He's too busy with the war effort. Why do you ask?' She gave a happy laugh, 'Oh, just we've all got to pull our weight at a time like this and, if it would be any help, I'd be perfectly happy to stay on of a Saturday afternoon, even come in Sunday, if he wanted any typing done.' I was impressed. 'That's very good of you. I'll most certainly tell him. Now when can you start?'

'Tomorrow morning suitable?' I assured her it would be. As she was leaving she said, 'By the way Mr Twist, I will of course be properly attired as a secretary should be when at work. I can bring suitable clothes and change in the washroom.'

Kay settled in well, her work was exemplary and she ingratiated herself with all the household. Ethne remarked one day that Kay was a great girl and seemed to be a tremendous admirer of her father, for she was always chatting about him and the work he did. She'd been with me for just over a week when I discovered she had a boyfriend. Apparently he was tall, bearded and, according to Ron Chamberlain 'a scruffy looking cove'. He waited for her most evenings on his bike, just a couple of hundred yards beyond Ron's cottage. So what? It was none of my business who her friends were, she was turning out to be damned good at her job and if she liked her boyfriends rough and scruffy it was no concern of mine. About a month after I'd taken her on I had just entered the house for lunch when the phone rang. I answered it and a voice enquired, 'Is Mr Michael Twist available?' I said I was and asked who was speaking. The reply was, 'One moment, I'm putting you through to Colonel Warren.' I had known the Colonel since I was a small boy. He was the Chief Constable of Buckinghamshire and a great friend of Edward Clifton-Brown, whose estate father managed. Seconds later I heard his familiar voice, 'Michael, there will be a Detective Inspector Taylor with you and possibly his Sergeant, in three quarters of an hour. I want them to meet you at the house. You are to tell no one who they are, I repeat no one and above all else not your secretary. Understood?' I was left speechless for a few seconds then said, 'What's this all about sir?' I was quickly told I would know very shortly and to do what I was told, then the phone went dead.

When lunch was over Rose and Ethne said they were going off into Aylesbury immediately. I told nanny that friends of the Colonel were coming shortly, I didn't say which Colonel and would she keep the children in the nursery until they had gone. Ten minutes or so later a rather ancient car drove up to the front door and two very casually dressed men got out. I did not go out to meet them, but let them ring the bell and then waited a couple of minutes before I answered it. The taller of the two just said 'Taylor' and brushed passed me, followed closely by his companion. I led the way into the living room and then to the chairs at the far end of the room. Turning to Taylor I said, 'What on earth's going on?' As an afterthought I asked, 'Have you any identity?' The smaller one, presumably the sergeant, nodded in approval and as both reached into their pockets, he pointed to the serving hatch through to the kitchen. 'What's that?' I was becoming slightly irritated by all this cloak-and-dagger stuff. 'What does it look like? It's a serving hatch through to the kitchen of course and, before you ask, yes there is someone through there, Verna, the cook/general who should be washing up the lunch things. And no, she can't hear our conversation, unless you shout and she has her ear pressed to the door the far side.' I looked at their identity cards. It seemed that they were who they claimed to be but were not members of the Bucks Constabulary. They were members of some special unit based at Scotland Yard. I wasn't feeling happy, but tried to put a good face on things and waved them towards the settee. 'Now gentlemen, please sit down and tell me what this is all about.' Stony faced both settled back comfortably before Taylor cleared his throat and said, 'Is it right Mr Twist, that you engaged a new secretary recently, here on Colonel Devereux's farm?'

'Yes, what of it? Kay Browne and a bloody good worker she is too.' Both men smiled. Taylor said, 'So that's what she's calling herself now?' He then produced some photographs and said,' Is this your Kay Browne?' There was no doubt about it, it was Kay. 'Yes. So what?' Both men remained silent for a moment, then Taylor shook his head. 'I'm sorry, her name is not Kay Browne, she is …' He gave a name I've long since forgotten. He went on to say, 'She is secretary of the Communist Youth Movement in this country and a very dangerous young woman. Further, she has a boyfriend, who is a known anarchist. Both are suspected of being Russian agents, but as yet nothing can be proved. Kay, as you call her, obtained a job with one of our leading aircraft manufacturers, that was where we first caught up with her when keeping surveillance on her boyfriend – a tall scruffy looking bugger with a beard. Have you seen anything of him?' He stopped and looked at me. I don't think I would have make a good poker player, for he said, 'Ah, I see that's rung a bell.' I sat quietly for a moment, digesting what I had been told. I looked Taylor straight in the eye, 'No, I haven't seen him, but the description you have given fits that of a man whom I am told meets her most evenings just a few hundred yards down the road.' Taylor nodded, 'That fits. However, the point of this visit is to tell you that you must get rid of your Kay Browne immediately.' I gasped, 'You must be joking. I was desperate for a competent and efficient secretary, she's super at her job, pleasant and I most certainly won't get rid of her. Further, she had excellent references. I spoke to all three of her previous employers. All said what an excellent worker she was and how sorry they had been to lose her.'

Taylor shook his head, sighed and said, 'No they weren't previous employers, they were all phoney and you spoke to members of her organisation.' He then named the three bogus companies and continued, 'Colonel Warren said he'd known you for years, that you were intelligent, would immediately understand and fully cooperate. Before you say anything more, she tried to obtain a job with Colonel Devereux's firm, High Duty Alloys, at Slough. Fortunately we were able to put a spoke in her wheel there. Then she tried to worm her way into your boss's firm at Aylesbury, International Alloys. Again we were able to thwart her, then she disappeared and it was only a couple of days ago that we discovered that she is now actually on Colonel Devereux's payroll. Doesn't that give you food for thought?' I remained silent. He continued, 'I'd have a sizeable bet that she often makes enquiries about the Colonel and has probably even offered to come in any weekend he's here to do any typing he requires doing urgently.' It was now obvious that I would never make a living as a poker player, for Taylor smiled for the first time and added, 'I see I've hit the nail squarely on the head. Now as you are aware there is a non-aggression pact between Russia and Germany. We think that she and her boyfriend could be – and I repeat could be, we aren't as yet certain – agents for either or both countries. You have to safeguard your boss's interests and get rid of her – how is up to you, but under no circumstances is she to know that we are involved.' I buried my head in my hands, this couldn't be happening. Kay was outstanding at her job, pleasant, everyone liked her. I looked up, 'How can I sack her? She's as near a perfect secretary as one could get, she doesn't make mistakes. Why can't she stay here, where she can do no harm? It really doesn't matter if Stalin or Hitler know how many cows we have, or pigs for that matter.' Both men laughed and it was the Sergeant who spoke, 'Mr Twist, you don't understand how these people work. Colonel Devereux is a very important person as far as this country's war effort is concerned, we cannot take even the smallest risk.' Taylor stood up, 'We must go, so must Kay Browne. How and why she goes is up to you, but in no way must you involve us.' With that they walked out.

Ten days had passed since Taylor's visit. On reflection I had realised, if what had been said was true, then Kay had to go, but what grounds could I find for sacking her? There had been one development, the boyfriend openly met her outside the farm gates, but that was no crime, nor was it one when I walked over to the farm from my office and said good afternoon to him as he waited at the gate and he totally ignored me. In the short time since Taylor's visit, the Chief Constable had been on the phone to me three times wanting to know if I had fired Kay. The whole business was getting me down to such a degree that I was seriously thinking of packing the job in. It was then that Lady Luck shone on me. I had been going through some accounts with Kay just before lunch, preparatory to her writing out cheques for the Colonel to sign at the weekend. As it came up to 1.00pm we hadn't quite finished, so I told her I would be back after the lunch break to finish off. As I walked across to the house I spotted the boyfriend virtually hiding behind a tree up the road towards Kimble. I went on into the house and asked Ethne if she would be kind enough to tell Verna to keep my lunch warm as I had to go out again. She asked what for and I replied, 'Oh, just playing a hunch.' I went into my office and collected a rather nice blackthorn stick I had been given. It was much like an Irish shillelagh and I frequently took it with me when I was walking around the estate, for a stick can have many purposes other than to help the aged walk. I made my way along the drive into the little shrubbery by the gate, just in time to see the boyfriend go through the wicket gate. I headed off to the field to the left of the buildings, came round the back of them and quietly up through the yard and, equally quietly entered the office and caught the couple on the floor, *in flagrante delicto*. The boyfriend positively snarled and as he got to his feet made a lunge at me, but it was no match. Apart from the fact that I had a very substantial weapon in my hand, which I was more than prepared to use, he was hobbled by having his trousers round his ankles! I quickly removed him from the office. Meanwhile Kay adjusted her clothing, looking daggers, but not saying a word. I took out her insurance card, went to the petty cash and took out two weeks' wages, turned and said, 'I'm most disappointed in you Kay. Give me your office key, because you're fired.' She took her money and card, handed over the key and headed for the door. Then she turned and exclaimed, 'You bastard, when we win I'll personally see you go through hell.' With that she departed. I sat down and after a moment put a call through to Colonel Warren. He was out, but I left a message which was simply 'problem solved'. That was true as far as he and DI Taylor were concerned but, once again, I was left looking for someone competent to take over the office. Feeling sure I was wasting time, I picked up the phone with a sigh and gave Renee the number of the Aylesbury Labour Exchange, telling her when she put me through to get off the line. It was my lucky day. The man who answered recognised my voice and said, 'Mr Twist isn't it? If you are still looking for office staff I think I've the very person for you. An experienced young lady, she has literally just come in. Apparently she had to go into hospital for a fairly major operation, from which she has now completely recovered. Regrettably her previous employer did not keep her job open for her, so she's looking for a position. Would you like to speak to her. An hour later I collected Megan Pring from the station. She had all the necessary qualifications, turned out to be a tower of strength and worked at Round Hill until the end of the war. I had one shattering moment, about three days after she started. I was in my office and a police car drove up. I panicked – surely not again. But on this occasion it was a very pleasant sergeant with a message from the Chief Constable. Firstly, he wanted to let me know that my friends were now in Newcastle and, secondly, he felt I should be armed with more than a twelve-bore shotgun and so was sending me a .32 revolver with fifty rounds, together with the appropriate Firearms Certificate.

10. The Calm Before the Storm

Whilst I had been coping with all the mayhem in the office caused by Harrison being called up, much had been happening outside. As I had suspected when I first met Bonner, the storeman at the piggeries, he was not a farmworker and hadn't lasted two weeks in such a capacity when he tried to adapt. He gave his notice in and said that he and his family were going to move back to London. As far as Bonner himself was concerned this was no loss but his son, who had been working with the dairy herd under Ron Chamberlain's tutelage, was rapidly developing into a very useful and reliable under stockman. I asked him to stay on, but he decided to return with his parents and said that anyway he'd soon be called up for the forces. However, once again luck was with me. Father phoned and in the course of conversation happened to say that the brother-in-law of one of the key workers on the Burnham estate, currently employed on a farm in Hampshire as a tractor driver, was most unhappy where he was and wanted a change. With Bonner's cottage to be free within a week, I quickly contacted him, for things were moving rapidly on the grass-drying front but a drier without staff to work it was not going to be a lot of good and would undoubtedly leave me open to a right dressing down from the boss. As a bonus, he had a seventeen-year-old son, Gordon, who had been working with dairy cows and proved to be an excellent lad.

To say that things had moved rapidly on the grass-drying front would be something of an understatement, for within seventy-two hours of my inspired answer as to how the drier was to be accommodated, Mr Bertelli, the managing director of Templewood Engineering, arrived. He inspected the cattle yard and together with a minion he had brought with him, measured it and assured me that it was ideal. They then set to work to peg out the site and that of the concrete road leading to it and what would eventually be the unloading area. It was patently obvious Bertelli was near terrified of the Colonel, a trait I noticed in a number of his co-directors on the boards of the various companies where he was unquestionably the supremo. It was something I first discovered when I had accompanied Ethne over to her father's beautiful home, The Meads at Stoke Poges. When we arrived there was a meeting going on in the study and we joined Dorothy Devereux in the drawing room. Suddenly the roars of the chairman were clearly discernible as we sat talking about a vegetable garden which I had suggested should be developed at Round Hill. Ethne looked across at me and laughed, 'The old man's in good voice tonight. I'll bet some poor sod is nearly peeing himself.' Dorothy looked crossly at her stepdaughter. 'Really, you shouldn't talk like that.' Ethne's reply was immediate, 'Why not? If they stood up to him as mother used to, he'd pipe down at once.' I wasn't too sure about that, but Ethne's Irish mother reputedly had a very fiery temper and was well able to upstage her husband in an exchange of words should the occasion arise, which was seldom. Dev always declared she saved his life in the ghastly road accident that killed her.

The days of the phoney war were gone, as became very apparent when Germany invaded both Norway and Denmark in April, driving out our meagre forces trying to help, whilst the U-boats continued their attack on our merchant shipping with ever-increasing ferocity. This led to the government urging farmers into even greater production than they had already asked. Having been ignored between the wars, forced into a situation where the majority were undercapitalised, farmers were somewhat bemused to find they were now important.

The beginning of May brought some cheer to the nation when the bungling Neville Chamberlain, who had been totally hoodwinked by Hitler at the time of the Munich Crisis, stood down as Prime Minster and Winston Churchill took his place at the head of an all-party coalition government. But any cheer was short-lived, for on 10 May, the same day as Churchill was appointed to head the government, Germany invaded the Low Countries and attacked France, circumnavigating the much vaunted Maginot Line. Colonel Devereux and the managing director of one of the country's leading aircraft manufacturers had told the cabinet this would happen after visiting Germany in 1937. Neither had any doubts that Hitler was preparing for war and said it was obvious that Germany could invade France by simply going through Belgium. He and his companion were accused of being warmongers (except by Churchill) but nevertheless they immediately started to gear their factories for what they considered to be the inevitable.

Shortly before Hitler's invasion of France, the Local Defence Volunteers were formed. This led to my receiving a phone call from a retired Air Vice Marshall, who lived at Wendover, saying that those of us who rode should do our bit by patrolling the Chiltern Hills within our areas. He had been in touch with the powers that be who thought it an excellent idea and had asked him to organise it and take command of the overall operation. In addition he would also be responsible for patrols for Coombe Hill and the surrounding Wendover area. He wished me to be in charge of the hills overlooking Kimble and Monks Risborough, the chief of which was Pulpit Hill which was actually on part of the Chequers estate and from where one could have a commanding view of the Prime Minister's country residence. According to the AVM this was undoubtedly a most strategic position which, should there be an invasion, the Nazis would be anxious to control. He then told me he'd be with me within the next twenty minutes and was true to his word. I asked what he thought we could do. His reply was, 'Report any shady-looking characters you see in the woods.' I then enquired what could we possibly do against German paratroopers landing on Pulpit Hill as he felt sure they might. His reply was, 'Ride like hell for help', but failed to say where this would be available. However, it certainly gave the 'commander' of the LDV Scouts a feeling that he was doing his bit. He left, instructing me to start recruiting and said he would contact me in the very near future. The Kimble Section, as the AVM referred to us, was not exactly overwhelmed with volunteers. It consisted of myself, Phil Oliver, Bob Hitchcock (very reluctantly), Ethne and a Land Girl, known to her mates as Deane, who had just joined the staff and proved to be an excellent horsewoman.

The weather was kind and about every third evening up to dusk I went for a pleasant hack up into the hills – but shady-looking characters or enemy we saw none. It had become a regular occurrence to hear the drone of German bombers flying overhead, but they would all be monitored by the Observer Corps. One morning, when I'd only just got back to the house for breakfast, the 'Commander' phoned in great excitement. Apparently the LDV in the Monks Risborough area had, for two consecutive nights, seen someone signalling skyward with a torch as German planes flew over. The AVM ordered me to take a patrol and capture the offender, or if that wasn't possible drive him down the hill into the arms of what he described as the waiting infantry and police. Apparently, each time the signalling had been spotted it was just after dark. This meant there was no question of a cavalry charge across the top of the hill, the final operation would have to be on foot. If the signalling was really happening it sounded as though it could be a fun evening, but it was important to get the lie of the land. So together with Ethne and Bob Hitchcock, the latter giving no indication that he thought it might be a fun evening, we drove as far as we could and then walked on up the track to a spot where we thought we could leave the horses with Ethne and Deane. We then made our way along the hillside to where there was a lone and very big beech tree, just beyond an old broken-down barbed wire fence. It was decided that Bob was to wait there and should the signaller appear and make a run for it down that side of the hill, he was to trip him up, grab him and shout for help. If nothing happened he was to wait there for me. Poor Hitchcock, he didn't look at all happy. Ethne, who had much of her father in her, said 'Don't worry Bob. Yell like hell if you grab him. I'll leave the horses with Deane, risk showing a light, run across and kick him in the goolies.' Bob gasped, 'Miss Ethne – really! For a young lady your language is not very nice.' Ethne laughed, 'You've often heard me use worse when I've taken a gutzer when schooling a horse over fences.'

I suggested to a somewhat disconsolate Hitchcock that he

could either make his way back to the car, or, alternatively, he could come up to the top of the hill with me to see what the going was like and what cover was available. He chose the car, but Ethne accompanied me. Near the decent down to Monks Risborough were some bushes that would provide the cover I needed. As we walked back we discussed the plan of action. We decided we would ride up on to the hill, as we had frequently done, just before dusk to where we could easily be seen, turn and ride back as normal. As soon as we were out of sight of the road and houses below, I would dismount and, as it would be getting dark, make my way back to the place where I intended to hide. Ethne would take my horse on to where she and Deane would wait for the return of Hitchcock and I. The signalling had been early in the evening and there would be a good moon, about an hour after nightfall, so if nothing had happened by 11.00pm we'd head for home. Finally, I told Hitchcock that if nothing happened and I decided to abort the plan, I would make my way down the hillside and when I neared the beech tree I'd call his name. Laughing I said, 'I don't want you doing a rugger tackle on me, calling Miss Ethne and her kicking me where it hurts most.' The response I got was nil.

I was comfortably hidden in the bushes, certain that no one could have seen our little subterfuge and had even told Deane and Hitchcock to stay back out of sight, as normally we only patrolled in pairs. Bob had been much cheered, when we had set out from the stable yard, after I mentioned that I had the revolver with me that I had received from the Chief Constable. An hour passed and nothing happened to disturb the quiet other than the hooting of a pair of owls in the trees behind me. The moon was coming up and with it came the familiar drone of a Junker overhead, then another. I did not look skyward, but gazed intently towards the edge of the hill. My heart raced as suddenly I saw a flash of light, then again, again and again. Undoubtedly someone was signalling to the planes. I moved swiftly forward and as I neared the flashing light I could see a person about twenty yards away, still busily signalling. Then I must have trodden on a piece of old dead wood which cracked loudly. I heard my quarry gasp, half turn and then run off down the hill towards Monks Risborough. I shouted as loudly as I could, 'Halt, or I'll fire' several times. I couldn't see anyone, but hoped my voice would be heard by those at the bottom of the hill and alert them to the fact that the flasher was on the way down. Cursing my misfortune of having stepped on a stick and made my presence known, I started on my way back to join up with Bob Hitchcock.

I found the going was nothing like as easy in moonlight as it had been when the sun was shining in the middle of the afternoon. Eventually I spotted the beech tree and when a few yards from it called out Hitchcock's name. There was no reply. I called again. Still no reply. I bellowed 'Hitchcock, where the bloody hell are you?' This time I was just able to hear a gasping, terrified voice reply, 'Here. Watch it sir, he's got me by the legs.' Quicker than a Western gunfighter my revolver was out of my pocket, cocking it as soon as it was clear, at the same time switching on my torch. A moment of extreme tension, on the flick of a torch switch, turned to one of hilarity, for there, lying face down on the ground was poor Bob, having caught his legs in the old barbed wire fence. I released him and helped him up, he was shaking like a leaf. Poor chap, I felt truly sorry for him. I had a small flask of brandy in my pocket and made him take a couple of good swigs at it. It was twenty minutes or more before I deemed him to be in a fit state to rejoin the girls. One thing was certain Bob, who was a very good studgroom, was no soldier. As we made our way towards the horses I told him that his capture would be known only to the two of us, for which he was truly grateful.

The next morning I had an ecstatic AVM on the phone. The lads at Monks Risborough had caught the fifth columnist and I and my section were to be congratulated on flushing him out. I enquired what would happen to the prisoner. 'Don't know', came the reply, 'I think they should shoot the bugger. It's war you know, total war and there should be no mercy on traitors.' That was the last I heard of the event. The only other outcome was that Hitchcock came to the office the next morning and asked if we were part of the LDV. I replied, no, not officially, just a patriotic body trying to help in the war effort. He gave a sigh and informed me that he was withdrawing his services for family reasons – his wife didn't like him being out at night. The AVM was a bit miffed about this, for he had become even more enthusiastic about the patrols since we'd chased the man off the hill.

Several days later the telephone rang at lunchtime. Ethne answered it. It was the AVM wanting to know if the Kimble Section could spare a volunteer to go on patrol with him that evening. He could provide a horse. Ethne volunteered and drove over to Wendover on what was a lovely warm late spring evening, just the sort that would encourage courting couples up on to Coombe Hill, to enjoy the views across the Vale of Aylesbury and the love light in each other's eyes. When she returned Ethne was grinning from ear to ear and when I asked what sort of a patrol she'd had, she started to giggle like a silly schoolgirl. At last, wiping her eyes, she said you'll never believe this. Apparently when she arrived at the AVM's house the horses were saddled up ready to go, his two oversized and totally untrimmed Airedale Terriers leaping around in great excitement. She was to learn that they regularly went on patrol, but what really intrigued her was the fact that the AVM had a hunting horn protruding from between the top and second button of his jacket, as would a pukka huntsman of a pack of hounds. As soon as they got on the hill, the AVM pulled out his hunting horn and, cantering on, started blowing hounds on in the traditional manner, the Airedales racing on ahead and into the bushes. He then pulled his horse up, turned to Ethne and said, 'Soon find any suspects this way, my dogs will hunt anyone out.' At that moment, about 100 yards ahead, there was a sudden and sustained barking. Off went the AVM hollering as though he was encouraging a pack of hounds that had just found a fox. He rode into the bushes, closely followed by Ethne to see what was happening. They found a terrified young couple, somewhat scantily clad, were clinging to each other backed up against a bush, confronted by two large dogs barking frantically. Their owner called them off, shouting to the youngsters, 'Sorry, we're looking for fifth columnists.' Then to

Ethne's utter amazement he blew 'gone to ground' as if fox hunting when the quarry had done just that. He turned his horse and rode away. As soon as they were clear of the bushes, he set off again, his dogs galloping on ahead hunting out the cover. They finished the evening with three more 'finds' – three more terrified young couples – each pair on discovery causing the AVM to blow gone to ground. Finally the Commander of the LDV Scouts declared the light was going and that they should return to base, assuring Ethne that no Nazi sympathiser would loiter in his area.

That was the lighter side of life during a very tense period, for things were going badly in France. Only four or five days after the hunt on Coombe Hill the evacuation from Dunkirk commenced and yet, as far as I can remember, there was no sense of panic or defeat, rather a feeling of grim determination for everyone to put their shoulder to the wheel and win in spite of the odds being heavily against us. Around the middle of June the Air Vice Marshall called at the house, soon after midday, to inform us that he been recalled to the colours and told his services were required at the Air Ministry and, he added, it was about time too. He couldn't understand why he hadn't been sent for before. Ethne, poor dear, suddenly had an awful choking fit. When she recovered, eyes streaming, she gasped that some sherry must have gone the wrong way. As he left the AVM shook me warmly by the hand and said it was now up to me to ensure the honour and vital work of the Scouts was maintained – Ethne had another sudden choking fit. The LDV Scouts died a natural death, for shortly after this the Volunteers became the Home Guard in which women were not allowed and without the girls we couldn't muster enough 'men' to carry on. There is no doubt that 'Dad's Army' as the Home Guard is now affectionately known, were a very serious force and would have fought to the last man with the antiquated arms with which they were issued. They were an expression of the country's mood of no surrender.

11. Blood, Toil and Sweat

Blood, toil and sweat was what the Prime Minister promised, he wasn't kidding either, at least not as far as the latter two were concerned for farmers who had had many years of experience of these two ingredients just to exist. Between the wars cheap imported grain, particularly wheat, had been allowed into the country in vast amounts making the growing of cereals, with our weather conditions, akin to a lottery – only with perfect weather was a reasonable return possible. On the meat side they had to compete against huge imports of New Zealand lamb, Danish bacon and Argentine beef. Life was not easy, the situation not having been helped over the years by the media, and urban population in general, deriding farmers and their staff as brainless yokels. Suddenly these yokels were all that stood between them and death – not necessarily from a German bomb or bullet, but a slow and dreadful death from starvation.

In 1939 British agriculture was grossly undercapitalised. Machinery that should have been used to extract the full potential of farms was not, purely because such an outlay in many cases had, for a number of years, been an uneconomic proposition. Farming in the 1920s and 1930s due to financial incentive just didn't exist. Farming was a way of life and the majority involved were born to the life that incorporated a love of the countryside, its traditions and sports, from which, through sheer hard work – frequently seven days a week from dawn till dusk – it was possible to scratch a living. Generally, it provided a tolerable, if not financially rewarding lifestyle, largely untroubled by bureaucracy. The outbreak of war and the establishment of the War Agricultural Executive Committees (WAEC) throughout the counties of our once peaceful, if not prosperous, land quickly changed all this.

Ironically it wasn't until the harvest of 1943 that the output from the land reached the level it could have been at the outbreak of war had successive governments paid the same attention and given as much support to agriculture as they had to industry. After the fall of France and we stood alone, what British agriculture was asked to do might be compared to the feeding of the 5000 with five loaves and two small fishes, for it is a fair analogy of what this industry, depressed for two decades, was expected to do. The fact that somehow this was achieved was in itself something of a miracle and certainly gave credence to the maxim that all things are possible.

The powers of the WAEC were draconian – land had to be farmed to its maximum potential; if the War Ag (as the WAEC was known) said ploughing, draining or fencing for example had to be done, then it *had* to be done. There were subsidies for ploughing up grassland, draining, all sorts of things, but they were only paid when a job was completed! Farming had been allowed to become so impoverished that, however willing the owner of the land might be, sometimes he was unable to comply with instructions purely on financial grounds. If he didn't his farm was taken over by the War Ag and he received no compensation. Further, there were a number of cases where a farmer, his land already having been appropriated, was subsequently turned out of his house on the basis that it was for an agricultural worker, which the owner no longer was. Some, I believe, never got their property back after the war.

One unfortunate man who owned something a little short of 130 acres known as The Grove, adjoining Ted Clarke's land and only two small fields away from Marsh Hill, had not farmed it properly since the 1914–18 war. He had neither the machinery to plough it himself nor the money to pay a contractor to do so. He was given two weeks to either sell it or start ploughing it. He came to me to see if the Colonel would buy it, but he was in the USA and would not be back within the prescribed time limit. I walked the land, all was basically good, but one fifty-four acre field was so rough with old waist-high grass and rubbish in general that it nearly always produced one or two foxes when we drew it hunting. I walked it several times and got the price down to £17 per acre. The owner was desperate to sell, for if he didn't he would lose his land and get nothing for it. Even in those days, at that price, it was for nothing. I explained that if I did do a deal on behalf of the Colonel I couldn't pay him in full, but would get the estate's solicitor to draw up a legally binding contract, which I would sign as the Colonel's agent and pay him £500 on account – five separately dated cheques of £100 each, the maximum I was allowed to draw in any one day. The owner jumped at the chance, the deal was formally agreed and the War Ag were no longer involved. To begin with the Colonel was inclined to think I had taken too much upon myself. However, when I suggested that having ploughed it and having deducted the cost of the latter I could double, possibly treble, his money he said no more, except that we should ride out and look at it.

Just after the fall of France I set off to visit Colonel Pollitt in Shropshire, to keep a pre-arranged meeting. The journey had to be by train, for it would have used up too much of my supplementary petrol allowance to have motored. We were so frantically busy that I decided to travel overnight, feeling confident I would sleep quite well on the train. I did not arrive in London until after 10.00pm and made my way across to Euston on the underground. It was my first visit to the capital in the evening for some months and I found that in places I had to literally pick my way through those who were settling down for the night all along the platforms. It was an awesome experience, but the banter and general backchat that seemed to be everywhere was wonderful. It made me feel that we, the farming fraternity, must bust a gut to somehow feed these people. I almost felt I was intruding as I made my way through the maze of mattresses and other improvised beds, to a position where I could board my train when it arrived in the station.

I reached my destination soon after 8.00am and was met by Col Pollitt, who drove us back to his house for breakfast. We started with porridge. There was a large silver sugar bowl on the table but its contents were green – dried grass. My host lavishly sprinkled it over his porridge and passed me the bowl, urging me to try it, telling me how good it was for one. I wasn't over keen, but it had to be a case of 'when in Rome'. However, after the first mouthful, as far as I was concerned the cows could have it. Fortunately, this was followed by eggs and delicious bacon, which the Colonel told me was home cured. I really enjoyed it as I was famished, for apart from a cup of very watery tea I'd been lucky enough to get at some station where we had had a long wait to let a troop train pass through, I'd had nothing for nearly the past twenty hours.

After we had breakfasted we set out around his farms, first going to a field where there were two Wilder Cutlifts at work, which cut and loaded grass straight on to the trailer. We then moved on to his two driers, both were working. The grass for the Templewood drier had to be forked from the trailer up on to a platform, eight or nine feet off the ground, then again across the deck and finally into the pre-drying trays. To me it seemed an awful lot of manual work. When the drum was emptied a panel, one of a pair sited in the top of the drum, would be opened, a pre-drying tray would then be cranked up and the grass slid down into the empty drum for the final process. When ready the front of the drum was opened, the dried grass raked out and fed into a hammer mill, which in turn blew it through to a bagger. The furnace was coke fired, so the operator, at ground level, was kept on his toes. He had to stoke the furnace, watch the temperature and when he thought the load was ready stop the drum and fan, open up the two sets of doors, rake out the dried grass, close up the drum's loading door when the pre-dried grass was in the drum, close up the front and start it up again. Whilst the new load was drying, the operator had to fork the previous load into the mill, then take off, weigh, fasten and stack the bags. I remarked to Col Pollitt that I thought it was a hell of a lot to expect from one man. He airily replied that once trained the men were on piece work. Each gang got paid on the tonnage produced on their shift and it was entirely up to them how many were in a gang. I had made lots of notes and by lunchtime we must have discussed every possible aspect of grass drying. We had an excellent lunch of roast leg of lamb, it looked about the equivalent of six people's ration for a month. The Colonel passed me a sauce boat, I inwardly prayed it was not more dried grass, but thankfully it was traditional mint. The Colonel gave me a wink, 'You know sheep do the daftest things. This silly bugger tried to climb up a tree of all things, fell and broke its leg. Couldn't let it go to waste of course. In the past I'd have phoned the kennels to collect it, but not now. Have some more?' I did, it was delicious. After insisting I have a glass of port with him after we'd finished our meal, Col Pollitt said he would drive me to the station. Like me he had no idea as to when there would be a London train, but he assured me there'd be one along sometime. I was lucky, not ten minutes after I arrived at the station a train pulled in heading for London. Again there was a long delay, after we'd been going for about an hour, to allow a munitions train through and later we had another long wait, for what reason neither I nor anyone else knew. It was just on midnight when I arrived back at Round Hill, Ethne having met me at Stoke Mandeville station.

A couple of days later I went over to the Templewood factory and had a long talk with Bertelli about my concern at the amount of grass handling when it was brought in from the fields and before it was in the pre-drying trays and told him how I thought it could be greatly reduced. He listened to what I had to say, said it made good sense and that he would develop my ideas. The result was an overhead gantry with an electrically operated travelling crane being installed. Strong angle-iron frames were made up to fit into the bottom of the Wilder trailers, with four lengths of steel cable, one being attached to each corner, fitted with rings at the ends to hook on to the hoist. The tractor driver drove into position, jumped up on the load, drew the four rings into the centre, hooked on, rode up on the load in over the deck, stopping opposite the centre of the two pre-drying trays. All that then had to be done was to lower the frame, unhook the two cables nearest the drier and raise the frame which would nicely deposit the grass so the man filling the trays could just stand and fork it in. The tractor driver then hooked on all four cables, travelled back over the trailer and lowered the frame into position. I was to learn in due course that this took five to six minutes at the most for turn round. At Col Pollitt's, where I had surreptitiously timed the procedure the manual unloading on to the deck took twelve to fifteen minutes, but then had to be again forked across into a position to fill the trays.

I had been instructed by Colonel Devereux to prepare a report, in the greatest possible detail, on all my findings and thoughts arising from my trip to Shropshire. This I did, even going to the extent of taking the old International tractor, one Sunday afternoon, and driving from various named points on the estate and timing how long it took from these to get back to the drier. When it was complete I was, to say the least, impressed with my own efforts. I posted a copy to the Colonel and awaited his comments. These came the next time he visited the estate. We went into the office, he settled in the armchair and we discussed various matters for about half an hour. Then he said, 'Grass drying. I've read your report on your trip to Pollitt's and your various suggestions that have evolved from this, but there is one major mistake on your part.' My heart sank. I'd been so careful, checked and double checked every point over and over again. The Colonel continued. 'Is this the first report of this type you've prepared?' I nodded – what the hell had I slipped up on? Dev started to laugh, 'I thought so. Never give your superior a report without making a deliberate mistake so he can say, "Ah, but if you did so-and-so, wouldn't that be better?" You didn't do that and I if was your senior in an office staff, I'd begin to wonder if you were about to make me redundant.' It was advice I never forgot and a ploy I used, tongue in cheek, in the years to come on a number of occasions – sometimes causing me much amusement when the deliberate mistake was not spotted!

12. Things Begin to Take Shape

It was the last week in June and I was riding along the new concrete road that let to the grass drier. My mount was a magnificent thoroughbred heavyweight hunter that I had recently acquired for the Master as a second horse to replace The Priest. His manners were impeccable and he would jump a five-barred gate off a road into a field with the greatest of ease – a test any horse bought for Dev had to pass. After the plundering of stables for Remounts, it seemed the War Office had finally realised that the cavalry was outdated and the acquisition of horses ceased. Further, it appeared that the War Office now realised that, like the poor Tommys (a nickname derived from the name Thomas Atkins used in specimen forms for British infantrymen in the 1914–18 war) officers had legs, could march with their men and no longer needed chargers. What happened to the horses commandeered in the early months of the war – and there were a considerable number – only those in high places knew. However, this lawful appropriation, together with the reduction in number due to the lack of land to keep and feed them had made the younger ones that remained, particularly heavyweights, once again quite costly.

I reined my mount to a halt opposite the drier. The last few courses of bricks should be in place by evening, completing the storage area, and I had been assured the doors to the latter would be fitted by the end of the week. Vic Wells, Templewood's chief fitter and operational instructor was busy working on the installation of the drier with two helpers. He saw me, waved, and wiping his oily hands on a rag walked over to me. 'Not long now Mr Twist. If all goes according to plan I should be ready for the first load of grass immediately after lunch next Tuesday. I'll want George and the other operators here first thing in the morning to take them right through the procedure.' George had been an under gamekeeper at my home. He had not been accepted for the army because of hammer-toes. He was a highly intelligent man and as father had no place for him, I offered him a job on the Roundhill estate, to be trained and then run the grass-drying plant throughout the season and work where required during the winter months. I was able to offer him and his wife a nice cottage. Prior to engaging him I had run an advertisement in both *Farmers Weekly* and *Farmer & Stockbreeder* for a grass-drier operator, or someone prepared to learn. The only reply I had was from a pensioner, who was willing to come out of retirement and do his bit, if suitable. He assured me in his letter that there was nothing he did not know about haymaking and could still use a scythe with the best of them if things got really bad. It was an indication as to how low the pool of farmworkers had become, for a modern three-bedroomed cottage with bathroom etc and good wages for a farmworker was very far from the norm in those days, at least as far as the accommodation was concerned.

The younger generation may think that riding around on a horse is far removed from toil and sweat and if purely for pleasure that would be true. However, four-wheel drive vehicles, such as Land Rovers, that could take one across rough countryside were still very much in the future. A horse was by far the easiest way for me to get around the estate to plan and oversee jobs. Having said cheerio to Vic I walked my horse forward about fifty yards through a gate into the grass field beyond. Tom, who was standing just inside to the right watching, smiled when he saw me. 'Reckon she'll be OK now. She's really got the hang of the job.' She was Eileen Cattle, one of the six Land Girls who were now part of the regular farm staff; an attractive little slip of a girl, with a bubbly personality, she was rapidly becoming an excellent tractor driver under the tuition of Sudden and Tom. Currently she was mowing a meadow for hay, using an old converted horse mower, with a four foot six inch cut. The trouble was that it had been designed for use behind horses, with a carter riding on the seat from where he was able to lift the cutter-bar with a lever when turning at the corners. The design was such that it couldn't be fitted with a trip to do this, which was standard to all tractor mowers and so an extra pair of hands were needed – on this occasion old Harry Montague's.

When Tom had assigned him the job first thing in the morning and told him he had to keep an eye on Eileen, he replied, 'Aye, reckon that's about all I can do now, but if I were fifty year' younger it'd be more 'an eye I'd be keepin' on er.' I don't know how old Harry was, age didn't seem to come into the equation in those days. If a man was fit and good at his work, he just carried on. A large number of those who had been on the same farm for decades were dedicated to their job and to the land they tended – it became as much their farm as their governor's. Harry was a very likeable and interesting countryman and in his day must have been a remarkably striking young man who surely turned many a maiden's head. He still retained much of his past looks, which were now partially concealed by a vast grey handlebar moustache.

On several evenings when he and others had been working overtime thinning root crops, he'd called at The Prince of Wales for a pint when I happened to be there. With a little aid from me this had often become three and once four. He told me many stories about his youth and how, back in the 1880s, he'd left school when he was about eleven or twelve and gone to work on a farm where his father was one of the horsemen. He recalled that his first job had been in the spring, rook scaring, keeping them off freshly sown corn. He had to be out in the field, having had a bite to eat, by dawn – between 4.00 and 5.00am. Each day, around noon, the farmer, or sometimes his wife, would bring him a lovely new home-baked loaf of bread, often still warm from the oven, probably about 1lb in weight, and a large jug of milky tea, or if the mistress had been making butter, then it was likely to be buttermilk. Often he would get an apple and, very occasionally a big wodge of home-made cheddar cheese. That was his lot for the day. He was supplied with an old tin tray that he used to bang with a piece of wood to scare the rooks, but, he claimed, they soon became accustomed to this, so he was frequently chasing around the field to keep them off. He had to remain at his post until the rooks started to head back to their roost. That he assured me was easy to tell, for they'd fly higher than throughout the day, cawing to each other as they headed for home. For this he was paid a shilling a day, seven days a week, half of which he had to give his mother to help towards his keep. However, on Sundays he was given an hour and a half away from work to go to church. This wasn't optional, the farmer he worked for was a churchwarden – so church attendance became an order. Harry didn't mind this but there was one major snag, namely if the pastor preached too long a sermon, which apparently he frequently did, Harry had to run like hell to get back to beating his tray by the time his ninety minutes were up. On a number of occasions when he'd only been seven or eight minutes late getting back to his rook scaring, his employer had docked a threepenny bit from his wages at the end of the week. This meanness turned Harry against his boss and so, come Michaelmas he had spruced himself up, gathered his few belongings together and gone off to a hiring fair, where he landed a job as 'the boy' on a big place. His new governor told him, before he actually hired Harry, that he'd be the only lad, for he believed in the old adage, namely, if you employed one boy – then you had a boy. If you took on two, then you had just half a boy and if you were foolish enough to take on three, well then you had no boy at all. Harry had lived in the attic of the farmhouse, got his feet under the kitchen table three times a day and, as he put it, filled his belly with bloody good grub, causing him to grow nigh on four inches in the first year he was there. He stopped, grinned and added, 'An' I tell you what, governor, there was a tweeny working there, mostly in the kitchen, who didn't make staying there too difficult.' Harry remained in the job, well content, until the outbreak of the Great War, at which time he immediately joined the army and came right through unscathed.

The tractor came round to the side of the field where I sat watching and discussing various matters with Tom. It was a 1938 Fordson on pneumatic tyres. It was painted a pleasing shade of green and had been found for me by Phil Oliver. Apparently he had bought it from some golf club, who presumably had it for cutting the rough either side of the fairways. The course had been taken over by the War Ag and was to be farmed by a neighbouring land owner, who it seemed did not know of the tractor's existence. Phil, I was to learn, always had a money belt buckled around his waist under his shirt and seldom carried less than £500. He always claimed there was nothing like 'the readies' to quickly make up a seller's mind. I thought £180 was pretty steep but it was a case of beggars can't be choosers. We started out with Phil asking £240, saying, which was probably true, that it was barely run in and it took me about twenty minutes to beat him down, for Phil was an experienced horse-coper. Along with thousands of others, I was frantic for all forms of machinery and when the opportunity arose to get what you wanted you grabbed it – quick. As she passed Eileen waved, whilst Harry sat, grim faced, on the hard iron seat, tightly gripping the edges as he was bounced along on an implement designed to go at less than half the speed at which it was travelling. However, both Tom and I knew Harry could be trusted, for there was no job on a farm to which he could not turn his hand, although sometimes his approach to it had not exactly progressed with the then current modes – such as dry-hand milking. Like virtually all farmworkers he could milk a cow, but in the old-fashioned way, namely a couple of good squirts of milk on to both hands and away he went. At some time before I arrived on the estate, they were short of help with the milking, so Tom had sent old Harry along to give a hand. He'd taken a bucket and stool, ignored Ron's instruction about washing each cow's udder and his hands before he started, sat down to a cow, given a good squirt on to each hand and he was away, the cow happily letting her milk down. Ron had remonstrated with him, telling him to wash both his hands and the cow's udder as instructed. Harry had got up off the milking stool, told Ron that wet-hand milking was the right and natural way – a calf's mouth wasn't dry and rough like bloody sandpaper as his calloused and work-hardened hands were and with that he walked out. I had to admit that there was a certain logic to support Harry's argument.

Phil finding the Fordson had been a stroke of great good fortune, because it seemed, momentarily at least, that new tractors weren't being made. I contacted numerous machinery merchants, but could find none with anything in stock in which I'd be interested. However, I did get lucky with one firm, for I was offered a Caterpillar D2, but it was very pricey when compared to a Fordson or an International. The asking price was around £500 so I felt I should consult the Colonel, but all I succeeded in doing was getting my ear filled and being told I was managing his farms, if it was a viable investment buy it, if not forget about it. With that he put the phone down. After finding out a little more regarding its potential, I bought it. I was told it could plough four furrows on really light land, three on medium to heavy. Our only plough was a two-furrow Ransome. I phoned their works at Ipswich to enquire if it was possible to convert the two furrow into a three. I was told this was no great problem, but they had a new three-furrow plough in stock. I bought it, which meant that with the new plough, plus the existing one and the old International tractor, we would be able to plough up to as much as ten acres a day – the equivalent to what could be achieved by ten teams of horses and ten men, which was the way the majority of land was ploughed in the 1930s.

The enthusiasm of the six girls for the work they had undertaken was quite amazing. I'd selected them from several dozen who had been sent, or brought out for an interview. Two sisters were local, from Wendover. Their father was a Squadron Leader, I believe attached to Horton Camp. The elder one, Molly, became dairymaid, which soon included milking, calf feeding and even leading out one of the bulls, who were taken out for exercise every day. Her sister Barbara, was a good hard worker, cheerful and didn't mind what she did. Florry, who came from London, developed a great rapport with the pigs, helping Fred Goodchild when necessary and when the herds became fully established, worked full time in a job she was not only good at, but seemed to thoroughly enjoy. Grace and Deane were great workers, cheerful, quick to learn and could soon turn their hand to many of the everyday jobs around the farms.

Having left Tom I rode around the back of the piggeries and along the edge of the adjoining field, which Tom had told me had had so much slurry spread on it. I took Tom's advice, which basically was that it had received so much pig muck that if we sowed a cereal crop it would almost be blown out of the ground. Therefore, it was planted with marrow stem kale, which had already reached a phenomenal height and was going to be a tremendous crop.

I then cantered down what was known as Great Ground and on to a field at Little Marsh, where the nucleus of both new herds was being penned over an old pasture scheduled to be ploughed in the autumn. It seemed at one stage that these herds would never materialise because legislation had been brought in, soon after I had cleared out all the diseased pigs, stating that feeding stuffs for pigs were to be rationed from a designated date. The allocation was to be based on the number on each holding on the date in question. On the Roundhill estate that was zero – two months previously, if one included piglets it would have been around 2000. To begin with I wasn't too concerned, feeling common sense would prevail and applied for an allocation for 1000 pigs, which I sent with a covering letter explaining the circumstances, even referring those involved to the Ministry of Agriculture's vet who had advised at the time. The reply I got back was a curt note which simply said, 'No pigs on the designated date means there will be no food allocation.' I went to see Mr Walley, Chief Agricultural Executive Officer for the county. I even went to see Lord Addison, chairman of the Bucks War Agricultural Executive Committee. Both were sympathetic, and both realised that it seemed likely that what was probably the largest piggery within the county would remain empty and totally non-productive throughout the war. However, they had received instructions from Whitehall and there could be no exceptions.

Walley did try to be helpful and told me that an unrationed pig food was about to come on to the market, known as Tottenham Pudding. This was being produced by an enterprising gentleman who had contracted to collect all the leftovers from the majority of London hotels, army canteens, in fact anywhere within ten miles of his plant. The swill would be boiled, ladled into what can be best described as circular moulds about two feet in diameter and nine inches deep, in which the Pudding was delivered and tipped. Together with Fred Goodchild, who had already arrived, but as yet had no pigs to care for, I visited the plant and met the owner. He was a cheerful Cockney who could easily have doubled for Walker in the famous TV series *Dad's Army*. Fred and I talked it over and decided that with Tottenham Pudding as a basis and the addition of home-grown barley and dried grass, we should be able to manage. I entered into an agreement with 'Walker' to take a regular weekly supply which he would deliver. It was revolting stuff, but comparatively cheap and definitely nutritious. It also produced some interesting 'trophies' for Fred, which included a very nice sold silver half-pint tankard and, by the time the war was over, several sets of excellent, if not matching, cutlery.

To date I had bought twelve in-pig Large White gilts and four rather special young sows carrying their second litters. In addition I had been able to obtain eight in-pig Berkshire gilts, all but one descended from the Burnham herd which had been dispersed in 1937, when Fred Goodchild was head pigman. There had been no particular reason for the sale of the herds but the owner of the estate had almost casually said to father one day, 'I'm not really interested in pigs, sell them.' Both herds, but in particular the Berkshires, were internationally known and, apart from the commercial side of meat, breeding stock were regularly exported to all parts of the world, particularly Japan, Australia and South Africa where, due to their black pigmentation, they did not suffer from the sun in the same way as breeds such as Large Whites. I had also bought, for what in those days was a very high price, a boar sold in the Burnham Dispersal Sale at five to six months of age, Burnham Marjua Monarch 3rd, who was proving to be one of the leading sires of the breed in the country. As soon as the pigs had been penned right across the field we were going to bring the piggeries back into use. I had had further talks with the Ministry of Agriculture vets and they assured me there was no fear of any reinfection from the previous problems, for the precautions taken were equal to what the Ministry would have insisted on following an outbreak of Foot and Mouth disease.

Not long after I took over the management of the estate I realised that it was essential we employed a maintenance man. The question was where was I going to find a man who was a reasonable carpenter and could lay bricks etc. For some weeks I searched in vain, via advertisements and the Labour Exchange. Archie Andrews, with whom I had become quite friendly since buying Duke, rang me one morning, largely to have a chat, for he was very despondent about Miss Heap's health, which he said was deteriorating rapidly. I happened to ask him if he knew of a man who could fulfil my requirements, but he was no help. No sooner had he rung off than my phone went – it was Renee from the exchange. She apologised, in a giggly sort of way, for listening in, but, she declared, there wasn't much happening at the time so she was having a little listen, but she thought she knew of just the man I was looking for, Fred Spittles. He lived up the road, she told me, from Round Hill, in one of a pair of quite new cottages owned by a retired farmer, Stanley Rose. She said that she'd heard yesterday – hastily adding when she had got home – that he had packed his job in with a firm of builders and was looking for work. I thanked Renee for the information and having gently chided her for being a naughty girl and listening to my conversation, hung up. I got in the car straight away, drove the half-mile or so up the road and was fortunate enough to catch Spittles at home. He was somewhat surprised to see me, for apparently he had only picked up his cards the evening before. He seemed a very pleasant man and obviously knew his job. I made a note of the names and phone numbers of two previous employers, in order to check references he'd shown me. I was about to leave saying that if I was happy after I had contacted the two referees, I'd get Tom Burrows to drop a note in about him coming for an interview next day, when I passed some comment about the cottages. He said they were quite new and that Mr Rose had built them at the same time as he'd built his own new house, when he sold the main Kimblewick Farm to Mr John Robarts. Further, would I like to look over his as he thought Mr Rose was thinking of selling them. It was a nice three-bedroomed cottage, with a sitting room, good-sized kitchen and a bathroom with wc, mains water and electricity. Fred told me the one next door was exactly the same and he paid five shillings a week rent. Having left Spittles I visited the two firms who had provided him with references – I didn't want another debacle as there had been over Kay Browne. All was well and Fred Spittles started work the following Monday. The Colonel was down over the weekend and I told him about the possible sale of Stanley Rose's cottages. What were they worth? I replied that I thought they'd have cost about £600 to build the pair. Dev thought for a moment. 'They'll be worth more after this war. If they definitely come on the market, go up to £1000.' Only a few days later old Stanley Rose came to see me, he'd heard I'd taken on Spittles and he didn't see why he should provide accommodation for the Colonel's workmen, so would he like to buy the cottages. After much haggling I bought the pair for £700. Subsequently I learned that old Stanley had them built in 1937 for £600, so he made a nice profit. The next time I saw Renee, at The Prince of Wales, I bought her a large gin and tonic. Her behaviour was certainly unethical and contrary to regulations, but looking back to those days it was a hell of a lot better than all this business of 'if you have a star button please press it, then if you want so and so press on etc, etc.' Over the years Renee proved to be a tremendous help not only in getting calls on the ever more-crowded lines, but, if for some reason, Megan Pring wasn't in the office, I only had to let Renee know I'd be out and she would take messages for me. Further, if one had a really private call and said, 'Renee get off the line', she did.

13. More Haste, Less Speed

Following Dunkirk urban Britain realised that its main source of sustenance was going to come from the countryside which, until recently, had been looked upon as a place to go for a picnic, enjoy fresh air and in spite of objections from cranky yokels, wander without restriction. At the Burnham Grove estate just prior to the war, four of the estate workers were paid overtime on a Saturday afternoon and Sunday in the summer to help the gamekeepers dissuade urban visitors from picnicking in the middle of fields of corn or hay and leaving gates open so that cattle could wander into a field of clover, where they were in danger from bloat, which once led to the death of two cows. Such thoughtlessness was almost entirely due to ignorance and a deep-seated and erroneous belief that everything in the country just happened, with the whys and wherefores seldom given serious consideration. Now many from towns and cities were anxious to give a helping hand during their holidays with hay, harvest or wherever they could be of use. While this was both patriotic and well meaning, it was also an eye-opener to those who volunteered as they discovered there was more to farmwork than they had imagined, but one didn't have to be a townie to make this discovery.

The weather throughout the haymaking period of 1940 was, on the whole, above average but it was still essential to save every mouthful in good condition, in order to carry livestock through the winter. It was a time of long and, I suspect, tiring days, but there was really no time to think about the latter, at least not for me and I was amongst the majority. When my head hit the pillow, which, whilst we were getting in the hay and harvest was usually around midnight, I zonked out within seconds. Like most involved in farming, I was up every morning at 6.00am and, providing it wasn't pouring with rain, was off riding around the estate by 6.30am, checking on what was going on and what needed doing. I usually breakfasted around 8.30am and Tom would meet me at the office at 9.00am when we would discuss the day's work and plan ahead. One particular Saturday morning we were discussing a big field of hay which, providing it wasn't rained on, was going to be in excellent condition; we decided if it was turned with the swathe-turner a couple of times during the day, it should be ready for ricking the next day, providing the weather held. I knew there would be no trouble in getting the staff to work on a Sunday and, with a bit of luck we would have two-thirds of the field safe by the time the dew started, but with double summer time that could be quite late, for it was light up to close on 11.00pm.

Later that day the Colonel phoned to say that he would be down that evening and we were to ride out in the morning and discuss certain duties he wanted me to take over in connection with the hunt. I was prepared for an earful when I said that wouldn't be very convenient as I was anxious to get as much as possible of a biggish field of excellent hay ricked and had counted myself in as one of the gang to achieve this. There was silence for a minute, then Dev said, 'Quite right. Tell Hitchcock to have two horses ready by 6.30am. We can take a look around the estate and talk at the same time. Then as soon as you're ready to start, after breakfast, I'll help with the hay. What's more I'll round up one or two others to lend a hand but I won't be able to stop after about four o'clock.' With that he hung up. When he arrived at the house around 9.00pm he was in cracking form and told me he'd told John Herron, married to Dorothy Devereux's sister Violet and employed in one of the factories, that he was to come and help. Further, he said he'd talked Geoff Herrington, his second in command at High Duty Alloys to join the party, which was exactly how I felt the Colonel viewed the morrow.

On hearing this I slipped away for a few minutes and went across to Tom Burrow's cottage to give him the good tidings. Tom's immediate reaction came out with his usual forthright north country candour, 'Bugger me, what the hell are we going to do with them?' Eventually we decided we'd put the boss on the rick to help with the building. Normally the rick team was Joe Swaine building, Harry Montague forking to him and Left-Legged Harry clearing the hay as it fell from the elevator. In the field I would be loading the one big trailer we had, with Tom and Sudden pitching the hay up to me. When loaded Sudden would drive to the rick and join me forking it off the load. There were two smaller trailers and we'd decided that Eileen and Deane should drive the two other tractors, pitching on to trailers what they were able, together with Tom. Miles and the grafter Spittles should load them. Eventually I decided I would take John Herron with me because, for those times, it was a very long trailer (25 feet), and he should be able to keep out of my way. I felt Geoff Herrington had been truly railroaded into participating and so I suggested he should help Tom to whatever degree he felt inclined. After breakfast the Colonel changed into cords, an open-necked shirt and borrowed a sun-hat from Ethne, who told him he looked very becoming; whilst Dorothy worried he'd do himself an injury. It looked like being a real scorcher and I must say I was a bit concerned that my governor would attack rick building in the same way he seemed to face up to all work, and such an approach might not be too good for his heart. I suggested, that like me, he should wear a pair of string riding gloves, as his hands weren't hardened sufficiently to use a two-grained fork all day, for which advice I got no thanks. The two reluctant volunteers turned up soon after 10.00am and by 10.30am we had made a start. Joe and Harry had already marked out the size of the rick and put down a straw base to build on. Load followed load in quick succession. Dev really got stuck in and was forking hay straight to Joe, who was also being supplied as and when he needed it by Harry. Building a rick is quite an art, that is building one that is going to remain standing. John Herron kept out of the way when I was loading the trailer, but when we got back to the elevator he went mad, chucking it off at such a rate that poor old Left-Legged Harry was nearly buried, causing him to shout at John, 'You, yer daft bougger what the 'ell are you a trying to do, bury I?' Things were getting out of hand and I didn't know what to do. It had just passed noon as we finished unloading the big trailer. I told Sudden to pull clear and wait. I climbed up on to the rick, waded across to the Colonel who, judging by the grin with which he greeted me was enjoying himself, even though his face was scarlet, running with sweat and covered in hayseeds. I suggested he slowed down, not only for his own good, but to give Joe a chance to do a proper job building the rick. He roared with laughter, 'Not bloody likely. Don't you know we've a war to win? When you go back out in the field, tell old Geoff to go to the house, get a couple of churns off Rose and go down to The Prince of Wales and fill them up with bitter.' I gasped, they were two-gallon churns used for taking milk to the house dairy for butter making. 'That's thirty-two pints. We want the hay ricked, not the staff lying in it, sleeping off a gut full of beer in the sun.' The Colonel replied, 'All right, one churn and £1 extra for everyone if we clear this field today.'

At lunchtime Dev rang someone to cancel an appointment – told them he was busy on his farm building a hay rick. It was coming up to eight in the evening when Sudden pulled in to the elevator with the last load. The Colonel came stiffly down the ladder off the rick; as he passed the trailer where I was quietly unloading, he called up, 'I told you it could be done, but I must go. Make sure the gang get their bonus, they've done a great job.' Twenty minutes later the Bentley raced off up the road. When Tom and I then walked round the so-called rick I said to him, 'What a bloody shambles. What the hell can we do with it?' Joe Swaine was nearby, 'Sorry boss, but even when Harry was helping me to keep the sides straight the governor was throwing hay about as though there were no tomorrow.' 'I know Joe, it's not your fault, get off home now and we'll see what we can figure out in the morning,' I replied. Tom and I walked around the rick again. It had a definite tilt, thankfully away from and so, hopefully, out of sight of the road. Tom said, 'All we can do is put in four or five policemen (a common country term for big wooden props to hold up a rick) tomorrow, rake down the sides and ends and hope we can make it look half-decent. It would damned well be right by the road too, where everyone will see what a cock-up it is. I'm off, sir, I've had enough for one day. May God preserve us from bloody amateurs, however well meaning they may be.' With that he was gone. Alas, next morning was too late to get the policemen in position, the whole lot had slipped over and some thirty tons of hay was more vulnerable to the weather, should it change, than it would have been had it still been in swathes out in the field. Fortunately it stayed fine, but it took two days of back-breaking and unnecessary work to rebuild, but when finished it was a rick Joe said 'weren't too bad considerin' how the governor had bouggered things up to start with,' the sides being absolutely perpendicular and the corners as square as could be.

Looking at it a week or so later with Tom, after it had settled, I remarked that when thatched and the sides pulled it would be a rick of which we could be proud. Tom agreed, but added there would be no need to pull the sides, that is hand pull all the loose wisps that invariably protrude, however good the builder might be. I asked him why not, as it was just a matter of putting the finishing touch to a job well done. He laughed, 'Oh the fairies will come and do it at night.' I asked him what the devil he was on about. It transpired that old Gilbert, the sweep, would pull the sides of any ricks close to the road at night, bag up the wisps and take them back to store as winter fodder for his pony. Further, that he always made an excellent job of tidying up ricks.

I heard from Ethne, via nanny, who'd heard from Mrs Devereux, that on the Monday, after 'the haymaking party' the Colonel could hardly move he was so stiff from all the effort he'd put into his rick building. Further, that his hands were so terribly blistered he had had to get the nurse at the High Duty Alloys factory to put a dressing on them. Misguided help, but what guts! I can truthfully say that in all my reasonably long life he was without any shadow of doubt the greatest and most dynamic person I have ever met. When next the Colonel was at Round Hill and we set off around the estate he remarked, 'I could have sworn that rick I helped build was nearer the road.' I quickly changed the subject. When old Joe Swaine thatched it, a job he excelled at, he made a reasonably good job of fashioning a corn dolly in the likeness of a charging bull at one end of the ridge, whilst at the other there was, until the first strong wind, a most creditable likeness of a gate!

Much of the help that was forthcoming indeed fulfilled that role, for example the three youngish ladies who were taking a break from the traumatic life they led in London. I first encountered them one morning when I called at The Prince of Wales to see if Mrs Leversuch had any cigarettes. They were seated at an outside table sipping shandies, Mrs L leaning against the door frame, having a good old natter. When she saw me she said, 'Ah, here's a gentleman who might help you.' I was to learn that the three ladies were spending ten days camping on a nearby smallholding, but were finding, after the first couple of days, that time hung fire – was there anything they could do to help the war effort and fill their days? As it happened there was. I had bought in some 'once grown' wheat seed (the first crop produced from certified pedigree seed) and to my horror, whilst the wheat looked good and healthy, there was an abundance of wild oats, a most insidious weed, which back in the 1940s was a devil to get rid of, other than by laboriously going through a crop pulling it by hand and carrying it back to the headland. I told the ladies about this and they were all for it, particularly when I added that I was prepared to pay them. However, they did add a proviso, namely that they were on holiday and could work when they felt like it and weren't tied to hours. I suggested we went and looked at the field and agreed a price for the job, then they could come and go as they liked. This we did, a price was fixed and they did an excellent job. They also made friends with some of our Land Army girls and I gather there were a few lively evenings at The Prince of Wales before they returned to London.

Unfortunately, some of the proffered assistance was more of a hindrance than a help. None more so than the two young ladies, anxious to do their bit, wished on me by the Colonel two years after the summer of the famous, or perhaps more accurately infamous, rick. They were the daughters of two very big names in the world of aviation both of whom were knighted for the splendid and incredibly valuable contribution they made towards our winning the war. At the time there was a spare twin-bedded room free in the Land Girls' cottage and Dev had said they could stay there. Their ETA was given at sometime during the afternoon – not very helpful as life was becoming more and more hectic – and it appeared that these two girls were to be treated with the utmost deference. After a little persuasion Ethne, who was going to give Ann a riding lesson, agreed to do the honours. When I got back for tea Ethne told me our two new helpers had arrived in a chauffeur-driven Daimler and she'd taken them down to the cottage. She added she thought they had brought most of Fortnum & Mason with them in a large hamper and didn't seem over-impressed with their accommodation.

I had much to do and it was about 8.30pm by the time I returned to the house. After a shower and a quick change I suggested to Ethne and Rose that we walk down to The Prince of Wales for a drink. Rose declined, but Ethne said why not. As we neared the girls' cottage we could see our reinforcements, Sue and Betty, standing just inside the gate. They seemed to be prime examples of 'fish out of water'. We stopped and I introduced myself, thanked them for offering to come and help out on the farm and said the staff started at 7.00am, except with the dairy herd, where they began at 5.00am. The look of horror on their faces was such that Ethne started to laugh, which caused Sue to say, 'But we frequently don't get to bed until an hour or so before that.' I replied, 'Well there'll be nothing here to keep you up to that hour, unless Ron Chamberlain, from next door, calls you to help calve a cow.' Betty's face was a study – 'You're not serious?' I laughed, 'No, just leg-pulling. We're on our way down to the local pub, would you care to join us?' They looked at each other and Sue said, 'Yes, there doesn't seem much going on around here.' We walked on, both Ethne and I did our best to make conversation, but it was tough going. When we reached the pub, Ethne introduced them to old Mrs Leversuch and I asked them what they would like to drink. Looking at poor Mrs L Betty asked 'What cocktails do you do?' Poor old soul, she was totally nonplussed. Ethne explained it was a choice of bitter, mild, a shandy, or, when there was any, a gin and tonic. Sue wrinkled up her nose and said, 'How quaint.' They both decided on a shandy. Sue sniffed and sniffed again, then turning to Ethne asked, 'What's that extraordinary smell?' Ethne looked round the corner into the room and said, 'Hullo Gilbert, like a pint?' She didn't wait for an answer, for it was an offer never known to be refused. Sue looked into the room too, jumped back and almost yelled, 'Oh my God, what's that?' I answered her question and assured her that Gilbert was a harmless old sweep. Then, tongue in cheek, I added that she might like to make his acquaintance in case, when she got married she felt she would like a sweep to attend her wedding for good luck.

If ever two people struggled to make conversation it was Ethne and I. We could find nothing in common with our visitors and they made little effort to hide their boredom. Ethne did discover that the pristine light fawn slacks that Betty was wearing and which fitted snugly around her bottom had been purchased, just before clothes rationing commenced, from a sale at Harvey Nichols and she considered them suitable attire for working on a farm. At that moment a jovial, slightly rotund local character, Bill, walk in. He owned a few acres, would give a helping hand anywhere he could pick up a few bob, loved to get a singsong going in the pub whenever possible, which fortunately was seldom, and was a renowned poacher, but purely for the pot. Quickly eyeing Betty up and down he greeted her with a big smile, 'Hello love, not got your uniform yet? But don't worry, you look smashing as you are. Lovely little bum.' As he pushed past her, he gave the focal point of his admiration a quick tweak, then he called out to Mrs Leversuch, 'Usual please, love, and a half for that miserable old husband of yours.' Betty's mouth opened wide, but sound came there none – it was the only time I've ever seen anyone struck dumb!

Ethne's reflexes were quicker than mine, she downed the remains of her drink in a second and had the two girls out through the door before Betty's verbal explosion surfaced. I quickly joined them and was interested to discover that Betty who had featured in Tatler at major social events more than once, had a command of the English language which at that time was wider than the Oxford Dictionary. The storm having abated, we continued in silence. We were just approaching a bend in the road when four stirks, which I recognised as belonging to a smallholder, Rogers, whose property lay between Marsh Hill and Meadacre Farm, came racing round it. I shouted to spread out across the road and stop them. They had obviously broken out from their field. Ethne, like me, started waving her arms and leaping about in the road to turn the runaways. The stirks were not the only ones that could be so categorised, for, having been successful in our efforts, I realised our two companions had fled back towards the pub, but had stopped about 150 yards away and were standing like a couple of lame ducks in the middle of the road. I could see Ethne's Irish blood was rising – she had, at times, a very volatile temper. She called to the two girls to come and help drive the yearling back up the road. One shouted back something about them being bulls and that opened the sluice and Ethne gave vent to her feelings. At that moment Rogers and his wife arrived, thanked us for stopping their cattle and set off driving them home up the road ahead of us. It wasn't until they were out of sight that Sue and Betty joined us and we proceeded in stony silence to the cottage. I turned to the two girls, bid them goodnight and said I'd see them at Marsh Hill punctually at 7.00am next morning. I had already pointed out the way and told them it was only six or seven minutes' walk from the cottage.

Next morning there was still no sign of our two volunteers at 7.30am. I had decided with Tom that the only thing we could do was to set them off horse-raking the field opposite the cottage where they were staying. We had carried the hay two days previously, but there was enough left to make raking a worthwhile job. Originally Grace had been going to do it and Tom had in fact sent her to harness up the old shire mare, Smiler, and get on with the job, before I talked to him about Sue and Betty. I was in the car that morning and around 8.00am gave Tom a lift back to Round Hill. As we reached the cottage – Grace had just taken Smiler and the rake into the field – the two girls appeared. I glanced at my watch and, probably rather sarcastically, said 'Good afternoon girls.' Betty was the spokeswoman. 'We couldn't get to sleep for ages after being chased by those bulls.' To my surprise it was Grace who replied, 'Don't talk nonsense, they're little more than calves.' Betty positively bridled and demanded, 'What would you know about it.' Grace snapped back, 'Plenty. I helped the Rogers get them back in the paddock. As for being bulls, two are heifers and the others have no more balls than you two – they've been steered.' She turned to Tom, 'What now?' He told her to go and join the gang hoeing through a field of turnips down at Little Marsh. As she left she looked daggers at the two visitors. It was obviously going to be a blistering hot day and riding on a horse rake would have been far more pleasant than hoeing roots.

I left Tom to it. One girl was to ride on the rake and pull the lever when it was full to empty it, the other was to lead Smiler up and down the field. They could periodically change places. The last thing I said before leaving the field was, 'Now remember, which ever of you is leading Smiler, when you get to the end of the field turn her away from you. If you turn her towards you she could step on your foot and that could be very painful.' Three quarters of an hour later Tom joined me for our usual morning meeting. I asked how our recruits were getting on. 'Well, I went up and down the field with them and again impressed on them that they must turn Smiler away from them. I can't do more, but what the hell are we going to do with them for the remainder of the week?' I didn't answer, because I didn't know. I went into Aylesbury shortly after that, so stopped at the field for a moment. Smiler was obviously well in control. She was a lazy old thing and a sauntering snail could well pass her if there wasn't someone in charge who would make her buck up her ideas. As I drove on, one thought crossed my mind, if the weather stayed good old Smiler might partially solve one problem, for at the rate she was going she could well turn a short day's work into three. An hour and a half later when I returned, I stopped at the gate. Smiler stood about fifty yards out in the field, still between the shafts of the rake, happily munching hay, but no girls. I went into the field. I thought they might be sunning themselves under the hedge, but there was no sign of them.

I crossed the road, walked down the side of the cottage and entered via the back door. I called out and received a reply from the sitting room. I went through and there, stretched out on an old settee, was Sue, her make-up streaked from tears. 'Whatever's happened?' It was Betty who again took on the role of spokeswoman. 'That bloody horse, it ought be shot. It's crushed poor dear Sue's foot.' I kept my cool and quietly said, 'I don't think the horse is to blame. You did what you were specifically told not to. You turned Smiler towards you, didn't you Sue?' Betty was obviously about to deny it, but Sue nodded and gulped 'Yes'. I moved forward and knelt down beside her. 'Well, certainly your foot isn't crushed. Probably just a bit bruised.' I turned to Betty, 'Why didn't you get her shoe off?' She gave me a sulky look and replied, 'I don't understand about these sort of things.' I turned back to Sue and said, 'Right I'm going to take your plimsoll off. I'll be very gentle, but it could be painful just for a moment. Then I'll get your sock off and Betty can put cold compresses on it to reduce the swelling.' The shoe came off with only one squeak from Sue, but the ankle length sock seemed to be causing more of a problem. After several attempts to get it off over the heel, which were met by cries of 'No, please no' I pulled out my pocket knife, which I always kept near razor sharp, told her to keep still unless she wanted to lose her foot and quickly slit it down the front. Her foot was slightly swollen, but I felt pretty sure there was nothing broken. I showed Betty how to apply a compress, then I addressed them both. 'Sue you obviously aren't going to be able to do anything on the farm for several days, so I think I should phone your mother and ask her to collect you both.' Sue was fighting back tears but Betty's face lit up. 'Would you really?' I nodded and she continued, 'We never had any real idea of what is involved in farming and don't understand how, or, indeed, why anyone does it.' I laughed, 'Let's take the "why" first. The answer to that is easy. As far as I personally am concerned I love the countryside, the wildlife, the traditions, the people, the country sports and at this moment the biggest why is to help feed those of you who so frequently belittle what you don't understand. The 'how' is by the sweat of our brow and I'm proud to be a very, very small part of the job the British farming community are doing at this time – it's … it's glorious.' I paused for a moment, 'I'm sure you'll both think me mad, but in spite of the threat of invasion by the Nazis I've never been happier. It's such a challenge.' For the first time Sue gave a slight smile. I felt the cold compress was already doing good. 'You're a bit like my dad. He, too, is working all hours, but loving every minute of it.'

I bid Sue goodbye. As she walked to the door with me, Betty put her hand on my arm, and said, 'I'm sorry I was such a stupid bitch last night. I apologise and please give my apologies to Ethne.' I phoned Sue's mother who seemed to panic, but I assured her it was nothing serious. Soon after 5.00pm I saw the Daimler sweep down the road to the cottage, only to return ten minutes later when Sue's mother went into the house. A further five minutes and she was off again. I went to find out what was going on. Nanny told me that apparently brandy was required to revive the poor girl and she had grudgingly handed over two-thirds of a half-bottle which the Colonel had entrusted to her safe keeping. I thought this strange for when I left Sue had a bruised foot, but nothing more exciting than that. It was about an hour and a half later that the car returned and Sue's mother walked in. 'I've had a terrible time. The poor child was in such pain, but the brandy seemed to ease it.' Nanny interrupted, 'Can I have the brandy back please.'

'I'm afraid not, she drank it all, I left the empty bottle by the sink. If it hadn't been for that kind man from next door carrying her out to the car, I don't know how I'd have managed.' I joined in the conversation and asked, 'Does Sue drink a lot?'

'Oh dear me no. She's like me, seldom touches alcohol.' Somehow I refrained from laughing, instead I stepped forward, held out my hand and said, 'I'm so sorry that things have turned out like they have. I really think you should get underway and get poor Sue tucked up in bed.' When they had gone Ethne doubled up laughing, 'Silly old bat, she's made the poor girl absolutely pie-eyed. I'd have a bet that it'll be Sue's head that will be worrying her more tomorrow morning than her foot.'

I could fill many more pages about people who out of the goodness of their hearts wanted to help with various jobs on the farms. Some contributed much, others were more of a liability, but the spirit was willing and that was what counted and, as a nation, saw us through those memorable years.

14. A Time of Greatness, Grief and Glory

The end of July and into the autumn of 1940, when the Germans tried their damnedest to bring this country to its knees, but which instead culminated in the victorious Battle of Britain must surely rank as the nation's 'finest hour'. At the same time as the Luftwaffe flew sortie after sortie the U-boats kept up a relentless attack on our shipping, to an extent that in one week at the end of October we lost 88000 tons of vital food supplies to this country. This put an even greater strain on our agriculture, but at the same time stiffened our resolve to produce more and more.

It is a period that I remember well. Due to double summer time it was light up to nearly 11.00pm and, during hay and harvest, a sixteen- to eighteen-hour day became the norm when weather conditions were good. The wretched milking machine had long since gone – to my utter amazement I had been able to sell it for a little more than it had cost. The cowshed had been re-equipped with standings, fortunately those that had been taken out had gone no further than a small open-fronted cart shed at the back of the main farm buildings. A part of one of the open yards had been transformed into a second byre. Now all that was needed was the quality cows to put in them. I attended numerous sales together with Ron Chamberlain, but cows, or indeed in-calf heifers, of the quality we sought, seldom came under the hammer.

In the middle of August I had a phone call from a very distressed Archie Andrews who told me that Miss Heap had died two days previously and her heir was already asking how soon the herd could be sold. I asked Archie how many would be catalogued and he said twenty-four or twenty-five milkers and a further seventeen, being in-calf heifers, yearlings and an excellent stock bull, Arden Wildeyes Bellringer the 4th. I went out from my office into the stable yard, called for Bob to saddle up a horse for me and was quickly off around the estate. I have to admit that I wasn't concentrating too much on what was happening, for I had a thought going round and round in my head. The more I thought the more I liked what I was thinking. When I got back to my office I put a call through to the Colonel. Fortunately he was available and, for good measure, seemed in great form. I told him about Miss Heap's death and that the Diamond herd was to be sold. In spite of all that was happening in the war, he had lost none of his enthusiasm for building up a really first-class herd. I put my idea to him, namely that he should buy the Diamond herd in its entirety. He asked me how much I thought it might cost. I replied between 4000 and 4500 guineas. I was immediately told to get on with it. However, I pointed out that the new owner might think he could get more by holding an auction. I received a curt reply, 'I've agreed, so it's up to you to persuade him that it's in his interest to sell to me.' With that the phone went dead.

I telephoned Archie and said that Ron and I would like to come over that evening to have a look at the cows. He assured me we would be most welcome. We went carefully through all the milkers and with the exception of three old cows light of a quarter and used for calf rearing, there was nothing we wanted to discard. Then I told Archie of my idea. His face lit up like the rising sun, 'My God, that would be fantastic. The herd wouldn't be split up and you could go on building on the foundation I've laid.' I asked how he thought the new owner would react. Archie said he thought very favourably, as all he was after was the money and Archie had told him that to organise a successful auction would take several months. Further, with the herd gone the property could be put on the market within weeks. We then discussed how we should reach a valuation. I said that I thought Miss Heap's estate should pay for this on the basis of paying 1/- in the guinea, as was standard practice at auctions. Alternatively Archie might be able to agree a fee with a valuer beforehand. However, if having had the herd valued I felt the figure was too high and so would not continue the deal, then the Colonel would pay half the cost of the valuation. Archie thought this was very fair and equitable. The next thing to decide was to select a valuer agreeable to us both. We were in Archie's house by this time. He went to his desk and passed me a pencil and a piece of paper, 'Write down your first choice, I'll do the same.' The name on both slips of paper was the same, Harry Hobson, probably the most competent auctioneer and valuer of pedigree stock in the country at the time and noted for his honesty. Archie phoned me the next day to tell me that the new owner was delighted with the idea and again a week later to tell me Harry Hobson had been and I would be receiving a detailed valuation within the next few days. I was gratified to learn that the estimate I had given Colonel Devereux wasn't far out, for the herd changed hands for £4,180, the commission to Harry Hobson & Co being paid by Miss Heap's executors. Ten days later they were all safely transferred to Round Hill Farm. The grass drier was fully operational and turning out between two and three tons a day. The quality wasn't high, for the majority of the grass being cut at that time of year was no better than what would have made top-quality hay, so carotene content was low. Nevertheless we were getting from £21 to £23 per ton. The carotene, our agent told me, was extracted for medical purposes and the remainder sold on to manufacturers of animal feeding stuffs, including that prepared for pigs. We used it in our own mix for the dairy herd and, through necessity, for the pigs, finding that mixed with barley meal on a two to one ratio it supplemented much that was missing from Tottenham Pudding and the pigs seemed to be thriving.

Much to the Colonel's delight three of the Berkshires had farrowed, averaging eight to a litter, whilst seven Large Whites had pigged averaging eleven, with one of thirteen, and all were doing well. He told me that long before the various ailments struck the previous herd they lost more than a third of every litter before they were eight weeks old. As a result I happened to mention that there was to be a draft sale of one of the leading herds of Large Whites in the country, to be held the following week in the Midlands. Dev asked if I was going. I replied no, as we were just getting into the harvest and I didn't want to be away while such an important job was going on. I was asked whether I had faith in Tom Burrows. Having replied in the affirmative, I was then told to attend the sale, take Goodchild with me and buy eight to ten of the best in-pig gilts on offer. Further, he would send a chauffeur-driven car from High Duty Alloys to take us. He had a factory very close to where the sale was being held, so there would be no problem over transport. On the appointed day Fred and I set off in style around 7.00am, leaving a very delighted Florry to look after the pigs. It was a highly successful trip and, as Fred said on our way home, we could now quickly build up the Large Whites from home-bred stock. To add to the general pressure it transpired that Dev had been talking to Col Pollitt who had mentioned that he now kept a small flock of sheep on what had been a totally livestock-free farm and assured the Colonel they were a good investment. The only trouble was that occasionally one of the silly buggers would try and climb a tree, or do something equally daft and break a leg or its neck. Of course pre-war it would have been a case of sending for the knackerman to take it away, but ... well one couldn't waste good food, so it ended up on his and a few friends' tables. In early August Dev was paying a fleeting visit to the estate and casually asked, 'What do you think about keeping a small flock of sheep?' There was a look in his eye that told me something was more afoot than just the general economics of the farm, for there had never been any talk of sheep before and I knew Tom Burrows had tried to persuade him, before I ever arrived, to keep some. Suddenly the penny dropped, 'You've been talking to your friend Col Pollitt.' Dev roared with laughter, 'Maybe I have. I gather there is a bit of a risk that occasionally one breaks its neck or something like that.' Reading the picture quite clearly, I replied, 'Well that's a risk with all livestock – there can always be an accident.'

'Well as long as there can be, I think we should get a few nice breeding ewes. As far as what breed we have I'll leave that to you and Burrows.' When I told Tom he was delighted and suggested we get a truckload of about thirty-five to forty Masham two-year-old ewes from his home area, which would be the right number for one ram. Further, he claimed his dad would be just the man to buy them for us. I wasn't acquainted

**Colonel Wallace Charles
Devereux MFH.**

**The author (left) with R.C. Lee of Carters Seeds,
standing with a crop of Victory Oats in 1941. An
R2 Caterpillar tractor with a 'binder' can be seen
in the background.**

This picture of Stormont Prince, a point-to-point winner that had to be shot because of the war, was taken a few days before his death.

Diamond Wild Duke, one of the most successful Dairy Shorthorn sires of the 1940s.

The Champion Group at the November 1943
Reading Shorthorn Society Show and Sale. From
left: Roundhill Telluria Prince, Roundhill Wildeyes
Duke 2nd and Roundhill Telluria Duke 1st, the
Reserve Champion who sold for 900 guineas.

The Colonel enjoys a cup of tea with his wife and
daughter Ann whilst out exercising the hounds.

Land Girl Barbara Collinson, about to take a Hampshire Down ram out to join the ewes.

The quadruplets, the first lambs born at Roundhill, who were reared by their mother and helped by Barbara with a bottle.

'Sudden', about to take a load of muck out to spread, aided by Deane riding on the tractor mudguard.

Barbara Collinson, about to start raking oat
stubble with Smiler. Stooks of uncarted corn can
be seen in the background, but every grain was
precious - nothing was wasted.

Clive Haselden MRCVS, about to leave Round
Hill stables after a call.

The author (left), Clive Haselden and Emerys
Parry, at the Kimble AI Centre's first open day.

The author (left) and Phil Oliver, on their way to
Pairs Class victory at the OBH Hunter Trials in
1946.

The author receiving the cup for the
champion hunter from Lord Wigram at the 1944
Windsor Horse Show. Background, left: the
judge, 'Tidley' Lucas.

Ann Devereux receiving the cup after winning
the 12.2hh pony class at the 1944 Windsor Horse
Show. The disconsolate little girl in the background is Pat Moss.

A Massey-Harris 21 Combine in 1944. A man
can be seen bagging up the corn. As soon as
there were three bags on the chute they were
jettisoned to be collected by other members of
the harvesting gang with a tractor and trailer.
The sacks of corn weighed 1¹/₂–2cwt.

Wilder's Cutlift - a great labour-saving invention.

with Mashams, but Tom assured me they were very hardy hill sheep that produced lovely lambs if put to a ram of any of the Down breeds. I told Tom to contact his father and get some as soon as possible. Tom eventually got through to his father on the phone that evening and placed an order for the agreed number of two-year-old ewes. Apparently his dad charged a shilling a sheep commission for buying them, plus whatever he had to pay for help to get them to the station, loaded and, of course, the rail costs. Normally he didn't send sheep off until he was paid in full, but in our case he'd make an exception, for he knew the money was safe. Tom was really elated at the idea of having some ewes to care for again and even more so because the first major auction of breeding ewes was to be held at Penrith in a couple of days' time and so our order would be fulfilled in the immediate future.

It was six days after Tom had phoned his father that he supervised the unloading of thirty-eight Masham ewes at Marsh Hill, aided by one of the Land Girls, Barbara, who it had been decided should help Tom any time he needed an extra pair of hands with the sheep. Tom met me as I was leaving the house just after lunch and asked if I had time to come and take a look at the ewes – 'a grand quality lot' he described them. As I was heading for the piggery I agreed and told Tom to get into the car. We had decided they should occupy a field that bordered a brook dividing Marsh Hill and Little Marsh Farms where Tom had walked the hedgerows and declared them sheep-proof. As we walked down from the piggery I commented that I could see the field but no sheep. Tom airily replied that they would undoubtedly be tired after their long journey from Penrith and would be resting in the shade of the hedge nearest to us. When we reached the gate into the field it was easy to see that Tom had been wrong, for there were no sheep under the hedge nor anywhere else in the field. I heard Tom mutter under his breath, 'The rotten buggers.' I turned to the foreman, 'Tom, I don't think your Mashams think much of our lowland country. Do you think they've headed back to Cumberland?'

'I don't know where they've headed, but I do know we'd better find them quickly, there's a lot of corn left to cut yet and if they get into a field of that we won't be too popular. If you go one way, sir, and I'll go the other and maybe we can see where they broke out.' With that he set out along the hedge away from the gate, while I went the other. I reached the brook just about the same time as Tom did the other end of the field and we walked the bank towards each other. The brook was about fifteen to eighteen feet wide, quite jumpable with a good horse when hounds were running, if one stoked up well as one galloped at it and remembered the old adage, 'throw your heart over first, the rest will follow'. One thing about which I was certain was that no way could the ewes have jumped the brook, nor swum across, for the banks were almost vertical. I was about a third of the way along the section I was walking when I found the escape route and shouted to Tom to join me. Obviously many years previously a willow had fallen into the brook, which was low, for we'd had a very dry spell and the main of the trunk, normally submerged, was showing only three to four feet out from the bank where Tom and I stood, forming a most convenient bridge across to the far side. Our flock had obviously had no problem in making the short leap down and out on to the willow and across to pastures new.

Tom looked at me, what he said certainly would not be printable, but he finished by saying we'd have to go all the way back to Little Marsh Farm to cross the bridge, come back along the brook and pick up the trail. I laughed, 'Not likely. If a bloody sheep can get across there, I reckon I can.' I sat down on the ground, took my ankle-length leather boots off, tied the laces together and hung them around my neck. Tom looked quizzically at me and asked, 'What are you doing that for?' I pointed to the trunk of the willow, the bridge it formed was not more than twelve to fifteen inches wide and wet. 'That'll be pretty slippery and I've no nails, or even rubber, on the soles of these boots, I'll have more grip in my stockinged feet.' With that I turned, threw my heart over first and followed. I landed on the old willow, waved my arms around madly, but just and only just, kept my balance, made it to the far bank and scrambled up. Tom was obviously about to follow suit. I called out to him, 'Take your boots off, you'll slip otherwise.' Tom shook his head, 'No, I'll be all right, I've got nails in mine.' With that he jumped, the split second that followed was a blur of waving arms and legs before he crashed down astride the willow trunk. It might be verging on poetic licence to say that Tom was immersed in a blue haze, but certainly the language that floated up from the brook was colourful and it left me in no doubt that the breeding of the ewes was unknown. I advised Tom to stay where he was for a moment until the pain eased and he got his breath back. As he clung to the log I put my boots back on. When I'd done this Tom eased himself along until he could reach my blackthorn walking-stick which I held out to him to provide the aid he needed to scramble up the bank. I suggested he took his trousers off and we could wring most of the water out of them if we each took an end and twisted in opposite directions. It was a real scorcher of an afternoon and, as I pointed out, once we had done this he would soon dry. When Tom was ready to continue, albeit with him walking in a slightly stilted manner, we crossed a field of succulent young grass. It had been the first cut for drying and been immediately top dressed with Sulphate of Ammonia at a rate of $1^1/_2$ cwts to the acre, with a view to getting a second cut in September with a reasonably high carotene content. Tom, still intermittently cursing, remarked that if the ewes wouldn't settle in what we were crossing, God alone was the only one who would know what would please them. Eventually we found them, happily lying in the centre of a field of wheat that would be ready to harvest in a few days' time.

There was only one plus, which was that if they'd gone one field further they would have been in a field of wheat belonging to our neighbour, Mr Goodchild, a yeoman farmer, a most respected member of the community and a strong supporter of the hunt. Quietly we got the flock to its feet and they allowed themselves to be driven peacefully into the yard at Little Marsh and, to my amazement, meekly entered the old barn. Tom shut them in, saying he was coming up to Marsh Hill to collect some of the pig hurdles that we had used when the pigs were housed in arks, to make sure the Mashams couldn't cross the brook again. When we got to Marsh Hill I left Tom to his sheep, for I had much to do. He reported to me later that evening that he had our wandering ewes safely caged – there was absolutely no chance they would get out. I breathed a sigh of relief.

The following morning I rode out soon after dawn. I had arranged for Sudden and Eileen, the latter driving the old International, to be at The Grove as soon as possible after daylight to put in several hours ploughing before we progressed with the harvesting. Although we were having a wonderful spell of dry hot weather during the days, cold nights were resulting in a heavy dew which meant it was 10.30–11.00am before we could start either cutting or carting. This particular morning they were working in one of the two top thirty-acre fields. It hadn't been ploughed since the 1914–18 war, but several of the older locals such as Joe Swaine said it was heavy old three-horse land, meaning that it took that number of good strong workhorses to pull a single-furrow plough. Joe added that to break it down into a good seedbed there were nowt that could beat a few good early frosts, which in those days were a regular occurrence through October and early November. Time proved him to be right; without a frost the two top fields were the very devil to work, but the third, a fifty-four acre field, was quite different, with a nice friable soil that was easy to work. By the time I arrived both tractors had started and were at the far end of the field. Sudden had set Eileen's plough for her, both were the same model, so they were cutting similar furrows. Now it sounds ridiculous, in this age of multi-furrow reversible ploughs, but it was a very gratifying sight to see so many ridges dropping neatly into place and realising that in less than an hour they would have ploughed more ground than could be done with a pair of horses in a day. I waited on the headland for them to return and signalled to Sudden to stop. 'How's it going?' He was joined by Eileen, who had jumped down off her tractor and before he could reply she answered 'Great! It really makes me feel I'm doing my bit towards winning the war. I'm so very glad I joined the Land Army rather than going to work in munitions as Mum and

Dad wanted me to.' It was Eileen's first time ploughing and the first time she'd driven the International, but I heard on the grapevine that she now classified herself as a tractor driver. Sudden smiled, 'She's doing well. I don't think there was as much dew last night, I thought if we stopped ploughing around ten o'clock that would be about right.' I agreed and headed off towards Marsh Hill.

I had a quick look in at the grass drier, all seemed to be well and the first load for the day was being processed. I rode on down the lane towards Long Hill, as I neared the entrance to the few buildings Tom appeared. He looked hot, flustered and exceedingly cross. I greeted him cheerfully, 'Your sheep settled down now?' Tom used some language which again would not be printable and, to be fair, he was not normally given to swearing. 'The buggers have totally disappeared and how do you think they got out?' I thought for a minute, 'Well it must have been across the brook.' Tom shook his head, 'You'll never believe this, but they jumped the gate.' I really thought Tom was trying to be funny, for the gate was a standard five-barred wooden one, which would normally keep any form of livestock in. Tom went on, 'They must have come from a stone wall area. One can get some Mashams that'll jump onto the top of a wall and off the other side. It's easy to see where they landed on the top rail.' This sounded serious, 'Where are they now?' Tom told me he'd been all round Little Marsh, Marsh Hill and Long Hill Farms and couldn't see a sign of them. I told him to grab anyone he could and keep looking, but whatever happened meet me at the office at the usual time. I arrived back at the stables, handed my mount over to Hitchcock and went in for breakfast. Together with Ethne he had been out exercising four of the hunters, riding one and leading one, for the horses were up from grass as cub hunting was due to start in a week's time. Ethne had already started breakfast and was tucking into home-cured bacon and home-produced eggs. She greeted me cheerfully and said, 'John Robarts has just been on the phone, he wasn't his usual cheerful self and asked me to tell you to ring him as soon as you came in.' At that moment Verna appeared with my breakfast – I suddenly realised I was feeling ravenous. 'Well he can wait until I've eaten this,' I decided. I finished my breakfast and then went and shaved, as was my custom every morning. Feeling fresh and in good form I called John, wishing him a cheery good morning and asking what I could do for him. The reply was positively terse, 'I hear you've got some sheep.' My heart sank, 'Yes, that's right. They arrived from Cumberland yesterday. They're down by the brook at Marsh.'

'Not now they're not, they're in my cattle yard, the gate's locked and it'll cost you half a crown a head to get them out – no, more, because I'm not letting them go for less than a fiver and I've counted them, there's thirty-eight.' I got a nasty feeling in the pit of my stomach, these bloody sheep were more trouble than they were worth. 'Are you sure they're ours?' John was getting distinctly edgy, 'Of course I'm not, but who else has recently bought sheep in the area? You'd better come and see if they are yours, but you're not damned well getting them without paying up.' With that he rang off. I left the house to go out to the office and, as I crossed the drive, I saw Tom coming through the gate. I walked down the drive to meet him and told him of John Robarts' phone call, adding that I thought we had better go and have a look.

I drew the car to a halt in the yard of Kimblewick Farm. John was standing by the wicket gate that led through the wall to the back door. He walked forward, grim faced, 'Right, Burrows let's see if you recognise your sheep.' Tom was ahead of him going to the yard, he looked in, turned and said, 'What sheep Mr Robarts? There are no sheep here.' John's face was a study as he looked over the wall into the yard, for there were no sheep. 'Well they were here, look at all the shit.' Tom looked solemnly at John, 'Mr Robarts, I grew up with sheep, I can recognise the likeness for two, sometimes three generations back, but I haven't learned to recognise their individual droppings.' With that Tom turned and walked back to the car. I turned to John, 'I'm sorry, but I can neither agree that they were our sheep nor deny they were, without seeing them. However, they could have been, so I'm sure the Master would want me to pay you a fiver as you requested.' John looked at me for a moment, shook his head and walked off into the house. I joined Tom in the car, he had a big grin on his face, 'Aren't they buggers, they're worse than mountain goats. I wonder where they've got to now?' As we approached Round Hill Farm there they were happily grazing in the field next to the buildings. I told Tom to round up anyone he could find, including the cowmen, drive them up to the piggery and shut them in one of the weaner houses. And that is where they stayed until sold, a few days later, at an auction of breeding ewes at Thame. Tom tarted them up a bit as he put it and they made a few shillings a head more than they had cost. At the same auction I bought thirty-five very nice quality Cheviot half-bred ewes. They were very happy in the field by Marsh brook and probably even happier when they were joined by a nice, correctly trimmed ram lamb from the Burnham flock. All that was needed now was a nice crop of lambs the following spring, amongst which, hopefully, there would be one or two with Masham tendencies, like trying to jump gates, which undoubtedly would lead to a nasty accident.

It was nearly the end of the third week in September when we finished harvest and certainly as I pitched the last few sheaves of corn up to Tom and old Joe finished topping off the rick it was virtually dark. The rest of the gang had gone, but as Joe set off on his bike I called after him, 'Drop in at The Prince of Wales and have a pint on me, tell Mrs Leversuch I'll pay her the next time I see her.' I just heard Joe call, 'Thanks boss, I will.' I dropped Tom at the gate into the house, parked the car and for some reason I'll never know, stopped, turned and looked towards London. Although about forty miles away a red glow was clearly visible in the sky – the Blitz was still continuing. I went into the house to be greeted by Rose and Ethne. Apparently they had been waiting for me to go up to The Bernard Arms in Kimble, our posh local, at least it was when compared with The Prince of Wales, to celebrate the harvest being safely in. I was exhausted, but I knew they had a bottle or two of whisky under the counter for special customers and we came under that heading. I agreed, but I had to have a quick shower and a change first. In the meantime I suggested they went out on to the lawn and look towards London. Like me they were horrified at what they saw. I quietly prayed that all the poor innocent people whose homes Hitler was having flattened were safely down in the Underground stations. Such barbaric behaviour must surely eventually be repaid at least threefold in kind. However, in the interim, somehow, the people of London and other cities had to be fed and there were tough, hard, tiring, but glorious days ahead for Britain's farmers, who hoped to earn the respect of the urban population, something which had been conspicuous by its absence for the past two decades.

15. Mend and Make Do

Autumn passed and quickly we were into winter. In those days one seldom sowed wheat until the last week in October and if the weather was really good one could sow in the first week of December, but much had to be done before any seed was sown on the Roundhill estate. High on the list of priorities was getting the hundreds of tons of muck heaped around the place out on the land. Again this needed equipment and again Phil Oliver came to the rescue, finding two ancient muckspreaders in September which he had seen advertised for sale. Said to be in need of some repair to make them useable, this was a major understatement! What Phil paid for them, if anything, I have no idea, for he had them back to Meadacre before telling me about them. They were in pretty poor shape, but having taken a careful look, it seemed there was nothing a good mechanic backed by a large engineering business couldn't fix. The latter was something easily solved. I contacted Mr Bertelli at Templewood, explained the situation, and he kindly sent down one of his top men who made a careful assessment of what was needed. Both spreaders were in perfect working order within two weeks. Once the mechanic had said they could be repaired I did a deal with Phil. He asked £25 each but really until fixed they were valueless except possibly a few pounds for the scrap metal. However, as the mechanic had assured me they could be renovated and muckspreaders were absolutely essential, I eventually bought the two for £35. Fred Spittles replaced rotten wood on the sides and added a lick of paint and they were ready to go.

Sadly we had no fore-end loader to fit on any of the tractors, I'm not sure they were even available then, but with the three old hands, Joe, Harry and Left-Legged Harry, plus the two tractor drivers Sudden and Miles loading – grass drying had finished so the latter was available – the turn-round time was quick and a vast quantity of dung was spread in a very short time. Meanwhile Eileen started ploughing it in.

Under Sudden's tutelage she had learned how to set out lands, adjust the plough and was sufficiently capable to be left on her own to get on with the job.

As soon as we had finished spreading the muck on the fields that were to be drilled with winter corn, Joe and Harry started hedging and ditching – there seemed to be miles requiring their attention. Joe was the hedger, although old Harry could do a very passable job at laying a hedge too, but ditching was a major problem, for it had been many years since anything much had been done in this respect, particularly on both Marsh Hill and Little Marsh Farms. Although there was a subsidy for cleaning ditches, only when the mandatory single-strand barbed wire guard fence had been erected would the subsidy be paid. The amount that required doing would take Joe and Harry many winters and that sort of time was not an option. In various parts of the county, indeed through the whole country, the War Ag had set up labour pools, which consisted largely of conscientious objectors and very green and inexperienced Land Girls. I had great sympathy for the Land Girls; they were trying to do their bit towards winning the war, but I always thought putting them in a labour pool was somewhat derisory, for it seemed that those in charge frequently had little knowledge of what was expected of the girls. Conscientious objectors, on the whole, were lazy and of very little use, they seemed to be always moaning about the way they were accommodated and fed. Frankly, I had no sympathy with them although I admired the minority who stuck to their principles of not killing but did their bit in the Red Cross or became army hospital orderlies.

When government departments become involved then, as sure as night follows day, bureaucracy materialises – the War Ag was no exception. There were local committees, comprised of experienced farmers, who advised the civil servants. These seemed to sprout like mushrooms and were largely unhindered by talent. I can think of no better appellation for the drainage officer, Evans, who came to see me when I submitted an application for an extensive ditching programme, which had been accompanied by a section from an ordnance survey map, accurate distances being shown (carefully measured by Tom and I using an old-type surveyor's chain of twenty-two yards which I had bought at a sale just before the war for two shillings) and arrows indicating the direction of the fall. Evans was pleasant enough, but I felt, rather full of his own importance. We walked down across the fields beyond Marsh Hill and Evans chatted away happily about the hunt and how before the war started he loved to follow it on his bike. I discovered he was responsible not only for drainage, but also for the allocation of labour from the local War Ag pool and pricing the various jobs that were undertaken. This intrigued me, for it was obvious he was not a farmer and I could not help wondering how he was able to do this. However, after a little probing it appeared he was supplied with a tariff, presumably from the Ministry of Agriculture, giving a minimum and maximum charge for various jobs, such as flat hoeing root crops £2 to £4 an acre and singling £4 to £6. We reached the fields which required the hedges trimmed back and the ditches dug out, the latter being virtually non-existent. Evans produced the map, strutted around a bit, came back to me and said, 'I think you've got this map wrong Mr Twist.' I looked over his shoulder, 'I don't think so. Turn it the other way up and round, then I think you'll find it easier to follow.' He studied it carefully and said, 'Ah yes, now I can see – you want all the ditches to drain into the Marsh Brook?' I bit back a snide comment regarding water running uphill, which was the only other alternative to channelling it to the brook and just nodded agreement. He then set off to check the lengths of the ditches to be cleared. Eventually he returned all smiles. 'Only one problem Mr Twist, you've over-estimated the yardage to be dug out, but don't worry I'll adjust that when I send in the approval form.' I wasn't going to argue. I knew my figures were correct, but he was the government official and sometimes there are occasions when it is folly to be wise.

One morning about two weeks later Evans arrived at Marsh Hill with a truck full of pool workers. My first thought was how the hell is he going to keep that lot occupied, but that was his worry not mine. I had received a price for the work, which I had quickly agreed as it was way below my estimate and as long as the job was done who was I to worry with regard to the number involved in doing it? I asked Evans if he was staying to supervise the gang. He replied no, he was too busy, but he was leaving Pete, his new assistant. He called Pete over to us, a pleasant enough lad, who was quick to tell me he had tried to enlist in the navy, but they would not accept him as he had a deformed foot. I told him 'Make sure you finish up with the water running into the brook and not back up here.' Pete laughed, 'Don't worry, sir, I spent the previous eighteen months prior to the outbreak of war with a small firm of surveyors, but the boss was a captain in the Territorials and the junior partner quickly joined up, so the business has closed until after the war, that is if we all come through OK. I'd better muster my troops and make a start.' The mustering took some minutes, they didn't seem over-anxious to start work, in fact they looked a right motley and lazy lot. My sympathy was with Pete as they slouched off along the track through Great Ground, spades and shovels over their shoulders, but what the hell, we were getting deeper and deeper into a horrific war, so we just had to make do and somehow get results with what was available, be it machinery or labour. I counted twenty-three, excluding Evans, as they straggled apathetically down across the field. I did some quick calculations. If they were receiving the basic agricultural rate, then by the end of two weeks their wages would amount to more than the estimated cost of doing all the work for which Evans had contracted!

Having had my morning session with Tom and then, as usual, dealt with the mail with Megan Pring, I headed off for a village a few miles the far side of Aylesbury to interview a groom, for we were desperately short of help in the stables. In addition the Colonel had told me he wanted a good second horseman, that is a groom who could follow quietly round after a hunt with a second horse for the Master to change on to if necessary. I suppose there are now generations who must wonder how we could possibly concern ourselves with such pastimes as hunting when an invasion could be imminent, or one could be blown to bits by a German bomb, but life had to continue. In towns and cities it was theatre, opera, ballet, the cinema and nightclubs that gave respite from the toil, misery and shortages of war. Similarly hunting, shooting and gymkhanas run in aid of the Red Cross played an equivalent role in the country. One of the things we were fighting for was our heritage and man has been a hunter since time immemorial. We weren't going to be deprived of something that had been a part of country life for many, many centuries by a jumped-up German army corporal from the First World War. The determination to retain such deep-seated, time-honoured traditions did much to help keep up both morale and stamina when a sixteen-hour day was frequently the norm throughout hay and harvest time. Certainly the Colonel considered this no hardship, for he frequently called board meetings of his various companies at 6.00am, much to the fury of his co-directors. Apart from this there was a totally different approach to life then, such things as counselling for those who had suffered a bereavement, or witnessed some gruesome accident, was unheard of – and, thanks to Hitler, such happenings became commonplace. To use a modern idiom, one raised two fingers vertically and carried on; if people hadn't the Germans would have won the war.

The groom I interviewed, Harry Wingfield, had above-average ability and had been in charge of a stable of top-quality horses at a lovely country property of thirty to forty acres and a most lucrative sandpit. The owner, a Harley Street dentist, left the entire management of his country home to Harry. The latter loved horses, but unfortunately not just the ones in his care and he couldn't resist having a flutter on the races. Inevitably the bookies won, so Harry 'borrowed' a bit from his boss's account, then a bit more and still more, until one day one of the grooms and a gardener went to their employer and said they hadn't been paid for six weeks. Not surprisingly Harry's boss was not a happy man and phoned the police. Subsequently he regretted this and tried to have the charges against his studgroom quashed, but things had gone too far and Harry finished up in Oxford jail, his wife and daughter having left him. The story was well known by the hunting fraternity around the North Buckinghamshire area and it was Clive Haselden who told me Harry was out and looking for a job. I engaged him, as I knew I would when I set off to see him, found accommodation for him and he started work the following Monday. The fact that he'd let his employer down was outweighed by his undoubted ability and the extreme shortage of trained stable staff and, in any case, he would not have an opportunity at Round Hill to repeat his misdemeanour.

Everything seemed to be going along swimmingly. The contract drainage work had been finished some six weeks after it had started and, solely thanks to Pete, it was a reasonably good job. The winter drilling had gone well, although it was a tedious job with a converted horse drill to go behind the tractor. However, Sudden and Miles took a lunch break in the middle of the day at different times, so at least we kept going non-stop from daylight to dark. The Shorthorn herd was doing extremely well and although we had fewer cows than when I had taken over, the milk sales had doubled. The price was around 1/9 per gallon, of which either 1d or 2d was for quality. But the real excitement in this section was the fact that the Roundhill herd would be exhibiting at the Breed Society's Show and Sale at Reading in March. In all branches of livestock there are good herdsmen and exceptionally good ones, who are totally engrossed in their job and have that little bit of extra know-how that puts them in a class on their own – Ron Chamberlain was one of these. In the years that followed he was to prove that there were few who could equal him in the preparation of young bulls for the all-important show and sales, which provided a major source of revenue for the estate. Our one entry would be in the junior class for yearlings. He had one disadvantage, he was white and there was not a great demand for these, except to mate to red cows and heifers, producing nice roan-coloured calves. However, Roundhill Waterloo Wildeyes, his registered name, oozed quality and we were able to put QBF after his name, which indicated his dam had attained a standard worthy of note by the Breed Society for both the quantity of milk she had given and a high butterfat content.

It was about the middle of February that I awoke one morning feeling very far from well. When I went to shave and looked at myself in the mirror, I noticed spots on my face. I didn't feel like breakfast and phoned the only doctor available in the district. There had been an excellent one, but he'd either been called up or joined up and our only medic was a charming old gentleman who had practised, up to his retirement, in some African country, where he had lived most of his life. He took a look at me, said I had a mild skin infection, told me to take two aspirins every four hours and gave me the name of some cream to get from the chemist. The latter had never heard of it, nor was it listed in any of his catalogues. Having had previous experiences of the doctor's prescriptions, he said I'd probably be able to get it in Africa. I returned to the office and was feeling awful when Clive Haselden breezed in, took one look at me and said, 'When did you blossom with chickenpox?' I told him what the doctor had said. His reply was, 'Stupid old bugger, I know he's doing the best he can, but he hasn't practised for years. Now you get off home. I'm going to phone Dev, tell them in the house and Tom. Then phone your parents to say you are on the way so they can call your doctor.' Gratefully I stuffed a few things into a case before heading for the car. Ethne had come as far as the door to my bedroom, which was open, taken one look and said, 'God, you look awful. Would you like me to drive you home?' I asked if she'd had the wretched pox and her reply was no. I told her in that case to keep well away as I certainly didn't want her and the children catching it and, thankfully, none of them did.

I just about made it home and father kindly let me have his room as there was a phone by the bed and I would be able to keep in touch with Round Hill. The doctor arrived about half an hour after I had, said I had a temperature of 103.7° F, confirmed Clive's diagnosis and told me that I'd be in bed for at least a week to ten days. Could anything be more infra dig for a young, ambitious land agent-cum-farm manager who, on looking back, must have rather fancied his chances as what a few years ago would have been described as a whizz-kid? I was mortified. I don't think my recovery was helped, about four days later, when I received a phone call from the Colonel to tell me he had sacked Bob Hitchcock, but Wingfield seemed to think he could manage until I got back. Why he got rid of Bob he never told me at the time and I have long since forgotten. His final comment I found extremely galling to say the least, 'Don't you hang about at home because of some childish ailment, you're wanted on the estate.' The fact that I was fretting to get back there made me retort, 'Well I'm keeping in touch every day with Miss Pring and I speak to Tom twice a day on the phone. But I'll return tomorrow if you say so, sir, providing you will tell Mrs Devereux and take the responsibility. The doctor assures me I'll be infectious for another five to seven days, so I'd be putting both Ann and Marguerite and the rest of the household at risk if I return now.' There was silence for a moment, then he said, 'Yes, all right, but get back as quickly as you can.'

I had many reasons for wanting to return to my job, by no means least being the fact that whilst I had been away, the much rumoured Marshall Plan, correctly named the Lease-Lend Bill, was about to be signed by President Roosevelt. This would supply aid to Great Britain to be paid for at a later date. I was anxious to indent with the War Ag, who would decide as to who got what in respect of various farm machines which would be arriving, for a sixteen- or eighteen-coulter tractor seed drill, two tractors and a combine harvester. I knew I wouldn't receive all I put in for, because everyone was desperate for equipment, but, as a great fly fisherman friend of mine used to say, if you don't have a fly in the water you can't catch fish. By the time the doctor gave me the all clear to return I had been off sick for the better part of three weeks and, surprisingly, the childish ailment had knocked the stuffing out of me, but I set about getting fit again as quickly as I could. Apart from the business of Hitchcock nothing seemed to have gone awry. I had a chat with Harry Wingfield, offered him the job as studgroom, which meant an increase in wages, the cottage Hitchcock had lived in, free milk and a limited amount of potatoes. I also told him if he tried any fiddles he'd find himself back in jail. He laughed and said he had learned his lesson. Then he went on to say that he presumed I would want someone to replace him as second horseman for the Colonel. I confirmed this and he said he knew an excellent young man, who had not passed a medical for any of the forces and was looking for a job. Providing Harry and his wife could get together again, which they did, they would be happy to have him as a lodger, as he'd lived with them before' … Harry waved an arm 'during my holiday in Oxford.' That was another problem settled.

Roundhill Waterloo Wildeyes was looking superb. Ron had him all spruced up the day I returned and walked him out for me to see and stood him up – that is standing four-square. I was full of hope that we would get in the awards. As far as price was concerned, I hoped for 80 guineas. That sounds nothing now, but at that time it would have paid Ron's wages for the best part of twenty weeks and he was well paid. Apart from his wages, he had a new three-bedroomed cottage, free electricity, milk and a bonus of 6d in the guinea on the sale of all Shorthorns sold for breeding purposes. The afternoon before the Show and Sale Ron set off with his charge, bathed, horns smoothed, polished and rugged up for the journey in a cattle truck.

At Reading market by 8.30am the next morning, I quickly found Ron, who had our entry looking immaculate. He told me that Waterloo Wildeyes had caused quite a lot of interest and a number of people had come to look at him, including two well-known breeders. From my catalogue I saw there were forty-two in his class. It was the biggest in the show, but the junior class usually was. I went off to watch the judging; Ron would stay with his charge until called to the ring by one of the stewards. I joined two of the auctioneers, Harry Hobson, who I had known since I was a small child and one of his two partners, Billy Wiltshire, who I had also known for years. Harry used to deal with all their export orders and was a regular visitor to Burnham. With them was Leonard Bull, secretary of the Shorthorn Society, some might say a most appropriate name for the secretary of a cattle society. He was also secretary for the Shire Horse Society and Smithfield Fatstock Show. The other member of the foursome, who I came to know extremely well in years to come, was Henry Hamilton who managed the Duke of Westminster's farms at Eaton, just outside Chester, where there was a Dairy Shorthorn herd of over 500 head. I received a warm welcome from them all and I was asked by Harry Hobson, who would be doing the bulk of the selling, what, if any, reserve I wanted to put on the Roundhill entry. I said I thought 75 guineas, which he seemed to think was about right in view of the average the previous November.

At last the junior class entered the ring. The judge stood about fifteen yards from the entrance; as a bull came into the ring he stood so he could watch it walk towards him. It was then stood up, the judge went over it and watched it walk away. As it neared the end of the ring he gave a signal. If he wanted it for further comparison it went on round the ring, if not it was waved out by a steward and back to its stall until the auction. About halfway through the class Ron entered leading the first Roundhill entry to the breed's most prestigious event. Billy Wiltshire tapped me on the shoulder, 'Relax, there's been nothing to come anywhere near him for quality so far. You're bound to be in the cards.' He was right. Twenty minutes later Ron was handed the red card – first prize. I was over the moon and even more so when he changed hands in the sale ring for 135 guineas. I'm not absolutely certain, but there were only about eight bulls that made over 100 guineas at the auction. I sent a telegram to the Colonel who was obviously thrilled when he phoned me that evening after I had returned to the farm. It was equally obvious he'd been celebrating rather well, something I had noticed he was becoming rather prone to doing. But he was working almost ridiculously long hours and constantly under great pressure, for it was men of his brilliance and ability in whose hands our future lay, and their number was limited.

Only days after the Shorthorn Society Show and Sale Ron Chamberlain went down with a real bout of influenza and was in bed for several days with a high temperature. However, about six months previously I had taken on an experienced second in command to Ron, Sid Pullen. He was a good cowman, able to deal with the normal day-to-day routine of caring for a top-class dairy herd, but not too sure of himself if there was any problem. It was a Saturday evening and I had gone up to The Bernard Arms, around 9.30pm, with Ethne, Rose and her husband Duncan, to relax, have a drink and hear the latest news from Duncan about the Blitz in London, which seemed never ending.

I'd had a hectic but very productive day. I had gone into Aylesbury cattle market fairly early in the morning where I happened to hear of an elderly farmer, near Bicester, who had had enough of the War Ag and had decided to sell up. I gathered he had a quantity of machinery, albeit in a poor state of repair, which would be sold. I felt it was an opportunity not to be missed, got his address from my informant and drove over to see him. He was a very pleasant man, into his seventies so he told me, and couldn't put up with little whippersnappers from the War Ag telling him how to farm land that had been in his family's possession for over 100 years. I brought the subject round to machinery. Yes, it would all be sold and yes he was quite happy to do a deal now for any of it, providing the price was right. There was no question of it being in a barn, or under cover, it lay around all over the place. In the corner of the rick yard I spied two tractor power-driven grass mowers, both Albions, identical models, with a five-foot cut. Like the muckspreaders I had bought from Phil Oliver, they were in need of repair, but I felt one good mower could be made up from the two. I asked the price – £50 the two. It was one I would happily have given, but knew if I had agreed I would have left the owner worrying that he might have got more. I bid him £30 and we departed to the house to argue a price. He produced some sloe gin and a couple of tumblers and poured two liberal measures. I realised it was pretty potent stuff and sipped it gingerly. He was good company, a keen hunting man and appeared in no hurry to strike a deal. The phone rang just as I had increased my bid to £42 and he had to leave the room to answer it. Fortunately he was gone some minutes, for I still had about a third of a tumbler of sloe gin left, some of which I added to his glass and poured the rest back into the bottle. As I heard him returning I stood up and when he entered the room I greeted him with, '£45 and that's my final offer.' He looked at me for a minute, then nodded and held out his hand, 'It's a deal, providing you pay cash.' I assured him that was no problem and said I'd send the money with the man driving the cattle lorry that would collect them, hopefully on Monday, but I'd phone him and tell him when. I asked if he had any men around who'd be able to help load them. He said he had, so I left a 10/- note for them to have a drink on me. He was well pleased, so was I.

I had just ordered the second round, as we sat relaxed in the saloon bar of The Bernard Arms – the first whisky had done me good, for I was, to a small degree, still feeling the effects of the wretched chickenpox and tiring rather too easily as a result – when the phone rang. The landlord went through to his sitting room to answer it, quickly returning to say I was urgently wanted back at the farm – something to do with a cow calving. I downed my whisky, Ethne said she'd run me back and return for the McKellars. I was greeted by Sid Pullen – one of our best cows was having a difficult calving. He'd asked Tom to ring the vet (Tom had a key to the farm office), but he was out foaling a mare that was in trouble at the Mentmore stud. It was by no means the first difficult calving I'd had to sort out and duly attired myself for what was to come, a large, near full-length rubber apron being an important part of the kit. I soaped up, inserting my hand, then arm. Within seconds I realised this was going to be quite a problem. The calf was big, the head and one foreleg back. I quietly cursed as I knew from past experience that this wasn't going to be a ten-minute job. Eventually I was able to manipulate the head into the right position, as well as the leg. Then with the aid of Pullen and Tom Burrows pulling on the calving ropes attached to the forelegs, eventually a lovely roan heifer calf flopped out on to the straw. It was Tom who quickly cleared the air passages and the calf tried its voice out with a few bleats. When Sid had taken off the halter with which mum had been tied up, she turned and started to lick her baby. Tom and Sid Pullen cleaned up the loose box and put down nice clean fresh straw whilst I went off to get a warming and what I and numerous others thought was an excellent drench to give a cow after calving – Cataline, one of the many good things of the past no longer obtainable.

It was about ten minutes to midnight that I finally left the farm, the calf having suckled and feeling satisfied that both mother and baby were fine. Exhausted, I tumbled into bed and was asleep in seconds. The next thing I knew someone was banging on my door, I switched on my bedside light, glancing at my clock as I did so; it was five minutes to two. I called out 'Who is it?' It was nanny, to tell me the Colonel wanted to speak to me immediately on the phone. I put on a dressing gown and slippers and crossed over to the house. Nanny was waiting at the foot of the stairs, she nodded towards the phone, 'He seems in an awful mood.' With that she went upstairs. I picked up the phone, said hullo and got my ear filled. What over I have no idea to this day. His voice was slurred and it was quite obvious he'd had a couple of whiskies too many. I listened, but was unable to make sense of what was being said. I could hear Dorothy Devereux in the background urging him to come to bed, then loud and clearly came over 'You bloody fool.' With that I put the phone down and waited five minutes to see if it would ring again – it didn't.

The next morning both Ethne and Rose McKellar wanted to know what the call was about. I told them and it was Ethne who said, 'I wouldn't put up with that sort of nonsense from my old man, or anyone else.' I replied I had no intention of doing so and was resigning. For the first time for ten or eleven weeks I had arranged to go and see my parents and have Sunday lunch with them. This meant I could go via The Meads, the Colonel's home at Stoke Poges. I drafted my resignation, Rose typed it for me and I slipped it through the letterbox on the way to my home a few hours later. I had barely entered the house when the phone rang, it was the Colonel demanding to know what my letter meant. I replied rather icily, 'I think it's quite clear, sir. When I've been a bloody fool I'll be prepared to admit it and take the consequences, but when I haven't, I'm taking it from no one, particularly at 2.00am.' There was silence for a moment, then, 'Didn't think I'd called you that. I'll be going to International Alloys at

Aylesbury tomorrow, be at your office at 2.00pm sharp.' With that he put the phone down. Both mother and father were most concerned, much more so than I was, but I had no worries about getting another job, although it probably would be neither as interesting nor as challenging as the one from which I'd resigned, but there was a limit to what my self-respect could take.

16. A Time to Roar and a Time to Flatter

I was in my office at 1.45pm the following day, Monday, and it would be untrue to say there wasn't the odd butterfly floating around in my stomach, even though Ethne and I had nipped down to The Prince of Wales before lunch for a large gin and tonic each! The Colonel was a formidable and intimidating presence when roused, particularly to someone of my age and I had a feeling, come 2.00pm, that he might well display the more acrimonious side of his nature. But I was determined to stand my ground.

I heard the Bentley turn into the driveway. I could see, as I looked out from the office window, that Wren, the senior chauffeur at High Duty Alloys, who always drove Dev, was at the wheel. He didn't come up to the front door, but pulled up in the main parking area and the Colonel got out and bustled across towards the office – obviously this was going to be a short visit. The butterflies were becoming frantic. I moved towards the door and timed it to perfection, for I opened it just as he was reaching for the handle.

'Good afternoon, sir.' I thought I detected a slight quaver in my voice, but my gaze held those steely eyes, but they weren't steely, they were laughing. He almost pushed me back into the office, 'You cheeky young bugger. Do you know you're the first person that's stood up to me for years? Do you really want to leave?' The wave of relief that surged over me was so great that I retired to my chair behind my desk, as my boss dropped into the armchair. I cleared my throat, 'No sir, not at all. But if remaining means, that having put in an eighteen- to nineteen-hour day on your behalf, done nothing wrong, at least that I know of, will involve being got out of bed at 2.00am to be abused, then, much as I may regret it, my resignation stands.' The Colonel looked at me, it seemed like forever, before he started to laugh. 'Right, Michael, then we'll forget it. I had that bloody man Beaverbrook (Lord Beaverbrook, the Minister of Aircraft Production) with me for about three hours yesterday evening, turned up, unannounced, at around 10.00pm. Arrogant sod, drank most of my whisky, although I must admit I kept him company, but by the time he left I was in a stinking mood. Something Dorothy said, very minor, can't even remember what it was, except it was to do with the estate and I expect you got what I'd dearly have loved to have given Beaverbrook.' He stood up, held out his hand, 'All right?' I took it … 'All right.' He reached the door, stopped, turned and asked, 'How long have you been here?' I thought for a moment, 'Five days under thirteen months.'The Colonel stood silently for a moment and then said,'As long as that? Well, as from the first of next month your salary goes up £1 a week and we'll talk about a bonus scheme on profits. I'll confirm that in writing.' With that he was gone. £1 a week sounds nothing now, but its spending power then was equivalent to the current cost of ten to twelve gallons of petrol a week. For all the years I remained with him after that, whilst we often had quite strong arguments as to what was the right policy regarding various matters in connection with the estate, he never raised his voice to me again.

It was quite an eventful day, for the Colonel had only gone a few minutes when Tom Burrows arrived at the office, all smiles. 'Thought I'd let you know, sir, the first ewe's just lambed.'

'Great! What's she had, a single or twins?' Tom's smile became even broader, 'You'll never believe it – quadruplets. Nice level lambs and all four seem fine. Barbara's with them now, giving them all a suck at a bottle.We'll have to give their mum a bit of a helping hand. Of course if we have a dead lamb born, which I hope we won't, we can always give one of the quads its jacket.' Tom was referring to a common practice if one had a stillborn lamb.Whilst still warm and wet, one quickly skinned it, rubbed the head of the lamb needing a foster mother with the skin and then fixed the skin from the dead lamb on to it and the ewe, who had lost hers, would immediately take to it. Forty-eight to seventy-two hours later the lamb could be relieved of its jacket and the ewe would happily rear it.Without doing this it would be an exceptional ewe that would suckle and rear an orphan lamb. Normally any lamb that tries to have a quick suck from a ewe that is not its mother will be sent flying with a good head butt.

Still smiling, Tom added 'If you've got a minute, I've had a word with all those living on the estate about the pig scheme.' This was a plan whereby any one country household, providing it gave up its bacon ration coupons, would receive coupons for a small allocation of meal to help rear two pigs annually for their own use, or if they wished one assumed they could sell them. I had suggested to Tom, who was all for it, that he sound out the rest of the staff living in estate cottages. However, I had stipulated that there couldn't be any ramshackle, bodged up pigpens in the cottage gardens, but as we had no hope of completely utilising both the vast fattening houses at Marsh Hill to the full, they could each have a pen in one of these. The other condition was that they would have to buy their weaners, at the current market rate, off the estate. I wasn't prepared to take any risks of more disease being brought in by purchasing these from Aylesbury, or any other market. It seemed that the majority thought it a great idea, some wanting to know if they could buy Tottenham Pudding from the estate and dried grass to supplement the meagre allowance of meal they could purchase. To this I readily agreed. Tom had the necessary long trays, known as leads, together with the knowhow and experience to produce excellent home-cured bacon and ham. At what stage the owners killed their pigs was up to them, around 200lbs liveweight was when we packed baconers off to the factory, but a number of those for home consumption were run on up to 300lbs or more. This meant there was $1-1\frac{1}{2}$ inches of fat on the sides of bacon and a good three inches on the hams, something which would be spurned now, but was much appreciated and valued during the war years.

Unfortunately poultry was not allowed, simply due to the fear of avian tuberculosis being picked up by the cattle, a reaction to which, when doing a comparative test for bovine TB, could lead to an animal being classified as a reactor. However, with a number of smallholdings around the area, plus cottagers who kept hens who were always quite happy to barter a few eggs for a rasher or two of bacon I don't think anyone on the estate staff went short. As far as Round Hill House was concerned, soon after I took over I arranged for wire netting, posts, etc to put up a big poultry run at The Meads, bought twenty-four pullets on the point of lay and the farm supplied the food, in return for which we received eggs.

When I arrived at the estate there was no vegetable garden, although there was a space where a previous owner had obviously had one. It was impossible to get a plough in to turn it over, so when we had several days when there was nothing needing immediate attention, I set Joe, Harry, the grafter Spittles as Tom always called Dick Spittles, and Harry North to hand dig it. It didn't take long and from then on, when not urgently needed on the farm, old Left-Legged Harry became gardener and he grew a lot of much-needed vegetables. I remember reading a number of years ago how HRH the Prince of Wales talked to plants. That was nothing new, old Harry North had done it years before. He took great pride in what he grew and in particular cauliflowers, all of whom it appeared he had given names to. Harry did not like it when Dorothy Devereux stayed at the farm, which wasn't often. I remember on one occasion when she did and Harry was gardening. She went out, admired his cauliflowers and, pointing at one, said, 'That looks a nice one. Will you cut it please, North, and take it in to Verna, we'll have it for lunch today.' With that she returned to the house, just as I came across from the farmyard to tell North he would have to leave the garden as he was wanted for some job on the farm. This meant I walked across the lawn and down the centre grass path of the vegetable garden – Harry had his back to me and didn't hear me coming. He stood gazing at the cauliflower, knife in hand. The conversation went something like this, 'Belinda, me ol' love, the missus says I got ter cut you for 'er dinner. Bloody 'ard 'oman her be, but us all got ter go sometime.' With that, with one quick cut poor Belinda was beheaded. Harry looked up and saw me, he obviously knew I'd heard him and he equally obviously didn't mind.

He smiled and said, 'Them understands me yer know an' they all got names.'

There is no doubt that we fed better in the country than in towns, but then, providing one could afford it, in London and other cities there were restaurants and cafes where one could go. Over the war years I quite frequently had to go to London and never had a problem in getting a reasonable meal. One thing I found strange about the Roundhill estate, after the one I grew up on, was the dearth of rabbits. This was excellent from the point of view of the crops, but a small number would have been handy to supplement the meagre meat ration. We used the same butcher in Kimble who supplied Chequers and sometimes when the PM didn't arrive with the working party for the weekend, as expected, there was an extra allocation of meat available, but this did not often happen. The other source of food I seldom saw on the estate was woodpigeon.

Looking back it seems extraordinary how cheerful and optimistic everyone remained. The Blitz, not only on London but other major cities, seemed never ending. The Germans were as ever predictable and we quickly learned throughout the winter of 1941–42 that Thursday night was usually bomb night. Most loads carried by the droning Junkers – there never seemed more than two and frequently only one – did little harm. One night some incendiaries dropped in a field at the back of Round Hill Farm but did no harm to man or beast. Nevertheless we never went out on a Thursday night. If anyone suggested it, the usual retort was, 'Better not, Jerry might decide to call.' There was one hit on Kimble village, fortunately there were no fatalities but two, maybe three, small cottages were demolished. Ironically a young lad, of about nine or ten, had just been evacuated to the village, having been already bombed, so the story went, two or three times. He, I gathered, was the only person who had to be rescued from the rubble and when he did appear, he shook his fist in the air and shouted, 'Yer won't get me yer bouggers, 'ow ever 'ard you tries.' Nobody gave him counselling – he went to school the next day, was a forty-eight hour hero and developed an ever-increasing desire to grow up in time to shoot a bloody German! That was a common trait.

I'd been over to The Meads one evening in January to see the Colonel over a number of matters. I left around 8.30pm and called at a little pub on the edge of Farnham Common. I knew I'd find one or two of the Burnham Grove estate men there and a few other locals I'd known for years. I had a pint and a chat with various people and in particular old Bob, the retired studgroom from a small neighbouring estate. The air-raid warning had gone, but that frequently didn't mean a lot in country areas, life just went on – at least usually. I left around 9.30pm, Bob said he must get home, or the missus would think he was off sparking with some flippity-jibbit of a girl. He got on his bike and was off down the road as I got into the car. I hadn't gone fifty yards when there was a hell of a bang and the car leapt forward as though it had been shot out of a catapult as a few bits of mud and stone fell on it. I pulled up, got out and listened but there was no sound coming from down the road. There was about a three-quarter moon and I could just see the outline of the pub, it seemed all was well and as both search lights and ack-ack guns were busy it didn't seem a good spot to hang around. As I drove on I hoped old Bob had made it home before the bomb fell, but felt pretty sure he would have, for he was fifty yards or more down the road before I actually got into my car. Sadly I was wrong. A friend told me over the phone a few days later that the blast had largely gone east and west and one bit of shrapnel had just sliced Bob's head clean off, there wasn't another mark on his body. Renee must have been having a listen, for when I next went into The Prince of Wales old man Leversuch greeted me with, 'Hear you had a near one t'other night mister.' I laughed and said, 'You know what they say – a miss is as good as a mile. Like a drink?' It was a silly question, he'd never been known to say no.

Things were going well on the farms, but I had one immediate decision to make. We had used the marrow stem kale at the back of the piggeries – it had been an enormous crop – in time to get the field ploughed and sown with winter wheat. I'd bought enough seed, once-grown Yeoman

II, from father. It was a high-yielding variety, but like most that had been developed up to those times, it had the long straw that was so essential for thatching. The trouble with it and other such varieties, was that they were very prone to storm damage and, if flattened, they couldn't be successfully cut with a reaper and binder. It was common in the early part of the last century that if winter-sown corn became 'winter proud' – that is very lush with really too much growth for the time of year – then sheep would be grazed over it. Tom was terribly anxious that we should do this to the wheat in the piggery field, but I had other ideas. At one of our morning meetings around the end of the second week in April I told Tom to have George and Miles get the grass-drying equipment ready and the furnace lit and banked down so that we could starting drying in the morning. Tom looked puzzled, 'You're not going to cut that rye grass yet? I'd have thought we ought to wait at least another week.' We'd undersown a field of spring barley with Italian Rye Grass and some Dutch Wild White Clover. This had received a good dressing of phosphate and nitrogen with a view to getting two cuts for the drier and then ploughing in the lattermath growth as green manure in the autumn. 'No, Tom, not quite yet. We'll top that wheat in the piggery field and dry it. I think the carotene content will be out of this world.' Tom grinned, 'Well that's a new approach to managing a cereal crop, I hope you know what you're doing.' I looked at my foreman, for whom I'd developed a great liking and laughed, 'No, Tom, I don't for certain, but I can't really see that topping it with the cutlift is going to do it any more harm than grazing the sheep over it.' He shook his head, 'The sheep'll leave a lot of dung on it, which will all help the fertility, but you're the boss.'

I contacted our agent and told him I was going to have something very special for him in a couple of days, which undoubtedly would have a very high carotene content and he would have to get me an extra specially good price. He said he'd be down in about two days' time to get a sample of this wonder grass I was going to produce. I didn't tell him I'd be topping winter wheat. The result was quite an eye opener, for the carotene content was so high that the analyst tested the sample twice, still couldn't believe his finding and apparently asked a colleague to check his result, which proved to be correct. The sample also had a very high protein content. Our agent phoned me within the next two days to tell me he'd got £39 per ton for it; the best we'd had the previous autumn was £24. I wasn't over-enthusiastic, I had hoped for £40 a ton at the very least. I must have sounded disappointed, for it was then that the agent told me the buyers were only interested in the carotene for medicinal purposes, once that was extracted, as far as they were concerned, what was left was waste. So the deal he'd made was that we got the high-protein meal back for free. That was more like it. It was the most profitable crop of wheat we grew throughout the war. A really good yield in those days was 1½ tons an acre, most people were happy with anything over a ton. The crop didn't grow too high after its topping, we got it in perfect condition and ricked it on its own. When thrashed the following February, when the price was about as good as it was likely to get, it yielded just over 2¼ tons to the acre of good grain, plus the 'seconds'. That led to my having at least one field of winter wheat every year given a dressing of 1½ cwts of nitrogen to the acre in late January or early February, which produced a high carotene content meal, plus, on average 1½ tons of grain to the acre.

By May we were well into the grass drying and certainly on the estate front things seemed to be taking on a rosy hue. We'd had a nice crop of lambs and they were doing well. Every time the Colonel saw them I could almost see him licking his lips and thinking mint sauce. Unfortunately on the war front things weren't so good. At the end of April the British forces had been driven out of Greece by the Germans whilst raids by the Luftwaffe were becoming almost commonplace every night somewhere along the eastern side of the country. A particularly horrific one occurred on the night of 11 May, when there was yet another frightful blitz on London, badly damaging the House of Commons and killing over 1,400 Londoners.

Life is full of surprises and one of the most unexpected ones that ever occurred to me was when, one morning around the end of May, notification arrived from the War Ag that we had been allocated a tractor under the Lend-Lease agreement with the USA – a Minneapolis Moline. It was on pneumatic tyres and certainly a design we were unaccustomed to. It was high off the ground, tall with rather narrow rear wheels, but small twin wheels very close together in the front. In effect it was a three-wheeler. Three wheels or four wheels, it was still a real boon, for we were running out of power. I read carefully the sheaf of papers that accompanied the 'notice of allocation'. It was extraordinary that even as the country faced the greatest crisis in its history, bureaucracy still flourished. All that was needed could have been put on a postcard – we have a tractor, it is yours if you sign and return this form together with a cheque. Certainly we wanted it not tomorrow, but as of yesterday. I phoned Miss Moon, the Colonel's secretary, told her I wanted a cheque, the amount and what for. Further, I was leaving right away and would be at the office within three quarters of an hour. I was, however I didn't see Dev, he was in a meeting, but he had left the required cheque. I drove straight to Aylesbury to the offices of the War Ag where I asked to see Mr Knights, whose name was on the letter I had received that morning. The girl at reception glanced at a clock on the wall. 'Oh, he's at lunch.' Inwardly I cursed, 'When will he be back?' She smiled, 'Oh, he's not out. We take our lunch break in the office, sandwiches and a drink, that sort of thing, you know, all because of the war.' Casually I asked which was Mr Knights' office. 'First on the right at the top of the stairs.' I grinned at her, 'Thanks.' I was halfway up the stairs before she called out, 'You can't disturb him, he's having his lunch break.' I called back over my shoulder, 'Want to bet.'

I gave a cursory knock on the door as I walked in. 'Mr Knights?' A rather pimply-faced young man lolling back in a chair, his feet up on the desk, reading a paper, replied, 'Yes, but you can't come in here now, I'm on my lunch break. I'll see you (he glanced at his watch) in twenty minutes.' I took a firm grip on my rising anger, my fuse was getting very short. Quietly I asked, 'What time did you start work this morning Mr Knights and what time will you finish?' He looked quite surprised, 'Well 9.00am of course and the office closes at 5.00pm.' I leaned forward across the desk, 'Well I bloody well started mine at 6.00am and with luck usually manage to finish around 8.00pm, later by several hours when hay and harvest starts. Further, if you get off your backside and do some bloody work for a change I might just get fifteen minutes to have some lunch myself.' He started to display signs of a typical bureaucrat's arrogance. 'Look here you can't …' I cut him short, 'I can't understand why you're not in the forces. A young chap like you.' I heard him muttering something about being in a reserved occupation, but I continued, 'I'm sure my governor, Colonel Devereux, who I represent and who knows a number of very senior people in the Air Ministry, not forgetting the Prime Minister, will be only too pleased to get you fitted out with a uniform if you are unable to deal with this allocation of a Lend-Lease tractor to him immediately and, from experience I can tell you, in his world, immediately means yesterday!' He positively blanched and, without saying a word, reached out and took the papers I held, together with the required cheque. After several minutes, a rubber stamp and a bit of initialling, he handed them back, minus, of course, the cheque. 'Here you are, sir, I hope the tractor will be satisfactory.' I took the papers, 'When can we expect it?' He gave me a rather sickly smile, 'Soon, I hope. I'll have to phone the depot about it.'

I stood there and he gave me a somewhat perplexed look, finally asking, 'Yes, is there anything else I can do?' That was when something snapped, I leaned right forward across the desk, until my face was only inches away from his. 'Yes, you stupid idiot, use your phone. I want that tractor tomorrow. You may think you're helping the war effort, but you're just a waste of space, you're more hindrance than help.' Visibly shaken he reached for the phone. Eventually he put it down, 'Hopefully it will be with you tomorrow, but if not, definitely the following day.' I smiled at him and said, 'Now that wasn't too hard was it? Do you mind if I use your phone?' Without waiting for a reply I leaned across his desk, picked up the instrument and when the girl on the internal exchange answered gave her the Round Hill House number. Seconds later Ethne answered. I briefly explained I'd been delayed, but would be back within twenty minutes. I replaced the phone, smiled at a somewhat bemused Mr Knights and thanked him for his help. I got to the door and turned, 'By the way, I put in for a power-driven reaper and binder about ten days ago, we'll never cope with our harvest this year without another machine. I've been all over the place trying to buy a second-hand one, but can't find one anywhere. I hate to think what the Colonel would be like if, come harvest, we can't save the crops. He'd certainly have someone's guts for garters, but there you are. I've done my bit and grown the crops for him and, even more importantly the people of this country. I've a copy of my request for a binder to the War Ag. Can't do more can I?' With that I was gone. As I hurried through lunch, the others had all finished and, between mouthfuls, I regaled Rose and Ethne with an account of my visit to the War Ag offices. Ethne really chortled with delight, 'Dad will enjoy hearing about this. Bureaucracy is like a red rag to a bull with him and I think he'll consider he has a good up-and-coming convert in you.' Just after lunch the next day I arrived at Marsh Hill with Tom and purely by coincidence Miles was just about to leave the drier. Eileen had returned to the farm from scarifying a field with an old cultivator. The field was being given a bastard fallow, that is for the summer months only as compared with a full fallow of twelve months, in order to clean it before sowing it with winter corn. That afternoon she was to help draw grass to the drier, for where they were cutting was too far for Miles to cut, cart and keep the drier going non-stop. As they were both about to leave a lorry drove in, on it was a yellow tractor, looking vast before the lorry driver unloaded it – it was, of course, the new Minneapolis Moline. The sunlight seemed to rebound off its glossy paintwork. There was not a scratch, not even a speck of dirt. It seemed to me to look down its long steering-column at our dusty over-worked machines like a dowager duchess looking down her aristocratic nose at an aged general who has surreptitiously broken wind. Such stupid fantasising was broken by Eileen jumping down from what, up to then, had been her beloved Fordy, as she called the

Fordson, and running across to the new tractor. She ran round it, climbed up to the driving seat and sat there whilst I signed for it and received the manual, such as it was, from the driver. I gave him half a crown, for which he thanked me, adding, 'You must have a bit of pull governor. There's tractors at the depot been allocated three weeks or more and still sitting there. Yours only came in a few days ago.' I laughed, 'Luck of the draw I suppose.' With that he departed and Eileen came running over, 'Mr Twist, please, please can I take over Minnie?' I smiled, 'You're a bit fickle, I thought Fordy was the love of your life. I'll talk to Tom and let you know tomorrow. But if you don't get off down the field after Miles, you won't be driving anything, because I'll fire you for not getting on with your job.' She bolted. Tom was examining our new acquisition. He turned to me, 'Not what I'd have chosen, but beggars can't be choosers. I heard what young Eileen was saying. I think you should let her take it over, sir, next to the two men she's the most competent tractor driver we've got. Grace could drive the Fordson OK, but she can't plough or do anything like that.' I nodded, 'Yes, you're right. The only thing that worries me is that starting handle is very high. If the engine kicked back God only knows what it might do to her.'

'True, but both Sudden and I have told her if we ever see her swinging the starting handle with her thumb round it, holding it, she'll be off tractors at once. Anyway, like the rest of us, she could finish up with a bomb as a bedfellow tonight.' Tom was right, so Minnie would be Eileen's new charge. All tractors in those days had to be started with a handle, there was no ignition where one just turned a key. It was a hair-raising sight to see Eileen starting the new tractor. She would get the handle to its highest point, just about level with her chest and then literally throw herself down on it. Invariably Minnie fired and was running smoothly at the first attempt.

A couple of weeks later I was in my office when Megan Pring rang through to tell me, 'There's a Mr Knights from the War Ag on the phone, he would like to speak to you. I asked him what it was about, but he said he wished to speak to you personally.'

'Right, put him through.' I greeted him, 'Good morning Mr Knights. How can I help you.' Rather smugly the reply came back, 'Well actually I think it is me who can help you. I have a Massey-Harris binder for you, that is if you are still interested?' I didn't answer for a second, because I'm sure I'd have given away my amusement. 'Mr Knights! Interested? Of course I am. That's wonderful news. I never dreamed you'd be able to get it for us in time for this coming harvest. I wasn't looking forward to the flak that would have been flying around if the Colonel found out we weren't able to harvest the corn properly. I really am grateful.' A few more pleasantries and I hung up. I knew I'd been a bit devious and probably scared the pants off the wretched man, but I wasn't being paid to be nice to bureaucrats. I was being paid to run the Colonel's estate and, even more importantly, produce every ounce of food possible for our people.

17. A Time to Cry, A Time to Laugh

June saw more changes in the war, for Hitler turned on his ally, the Soviet Union, and sent his troops into Russia. The Colonel was jubilant over this for he claimed this had to ease the pressure on Britain and hopefully, give us time to recoup our loses and increase our air force.

His two eldest sons, Jack and Dean, were in the forces. Jack, who had been a good friend of mine at school, had joined the army as soon as war had been declared. On hearing that the Commandos were being formed he applied for a transfer and was accepted instantly. By the time I arrived at Round Hill he was somewhere in the Highlands of Scotland, basically learning two things: first, to kill by becoming superbly skilled in both armed and unarmed combat and second, to survive under the most adverse conditions. This I was to learn included being out on a Scottish mountain, at the height of winter, finding shelter and living off the land. Dev was tremendously proud of both his sons, as indeed he was of all his family, but I think deep down Jack was slightly his favourite, for he was truly a chip off the old block – what's more, he was an extremely good boxer. Sadly, Jack's career in the Commandos came to an unfortunate end.

Together with numerous companions he was eventually declared fully trained and given leave. Jack, together with three of his brother officers, hightailed it to London. They had been deprived of wine, women and song for months, so it was not surprising that they set about painting the town red. Having found a hotel and dumped their gear they first phoned their respective parents and then set off to enjoy themselves – first stop the famous Windmill Theatre. This was followed by much drinking, another trip to the Windmill and finally back to their hotel, accompanied or unaccompanied history doesn't relate, but I think it a money-on certainty the former. Later that evening they set off again and I seem to remember hearing, dined well at the Dorchester. From there they went to a nightclub. As the evening progressed they became livelier and eventually, for what reason I don't know, they were told, somewhat rudely, to leave. Had they been politely asked to quieten things down it is unlikely there would have been a problem. However, to be ordered out by a mere civilian was the wrong approach. When they wouldn't and had told the manager where he could go he threatened to send for the military police, to which the lads said, 'So what?'

In due course the Red Caps arrived, five in all, one, a sergeant, remaining at the exit in case any of them tried to escape. How misguided can anyone be? Far from escaping, Jack and his friends had the four military policemen stretched out on the dancefloor in a matter of seconds, having put a little of what they had been practising for over a year to good use. This activity seems to have sobered them up, for they paid their bill, helped the dazed military police to their feet and strolled over to the sergeant. He, wise man, realising they were Commandos, decided that discretion was the better part of valour and so took details of names, rank and numbers and said providing they would give their word as officers and gentlemen to report to the Provost Marshall's office the next morning at 1100 hours he'd not arrest them. All happily agreed.

Three did, but unfortunately Jack had found the girl of many dreams when bivouacking on a Scottish mountain side in the depth of winter. When he eventually arrived at 1233 hours, he assured the Provost Marshall that he found her more interesting than a visit to him and was in no way contrite. Tempers flared, ending, I was given to understand, in Jack being cashiered and it was fortunate probably for him that his father had so much clout. The others who reported on time got their knuckles severely rapped, leave suspended and were sent back to their unit – a year's intensive training to produce some of the fittest, toughest fighting men in our armed forces was not something to throw away lightly. Having a father in high places was a help and Jack was enrolled in the RAF and quickly found himself in North Africa. I never heard every detail, but I do know that Dev found the incident at the nightclub and Jack's subsequent meeting with the Provost Marshall highly amusing. He quite rightly claimed that if you spend months teaching men to react immediately to aggression and, if necessary kill at the slightest provocation, then, if you cross them, you must expect trouble. Sadly, after the war some of the Commandos reacted in Civvy Street in a way they had been brainwashed into doing automatically in the army, which landed a number of them in very serious trouble.

Dean was equally a great chap, but quieter than Jack. He was an officer attached to a reconnaissance unit of the RAF. It was towards the end of June 1941 that the Colonel phoned me, very distressed indeed. He had heard that Dean had been shot down on a mission somewhere off the coast of France and had been seen to bale out by one of his fellow pilots, but at this stage nothing more was known. Choking with emotion, the Colonel asked me to tell Ethne and Nanny, but not the children. He said he would be at the farm later that evening, hopefully with more news from his various contacts at the Air Ministry. It was not the easiest job I ever undertook for the Colonel. Poor Ethne, there was really no way one can break something like that gently. She turned white, threw her arms round my neck and sobbed her heart out. Then she pushed back from me and said, 'No, no, I know he's not dead, not Dean. He'll be all right. That evening I waited anxiously with Ethne but when Dev got out of the car he was laughing, great guffaws of relief. She was right. Dean had been rescued from the sea by the Germans and was a prisoner for the remainder of the War.

Things continued to progress on the estate. I was faced with one minor dilemma around the end of July. Our main entry for the Shorthorn Society Show and Sale in early November was to be a full brother to Diamond Wild Duke. A friend and partner of the Colonel's, Dr Leo Jakobi, in International Alloys, had purchased a farm not far away, just into Oxfordshire. Leo, together with his younger brothers Julius and Dave, owed much, no, correction, everything to Dev. They were German Jews and brilliant metallurgists with whom the Colonel was doing business before he went to

Germany in 1937. On realising which way things were going, the Colonel somehow got them and their money out of Germany and re-started in business in Britain. Leo had bought this farm and was building up a Shorthorn herd. He had greatly admired Wild Duke when visiting Round Hill and wanted to buy his full brother. When I heard about this I wasn't too keen on the idea. I wanted more success at the Show and Sale, I suppose partly for personal glory, but more to keep the herd's name in the public eye. I talked to Ron Chamberlain about it. We agreed that we had several outstanding bull calves coming along and if the price was right we'd let him go. There was no guarantee he'd win and we both knew he wasn't as nice as Duke. Ron thought if we could get 250 guineas for him it would be a fair price, for after all at the March sale the average price had been under 100 guineas. Leo, his two brothers and their stockman came over one evening just as we were starting harvest – they wouldn't come during the day.

They may well have been outstanding metallurgists, but they wouldn't have lasted long in the cattle-dealing business and an even shorter time with horses. As Ron paraded his young charge they all enthused so openly and obviously that they became 'lambs to the slaughter'. After about five minutes the good doctor called out, 'Yes, we must have him. What is the price?' On the basis that I had been taught that you can always come down but never up I glibly said 500 guineas. Poor Ron gasped, but fortunately all eyes were on me and not on the bull. I waited to be bid, but instead Leo immediately replied, 'Excellent, excellent, I will write you a cheque and we will send a lorry tomorrow.' I always wondered what would have happened if I had asked for more.

Having had a quick walk out through the dairy cows, Leo said he would like his brothers to see the grass drier, so off we set for Marsh Hill. Just before we reached the turning to the drier I stopped opposite the gate into a field where Sudden had just started to cut an exceptionally good field of Victory oats. I got out of the car and went to make sure all was well, the Jakobis joining me. Leo expressed admiration for the crop by rubbing out a head of corn and declaring it very good. 'If the weather remains fine you will have this field safely stacked by the end of the week.' I looked at him in amazement. 'Oh no. There's a very good and sound old country proverb, namely that oats, when cut, should hear the church bells ring three times before they're ricked.' Dr Jakobi's over-large belly seemed to bounce up and down as he gave vent to a loud and sustained laugh, guttural like his voice. 'Ah, you English country people are so superstitious. We cut a field of oats, the straw still a little on the green side so that it can be used for feeding in the winter, just four days ago and tomorrow we rick it.' I looked at the man he'd brought with him, who I had discovered was farm foreman, as well as head herdsman. He just shrugged his shoulders. I laughed, 'Well, now if you do that it will provide a great chance to see which of us is right.' Julius joined in the conversation. 'Without doubt Leo, he is always right.' If that was true then the ricking of the oats after just five days proved there are exceptions to every rule. The stack had been built in the somewhat isolated field where the crop had been grown. I heard three to four weeks later from Dev that poor Dr Jakobi had had an awful fire at his farm. A rick of oats had gone up in flames due, it was thought by the firemen, to internal combustion caused by carting crop before it was ready. I said nothing other than, 'That's hard luck, particularly with the shortage of feeding stuffs for livestock in general.' I never took to Leo Jakobi and it was a strange coincidence that he would eventually have a major influence on my future.

It was the last Saturday in August, every field that was ready had been ricked and the only major activity that afternoon, which would carry on into Sunday if the weather remained good, was the two binders cutting the wheat in the fifty-acre section of The Grove, with of course a team of men and a couple of the girls to stook the sheaves to keep them as safe as possible against a break in the weather. The latter seemed unlikely as it was very hot. I had been into Aylesbury market but hadn't stopped for a jar with my friends in the men's bar at The Bull's Head, which was where many of the farmers met on market day. However, I did drop in at The Prince of Wales for a much-needed pint of shandy. While I stood in the passage talking to Mrs Leversuch through the hatch, old Bill, the one who had tweaked the bottom of the volunteer helper who'd let Smiler step on her foot, breezed in. 'Hullo, sir, great weather.' I agreed, 'What'll you have Bill?' 'Thanks, a half if that's all right? I looked at him with surprise, 'Only a half, can't you managed a pint any longer?'

'Course I can, but I didn't want to seem greedy.' I liked Bill, he was a bit of a rogue. Once caught in the early hours of the morning digging himself a bag of potatoes from a very rich man's vegetable garden, recently rumour had it that Bill had 'got religion'. Apparently he was some miles from home, one bright moonlight night, hoping to see enough to shoot a rabbit or two to feed his kids, when a 'scare' bomb landed in a field he'd only vacated minutes before. Bill was convinced that it was only by the grace of God that he hadn't been blown to bits. So great was this conviction he attended morning service for two consecutive Sundays at Kimble Church. Bill raised his glass, 'Cheers! Did you know, boss, there's a fair few ol' pigeons workin' that wheat in the field way out the back o' Round Hill buildings?' He looked a mite wistful before adding, 'A couple of them wouldn't go amiss in a pie for tomorrow's dinner.'

'Now Bill don't you go getting any ideas about helping yourself. You know all the Colonel's land is private.'

'What, me? I wouldn't do a thing like that. Why that'd be poaching, which the last time I was up in front o' the ol' magistrate he said that were stealin' and stealin' is a mortal sin in the eyes of our Lord.' I asked Mrs Leversuch to fill his glass and give me another half. 'That'd worry you a lot you old reprobate.' Bill looked genuinely puzzled, 'Don't reckon I know what that is, but I tell you what, Mr Twist, you'll never catch me poaching.' I roared with laughter, 'That's probably true, because you're as crafty as an old fox. Anyway, Bill, don't forget what I've said. I must be off now.'

As I drove up towards the house I could see pigeons dropping in on the field Bill had mentioned, where about half an acre of wheat had been flattened by a recent thunderstorm. Thankfully the main of the crop was unharmed, for we had not caught the full brunt of the storm.

I decided that after lunch I'd take my gun and decoy pigeons and see if I could bag a few to help eke out the meat ration. Lunch, I well remember was roast stuffed lambs' hearts, which were delicious. Offal was not rationed, at least not at that time, but, having received one's allowance months went by before one came to the top of the list again.

My cartridge bag, which would take 150, was half-full, but I added two more boxes just in case the woodies appeared in big numbers. Cartridges were in desperately short supply. Farmers could get an allocation for vermin control from the War Ag, but even then distribution was strictly monitored. However, Phil Oliver, who did not shoot, regularly applied for his quota as did Renee's father and what they received they passed on to me for a small consideration such as a hare or a brace of partridges during the shooting season, plus of course the cost. Fortunately I had anticipated a shortage and had bought 500 before rationing started.

Duly equipped with gun, cartridges, decoys, plus a short-handled slasher to build a hide I set off across the dairy ground to the wheat field. As I approached the area where the corn had been flattened, which it so happened was conveniently close to the hedge, several hundred pigeons rose into the air. I stood stock-still as the majority flew off to some distant elm trees. Hastily I found a suitable place to build a hide. Having done this I put my gun and cartridges inside and quickly set up my decoys. As I was finishing this pigeons started circling overhead wanting to return to their feeding ground. I quickly entered my hide, which was ideal as an indentation in the hedge meant that all that was needed were a few leafy branches, which I cut from a nearby ash, to construct the front, providing all the cover and camouflage required. It was opposite a narrow neck of laid corn which led to the main area that had been flattened. Further, I could see along the hedge in both directions – perfect! All that was required now was the woodpigeons to cooperate.

I hadn't many minutes to wait before three were drawn to the decoys and I accounted for a brace. I hadn't done a lot of shooting since I'd moved to Roundhill, for the estate was quite different to the one I grew up on, which had a number of woods and spinneys. What shooting there was on the estate the Colonel said I was more than welcome to. He did shoot, sharing a large shoot at Limington, on the edge of the New Forest with John Howlett, the boss of Wellworthy Pistons, with whom Dev did a lot of business. I hadn't many minutes to wait before the pigeons decided to return in numbers and for a little under half an hour I had some really good shooting. Then for no apparent reason the flight stopped. I waited a few minutes then decided to pick up. When I'd finished the bag was twenty-three. I had just returned to the hide when I saw about thirty flying straight towards me, low over the corn. I was just about to raise my gun in readiness, when suddenly they jinked and climbed swiftly away to my right. Obviously something had scared them and I was certain they couldn't have seen me in the hide.

I glanced up the hedge to my left, where, crouched low and advancing slowly and somewhat unsteadily, was Bill, his old hammer gun held out in front of him at the ready. Quietly I swore under my breath, but I'd got the old varmint this time. He wasn't quite as foxy as he thought he was. As he drew nearer I could see he was, indeed, very unsteady on his legs, the barrels of his gun waving around all over the place. I felt certain it was cocked and I was equally certain that my friend Bill was as drunk as the proverbial fiddler's bitch. Annoyance started to change to concern, for as the barrels moved to and fro, I frequently came within their orbit. I quietly laid down my gun and then froze, for I felt the old fool was so drunk that if he saw a movement in the hedge, he might think it was a rabbit and blast off hoping to bag it. As he drew nearer my unease increased, for I could see the gun was definitely cocked and, worse still, he had a finger certainly resting on the trigger guard, if not the actual trigger. At last his slow faltering progress brought him to right in front of the hide and, it seemed with some difficulty, he straightened up. He was so close that, had he been sober he must surely have felt my breath on the back of his neck. I heard him take a sharp intake of breath as he spotted my decoys. Slowly, ever so slowly he raised the butt of his gun to his shoulder, as it reached it I stretched out my arm and grasped his shoulder, at the same time roaring in the deepest and most sepulchral voice I could muster. 'Sin not William.' Bill literally let out a shriek, accidentally discharging one barrel harmlessly into the air. He dropped his gun and followed it to his knees. Clasping his hands he cried out, 'Dear God forgive me. I didn't mean to sin - honest. I promise never to poach again.' He started to recite the Lord's Prayer.

I stepped out of my hide, 'Like hell you didn't, you old scallywag and I don't believe your promise for one moment.' I leaned forward to pick up his gun and took out the remaining cartridge. He was shaking like a leaf as he looked up, trying to focus. It was obvious that he was very drunk. I just stood there saying nothing. At last he staggered to his feet, looking owlishly at me. 'Thank heavens it's you sir. I thought it was the Almighty, or even old Nick himself come for me. I nearly died o' fright.' I grinned, 'You certainly did. That'll teach you to go poaching, particularly after you've been warned.' Suddenly his expression changed, he seemed to be sobering fast. 'Don't take me to court mister - please. Me ol' woman would beat the hell out of me an' it's more than probable I'd get sent down for a month or six weeks.'

'It's undoubtedly what I should do you rogue, but you're a likeable old devil and if you give me your solemn promise you'll never poach on the Colonel's land again, I'll let you off this time, but you won't get a second chance if I catch you again.' Poor Bill, he looked like a whipped dog. 'I'll come roun' to your office if you like and swear on the Good Book.' I laughed, 'No Bill that'll not be necessary.' 'I only wanted two or three to make a meal for the kids tomorrow. We've used all our meat ration to the end of the month an' the farms where I'm allowed to go to shoot rabbits - I share what I get with the owners - well I've pretty well cleared them out.'

'Strange though it may seem, I believe you.' I reached into the hide and picked out four nice plump pigeons and handed them to him. 'Here you are you old rascal and you can have your gun and this cartridge back. Now get out before I change my mind.' Bill seemed to have completely sobered up. 'Thanks, governor, you're a real gentleman.' He started to move away and then stopped, eyeing my open cartridge bag which he could clearly see just inside the hide. Turning he said, 'I suppose you couldn't spare me a couple o' cartridges? I'm gettin' terribly short of 'em.' I think I must have literally gaped from surprise at the sheer audacity of his request. Bill's face was a study – half-pleading, half-scared, he looked really comical. 'I could make it worth your while. I know where that fox hangs out that's been raiding the chicken roosts an' costing the hunt a deal o' money.' For sheer undiluted cheek he would take some beating, but poor man he was only trying to add to the meagre meat ration that he, his family and everyone else had to exist on. I asked and was given the information as to the whereabouts of the fox – it seemed plausible. I pulled out my cartridge bag, 'Right, I don't know why I'm doing this, but all right, just two handfuls and only two. If you drop one you don't have it, so don't be greedy.' Bill's smile spread from ear to ear. 'You're a real toff governor an' no mistake.' It was only then that I noticed the size of Bill's hands, they were like a couple of coal grabs. How many he managed to extract and get into his pocket I've no idea, but my bag looked considerably depleted when he moved away.

The sudden shock seemed to have had a great sobering effect on Bill, for he walked off as steady as a rock, in the direction he'd come in from the road. Bill loved to sing. When he'd gone about seventy or eighty yards he looked back, gave me a wave and started to sing a song from a Fred Astaire/Ginger Rogers film. The words of part of it were, 'they all laughed at Christopher Columbus when he said the world was round etc etc', the last line being 'who's had the last laugh now?' Those six words Bill positively bellowed, as he noticeably quickened his step. Just for a moment I thought of chasing after him and taking back both the pigeons and the cartridges, but instead I sat down by my hide and laughed until the tears ran down my cheeks. A good laugh was worth a lot, it helped relieve the tension under which we were living, so probably Bill would have claimed that his foray after pigeons had been therapeutic for me – that is if he'd known what it meant.

18. Of Bulls and a Baron

The Lend-Lease Bill, the lifeline thrown to Great Britain by President Roosevelt in March 1941, covered much more than just agricultural machinery, for it ranged from shipping through a vast variety of weapons and equipment, down to every man and woman's friend during those torrid years – the humble tin of Spam. A few derided it, but I can assure readers even they never refused it when it was available. Amongst the items that flowed into our country from the States were aircraft, mainly, I believe, the Tomahawk fighter. Of course these didn't have the range to cross the Atlantic under their own power and were therefore sent in packing cases, to be assembled in Great Britain. Large numbers of crated planes arrived and remained stored in numerous places, even along the grass verges of country roads. Those who saw them had no idea what they were, noticed, but said nothing. There were numerous advertisements advising people to 'be like dad and keep mum', or to remember that 'careless talk costs lives'. It was seriously important to keep mum; for fifth columnists most certainly were a reality and some were able to transmit spurious information to William Joyce, the notorious Lord Haw Haw, who became the voice of German propaganda.

Churchill, whilst fully appreciating Roosevelt's help, was quick to realise that unless arrangements were made to assemble these fighters immediately they might just as well have remained in America. Lord Beaverbrook, the Minister for Aircraft Production, was summoned post-haste to Downing Street. Naturally I do not know what was said in any detail, but I do know the essence, which was that Beaverbrook was to appoint the man he considered to be the most able in the country as his deputy, as Controller of North American Aircraft, someone with the drive and tenacity to set up immediately the necessary structure to assemble the planes so that they could become operational. It seems Beaverbrook was not slow in putting forward the name of Wallace Charles Devereux, managing director of High Duty Alloys and numerous other companies.

Shortly after this decision was taken Dev arrived at Round Hill one weekend and, in the privacy of my office, told me the news. He was naturally appreciative of the high esteem in which he was held, but not so thrilled that his appointment meant he had to hand over the chairmanship of HDA to Geoff Herrington, albeit temporarily and was, for twelve months, to forget about his businesses. He didn't like it, not one little bit, but as he put it, someone had to do the job and if Beaverbrook wasn't capable, he most certainly was.

One thing he had made quite clear to all was that he had no intention of giving up as Master of the Old Berkeley Hunt, in which I had become quite involved, acting on his instructions. His co-Master, Stanley Barratt, was back in the army, his interest watched over by his wife, Gloria. She and Dev mixed about as well as oil and water. We had a new kennel-huntsman, Tom Healy, David Griffiths having retired at the end of the 1939–40 season. We were very fortunate to get Tom. He'd been huntsman of the Glamorgan for several years, but at the end of the 1939–40 season, just when the OBH was looking for someone, the Glamorgan had ceased to exist, so Tom was looking for a job. The Colonel was sticking rigidly to his principles, namely that we must retain our country heritage, if we didn't what was the point of busting a gut to win the war? I had already started to act as whipper-in when we hunted in the Vale of Aylesbury on Mondays, deal with poultry claims and visit farmers who complained about a fence being broken down by the hunt and make sure it was mended in the minimum of time. In addition, on the Colonel's behalf, I paid regular visits to the kennels at Amersham.

One good thing the Colonel's new appointment brought about was that it gave him more time to spend at the farm at weekends, for he found the run-of-the-mill civil servants didn't take kindly to a seven-day week! Dev brought work with him, but he wasn't tied down by board meetings which he was used to calling at unsocial hours. That he didn't take to Beaverbrook became more obvious as the weeks went by and feelings were not improved when Beaverbrook visited The Meads one weekend and his car broke down. Apart from his two Bentleys, Dev had a magnificent Lagonda that he hardly ever used as it was a terrible gas-guzzler. He occasionally came to Round Hill in it, just to give it a run, otherwise it remained in the garage, carefully tended by Wren. However, to be rid of Beaverbrook he lent him the Lagonda on the strict understanding that it was returned within the next forty-eight hours. It was two months before he was able to get it back, Beaverbrook had taken such a liking to it. The fact that it did only about eight miles to the gallon did not deter him from going all over the country in it and, so the Colonel heard, refer to it as his new car ... which did not improve the undercurrent of animosity that had developed.

My only contact with the Minister was one wet Saturday afternoon when I was working in my office and the Colonel was in the house spending a little time with the girls. The phone rang, I said 'Hullo' and a voice, which had a distinct twang to it, came over the wire, 'Is Devereux there?' I politely replied, 'No you're on to the estate office. Who wants him?' The reply was snapped back, 'Beaverbrook.' The line was poor, as it frequently was, and the intonation of the caller's voice was such that I didn't catch the name. 'I'm sorry I didn't get your name.' My ear was blasted with, 'Beaverbrook. Beaverbrook you f*****g idiot. Have you never bloody well heard of me?' I replied that I had, gave him the house number and hung up. I didn't think I'd get on very well with Beaverbrook, he might have brains but he certainly hadn't any manners. When I went across to the house for a cup of tea around four o'clock Dev greeted me with, 'I hear you had Beaverbrook on the phone to you.' My reply was terse, 'Yes, he's got the manners of a pig.' Wallace Charles did not disagree.

I cannot think that the Colonel was over-popular at the Ministry, for as in his businesses he frequently called meetings at 6.00am, to which the bred-in-the-bone bureaucrats found it extremely hard to adjust, for they were not used to such an abnormal and disruptive mode of administration. I gathered that at the Ministry there was a long corridor, with offices on either side, culminating in Beaverbrook's. On the left, immediately before Beaverbrook's was that of the Controller for North American Aircraft, but between the two was the Minister's private washroom. Dev also had a private one, but it was about fifty yards away at the far end of the corridor. When he arrived early at his office and received the call of nature, to save time, as the Minister was seldom in before 9.00am, he would nip in next door. One morning, when this had happened, soon after 8.00am, Dev was enthroned on the Minister's private loo when a commissionaire knocked on the door, 'Colonel Devereux, Lord Beaverbrook wishes to see you immediately.' As quick as a flash Devereux replied, 'You go and tell Lord Beaverbrook I can't attend to two shits at once.' The commissionaire, being well trained in the ways of Whitehall, did as he was bid!

Geoff Herrington phoned me around 11.00am on the same day to tell me of Dev's gaffe, which he assured me had gone round the aircraft industry like wildfire, much to everyone's amusement – the only person who apparently did not see the funny side was Beaverbrook. Sadly, that instant retort, coupled with the naivety of the commissionaire, almost certainly cost the Colonel, at the very least, the knighthood which he so richly deserved, not only for the tremendous job he did in connection with the import of American aircraft, but, also, his overall contribution to the war effort.

One morning between hay and harvest I was closeted in my office, making plans for the 1942 cropping, seed and fertiliser requirements. It was a gorgeous day and I would far sooner have been out around the estate, but quality seed was becoming more and more scarce. Carters Seeds' rep for the area, whom I'd known since I was a child, as he had for more than twenty years supplied seed to the Burnham estate, had contacted me asking that I give him some idea as to what the Roundhill order was likely to be in the immediate future, so that he could ensure it would be met.

It was a job I did not enjoy and I had told Megan Pring not to disturb me with phone calls unless absolutely necessary. The window out to the path from the stable yard to the house was wide open. I was re-checking some figures when a somewhat distraught Nanny Hurst appeared at it. I'd heard a bit of a commotion from the house, crying and the coaxing tones of nanny just minutes before. I'd learned at breakfast that poor little Ann, who by then had her own pony and whom Ethne and I were teaching to ride, was not very well. Nanny was most concerned when I saw her at breakfast time, for Ann had a slight temperature and she had phoned the doctor. I'd seen him leave about fifteen minutes before nanny arrived at the window. 'Mr Twist, the doctor's just been, Ann's temperature has gone up since I took it earlier and he says she must have an aspirin every four hours. Unfortunately he said this in front of Ann and suggested I dissolve it in milk, which I've done, but Ann won't drink it. You get on so well with her, will you come and see if you can persuade her – please?'

When I first told my father that I wished to become a land agent-cum-farm manager, he warned me that there was nothing that did not come within the orbit of the former and he was speaking from years of experience. I was very fond of Ann and having had so much illness as a child I knew how miserable the poor kid would be feeling. So in spite of having so much to do, I joined Nanny in the hall who offered me the small glass of milk containing the dissolved aspirin. I took it, but said, 'Hang on a minute, if I'm going to be successful let me do it my way. I want two dessertspoons, an aspirin and a heaped teaspoonful of the finest sugar Verna has in the kitchen, preferably caster.' Nanny looked somewhat perplexed, but did what I asked. I ground the aspirin into a powder between the two spoons, then added the sugar and mixed it well. 'Right, off we go.'

As I entered the bedroom poor Ann gave me a wan little smile. She looked very flushed and miserable, propped up on her pillows. I put the spoon and the milk down on the bedside table, sat down on the edge of the bed and took her hand. 'You're a silly old sausage aren't you, being in bed on a lovely day like this? I was hoping to take you for a ride after lunch, but we can't now. You enjoy riding don't you?' She nodded. I picked up the glass and spoon and said, 'Now be a good girl and drink this, then you can have this spoonful of sugar. (I can assure readers that Julie Andrews as Mary Poppins was not the first one to think 'that a spoonful of sugar makes the medicine go down').

I held out the glass and in a rather stern voice said, 'Now, don't be a silly girl, drink this down and stop wasting my time.' I could see Nanny was about to intervene and gave her a warning look. Ann started to cry. I put both glass and spoon down and gave her a cuddle and when the tears had stopped, I said, 'Well, never mind. As you're my special girl I'll drink the milk and you have the sugar.' She gave me a watery smile, I downed the milk. I didn't need an aspirin but it wasn't going to do me any harm. I held out the spoon to Ann and down the sugar went. I leaned forward, gave her a light kiss on the forehead and whispered, 'I'll tuck you down now, you'll feel better after a little snooze and I think when you do wake up you'll find my taking your aspirin will have done you good.' She gave a little giggle. I sat with her for a few minutes, by which time she was asleep. Nanny and I left the room. When we got outside Nanny said, 'How did you think of that one?' I laughed quietly. 'My mother played that trick on me dozens of times when I was Ann's age, but when you do it in four hours' time, don't waste an aspirin in your milk.' With that I returned to my office.

On 29 September, Michaelmas Day, the tenants at Manor Farm vacated the premises. They held a clearance sale a week or so before they left, but anything that would have been of real interest to me had already been moved to their new premises. Nevertheless I attended the auction and bought anything which would be of use to us, which included some silage. Silage making was really in its infancy. One could buy sectional wooden silos, which when erected were lined out with rolls of strong waterproof paper. This could also be used together with a very strong type of wire framing and that is what the tenants at Manor Farm had done. The silo I bought contained about thirty tons, a useful addition to the winter food supply plus all the hay and straw stored in the Dutch barn. The acquisition of the farm, apart from providing some 250 more acres of good land, enabled me to start on something which was to the fore in the mind of many dairy farmers and particularly those with pedigree herds, namely to gain the 'Attested' status for these which would show they were tuberculosis free.

Having Manor Farm made this less of a heart-breaking exercise than it did for many with quality pedigree cows, who only had the one set of buildings. If a cow reacted to the tuberculin test she had to be removed at once from those that had passed. It was permitted to retain her on premises away from TB-free stock, calve her and when this happened the calf could be removed immediately to the potential Attested premises, providing it was not permitted to suckle its dam, not even to obtain colostrum – the all-important first secretions from the udder, rich in antibodies, passed from mother to offspring.

With this option available and my personal desire to have the first Attested herd in Buckinghamshire, I had the cow byre at Manor Farm thoroughly cleansed and a general clean up all round the buildings. Fred Spittles did some much needed decorating in the old farmhouse and, when this was completed, all that was required was a reliable and trustworthy herdsman, under Ron Chamberlain's control, to care for the reactors. I was under no illusion that when the time for the first test came the herd would be free of reactors, in fact I was dreading the day of the test. Strange though it may seem to those who have not been in the position to do so, one can become very attached to cows, for all have individual characters.

The problem regarding a herdsman seemed likely to be solved when Ron came to me one morning to say he might have the solution. He'd received a letter from his father, George Chamberlain, who had been head herdsman for Chivers the jam manufacturers who had farmed some 11,000 acres in Cambridgeshire, but was now currently herdsman-cum-farm manager at Dunmow in Essex. The farm was owned by a London businessman with no knowledge of farming, who had insisted on growing cash crops the previous harvest, with no thought as to how his pedigree Dairy Shorthorn herd was going to be fed throughout the winter. The result was that both the herd and the land were going up for auction, for the poor unfortunate cattle were existing on barley chaff and treacle (black molasses as used in silage making), plus a small amount of hay. Some had become so weak that a few had to be helped up if they lay down. His letter told of one particular cow that he claimed, with the right feeding, would be a very useful addition to the Roundhill herd. Further, he had a herdsman, John Saville, who was looking for a job. In George's opinion he'd never get to the top of his profession, but was a good reliable man. The sale was in a week's time. I sent a telegram to George saying I would be there and that if Saville had not already found a job I would like to interview him.

There was no basic ration of petrol any longer, one ran a car for business only, so Ethne could no longer use the super MG her father had given her for her birthday. As a result he had bought it at cost for me to use on the estate, as two vehicles were needed. Ron and I drove across to Dunmow, bought the cow that George had recommended for 140 guineas but the majority did not reach 50 guineas as they were skin and bone. I had a talk to Saville about coming to Manor Farm as herdsman, working under Ron, which he seemed anxious to do, so I engaged him and arranged he should move the following week.

There was nothing now to delay the initial TB test and at 8.30am one morning Clive Haselden started taking skin measurements and injecting the vaccine into two small clipped areas on the neck. It was a harrowing seventy-two hours at the end of which a number of the top cows that had come with the Diamond herd had failed and were moved to Manor Farm. But on the whole it could have been much worse, for most of the younger cows had passed, as had the young stock and the bulls. There was one problem – a quality stock bull for Manor Farm, we couldn't bring the cows back to Duke and the others we had at Round Hill.

Eventually I decided to move the most senior bull, who'd actually passed the TB test, to take up his duties with the reactors. His days were numbered anyway for, apart from age, the majority of the nice young heifers coming on were by him.

Clive murmured something about artificial insemination and research being carried out by Dr Joseph Edwards at the Cambridge University farm. There had been quite a few articles in the agricultural press in connection with this, but I hadn't paid too much attention except to look upon it as a threat to a serious part of the farm's income, the sale of young bulls and bull calves to be reared as future stock bulls. On one of his visits the Colonel commented on the fact that it was the way forward and eventually would be a boon to the smaller farmers who could not afford top-quality bulls. Certainly there were an awful lot of scrub bulls, as poor quality ones were known, in spite of the bull licensing scheme. All bulls used for breeding had to be licensed and, at around twelve months were inspected by the Ministry of Agriculture's Livestock Officer. If they were passed they were tattooed in the ear with a crown, if failed it was a large 'R' for rejected.

The Livestock Officer for our area was a very nice and knowledgeable Welshman, Emerys Parry, of good farming stock. I had several talks with him about Artificial Insemination. He was for it, except that it would eventually put him out of a job. He assured me I would share his view if I saw the rubbish he had to license. This comment eventually led to me accompanying him for a day. For the benefit of the farmers we were going to visit I was to take the role of a trainee Livestock Officer. This would enable me to inspect the young bulls brought forward without it causing any comment. Emerys suggested I should make a note of those I passed and those I failed and we'd compare notes at the end of the day. When he dropped me back at Round Hill we did this. He had inspected, as indeed I had, fifteen bulls. It turned out he had passed eleven, I, on the other hand, had only passed four and one of those had been a borderline case. Emerys explained if he was as hard as I had been, there just wouldn't be enough bulls around to get cows in calf. That day made me think there might, after all, be some virtue in Artificial Insemination.

19. Trauma and Elation

The winter of 1941–42 seemed to race by. There was so much to do and so little time to do it in, against the backdrop of the war which offered little cheer, although Japan's attack on Pearl Harbour in December had brought America directly into the conflict and we were no longer alone. However, we now had another enemy to face, for Churchill declared war on Japan just one day after they attacked the USA. We were still playing catch up – as far as agriculture was concerned, trying to raise production to the level it should have been even before the start of the war had successive governments shown even a modicum of interest in the rural economy, but undoubtedly, progress was being made. Hedging and particularly ditching, essential for the war effort, were being widely undertaken on many farms. There was a worthwhile subsidy for this, but it was only payable when a single strand barbed wire fence was erected to keep livestock from treading in the freshly dug ditches. At one stage that winter we had three gangs from the War Ag ditching, perhaps platoons might be a better description in view of the numbers involved, but it was up to Evans, who controlled the pool labour allocation, how many he sent, for it was all contract work.

The final inspection before the subsidy was paid was carried out by an ex-farmer who had been dispossessed, first of his land, because he hadn't the equipment and money to plough up his fields in accordance with War Ag instructions, and second of his home. He was a very pleasant and knowledgeable man and a great supporter of the hunt, his farm having been just on the border of the South Oxfordshire Hunt country. In fact he regularly followed hounds on his old cob up to the time that he was driven from his property. He retained his interest and was deeply concerned about the barbed wire guard fences, worried that when hounds were running, followers would jump a fence landing smack into the wire and cutting a horse to ribbons. Surprisingly I can only remember this happening twice and that was due to visitors not paying attention to what they were told. Thankfully the damage on each occasion was minimal.

Wire, however, in the much larger form of overhead electric cables, brought about some horrific and terrible tragedies, not only on the estate, but in other parts of the Aylesbury Vale. I'm not referring to the vast pylons and lines that criss-cross our countryside today, but poles, no taller than a telegraph one, carrying two cables, frequently not visible beyond a hedge. There were many such cables crossing fields supplying power to farms and housing. It was also an area in which the RAF chose to teach recently recruited pilots hedge-hopping, that is flying only feet off the ground, zooming up over a hedge then returning to their virtually non-existent altitude. That was fine providing there weren't cables crossing the field just beyond. On Round Hill and Manor Farm alone we had five planes crash. Of the five, three burst into flame on impact, one less than 100 yards from where I and several of the estate staff happened to be. There was absolutely nothing we could do, for in a fraction of a second it was a blazing inferno. The short-lived tortured screams of the poor lads as they were consumed by fire is something that will remain with me until my dying day. There is no doubt that such ghastly happenings strengthened the resolve, if that was possible, to see the end of the greatest evil that had ever beset mankind – Nazi Germany.

Ron and I attended the Shorthorn Society's Show and Sale in March 1942. The Colonel's instructions were still to buy any cow or heifer that I thought would enhance the quality of the herd, resulting in the Reserve Female Champion coming to Round Hill. As I watched the bulls being judged I put out a few feelers to various friends and acquaintances on the subject of Artificial Insemination, suggesting that it might be the way forward and lead to a general improvement of the national dairy herd. My comments were greeted by all to whom I spoke as positively sacrilegious and I suppose with good reason. Dairy Shorthorns were numerically by far the most popular breed in the country and were the backbone of the dairying industry. The sale of young bulls was a major source of income to those who had high-yielding pedigree herds like the one at Round Hill. Even suggesting that AI might have a future at one of the two most important dates in the Dairy Shorthorn calendar was probably ill advised. Certainly I received several very sharp rebuffs from those who were not only my elders, but very definitely my betters when it came to the question of breeding Dairy Shorthorns. The general opinion was that it would never happen and that it was just science again trying to interfere with nature. I hoped this was right, because the sale of young bulls and bull calves was an important source of income for the farm. However, since the Colonel's comments about AI it had been a niggling worry at the back of my mind and, whether I liked the idea or not, my day spent with Emerys Parry had been a revelation, for what I had seen licensed as future breeding bulls left much to be desired. However, it certainly was not going to happen in the immediate future and I put the question of AI from my mind.

Within days of the Shorthorn Show and Sale we had finished drilling the last of the spring barley and I concentrated on grass drying, although I also ensured that both kale and mangels were sown under the optimum conditions, together with the few acres of swedes grown to help maintain our small and successful flock of sheep throughout the winter. Although two or three lambs had, like Col Pollitt's, done stupid things, resulting in them finishing up on the dining room table at The Meads and Round Hill House, they more than paid their way. We also grew a few acres of potatoes to supply the two houses and the estate staff, leaving a surplus to sell.

However, a project that was breaking new ground, at least as far as I was concerned, was the planting of a thirty-two acre field on Manor Farm with a mixture of 20lbs of lucerne and 4lbs of cocksfoot grass to the acre. Although strictly speaking it was probably at the Colonel's suggestion, I had willingly joined the Grassland Association who were converts to the revolutionary work being done at Aberystwyth in breeding strains of grasses, coupled with grassland management, under the guidance of Sir George Stapledon. I had read everything I could lay my hands on regarding the work he had done and in particular that relating to the growing of the lucerne/cocksfoot mixture, which he strongly advocated as being ideal for silage and even more so for the limited number of establishments with grass driers.

With the enthusiasm of youth and an abundance of cheek, one morning I decided to place a person-to-person telephone call to Sir George. When I instructed Renee she was most intrigued and said she'd never put a call through to Wales before and it could take quite a while. For those who do not remember such old-fashioned service and are more used to the modern automated system of pressing buttons, then paying to listen to music one could well do without, interspersed with intonations that you are moving up the queue, I can assure readers such antiquity was bliss. I had of course to tell Renee what to say if, as frequently happened, she was asked who was calling. I told her to say 'the land agent to Colonel Devereux, Controller of North American Aircraft at the Ministry of Aircraft Production'. Having placed the call I started to get cold feet. Several times I reached for the phone to cancel it, but decided against it. The worst that could happen was that he either would not accept the call, or accept it and tick me off for wasting his time. I was wrong on both counts. After about forty minutes Renee rang to say she was through to Aberystwyth and they were trying the number. About a minute later I was speaking to Sir George. He was charming, listened carefully to what I had to say, then gave me the most concise and detailed instructions on the preparation of the seedbed, depth of drilling, naming the best drill he knew of to do the job and, finally, giving me details of the fertiliser he would advocate. It was most instructive. He told me to phone again if he could be of any further help, hoped to meet me sometime in the future and hung up.

The call had been most worthwhile, but it had also thrown up a major problem. Sir George had been adamant that the seed, if the venture was to be successful, must be drilled at a depth of $1-1^{1}/_{2}$ inches as opposed to being sown on the surface with a seedbarrow and then harrowed in. He told me that lucerne was extremely deep rooting, regularly reaching a depth of nine to ten feet and one plant was known to have attained a root depth of twenty-three feet. The problem was we had no drill even remotely suitable for such small seeds. I called numerous companies dealing in agricultural machinery, but with no joy. Finally I phoned the War Ag. Somewhat to my embarrassment I found myself put through to Mr Knights, who politely asked what he could do to help. I told him of my recent phone conversation with Sir George Stapledon, which obviously impressed him, my need for a drill and named the particular make and model that Sir George had recommended. There was silence for a moment, followed by a somewhat sardonic laugh. 'It's your lucky day Mr Twist, I have exactly the drill Sir George has proposed, it arrived with a consignment of Lend-Lease machinery and until now no one has been interested. Probably because it's a bit pricey.' I made some enquiries regarding the latter and then said I'd be with him inside half an hour, complete with cheque. Before I left I raided the house dairy, annexed half a pound of butter and cut off a couple of pounds of the delicious home-cured bacon, which Tom really excelled at producing. To my amusement, my converted bedroom and office/sitting room, as I had described the office and the washroom, was designated as separate accommodation to the main house and, providing I forfeited my bacon ration coupons I was entitled to kill two pigs a year for my own use, so we were seldom if ever short of bacon.

When I arrived at the War Ag office I was immediately ushered through to Mr Knights who couldn't have been more pleasant. We quickly concluded our business and he assured me I could expect the drill within a week. Having pocketed the receipt I told him I had a little present for him and gave him the bacon and butter. He was profuse in his thanks, for many things were becoming more and more difficult to obtain at times, even when one had the requisite coupons.

The drill arrived after four days and Sudden and Tom went into raptures over it. I had only considered it for sowing lucerne and grass seed, but it appeared that with a change of cogs and a few other adjustments it could be used to sow any normal farm crop. The weather couldn't have been kinder and a perfect tilth was achieved, the seed sown and rolled in. No sooner had this been achieved than we had what old Joe Swaine described as 'a bloody good ol' soak'. This was followed by weather, which these days, has become more traditional than factual – April showers with warm sunny intervals, real growing weather. It seemed as though every seed had sprouted. I was so delighted that I wrote and told Sir George about it and that I had carried out his advice in full, with an excellent result. I received a charming letter in reply saying I could phone him any time I needed his help.

Fertiliser and the proper treatment of the old pastures had produced some surprisingly lush growth compared to the previous year, to a degree that it was obvious that if we were going to dry all the grass available, two shifts would be imperative. The biggest problem was going to be labour. However, I had worked for the Colonel long enough to appreciate that problems arose only for one purpose – namely to be overcome. I had a chat to George Devonshire. He considered his platform man, Jim Hicks, the operator who filled the trays, was more than capable of taking charge of a shift. I had a talk to Jim, he was quite happy with the idea, so it was only a question of how we split the day. The obvious solution was from 6.00am to 2.00pm and from then until 10.00pm, to which both men agreed. There was one snag. I didn't want the drier to close down for a lunch break, at whatever time was chosen, for that would mean the furnace had to be banked down and by the time things were going again at full speed it would take a good half-hour or more. I had told George how Col Pollitt operated his drier, the men being paid on output and it was he who suggested we adopt a similar system. Jim was quite happy with the idea and said they could bring a snack to eat with them to see them through their shift. The other two men appointed as platform operators were equally happy. I suggested a rate which would mean they could earn more than on a fixed daily wage and this was readily accepted.

The final hurdle for this two-shift working was to ensure they didn't run out of grass, I hadn't enough staff available to arrange two separate gangs cutting and carting. However with the addition of a second Wilders Cutlift plus trailer, to give a boost when required and most importantly act as a stand by in case one broke down, we could manage. Sudden agreed to take over from Miles any evening from 5.00pm onwards if he felt like a break, providing he wasn't needed for some other job – so there were no problems over operating the Cutlift. However, we would need another tractor to ensure everything ran smoothly and that there were no delays when carting from the furthest fields, and we would need someone to drive it. Again Phil Oliver came to the rescue, by producing a very smart David Brown on pneumatic wheels. Apparently it had come from a stud farm which had closed down and had only done light work topping off the paddocks. It was ideal from every aspect, for apart from being in excellent condition, it was easily the fastest tractor we had.

Three of the original six Land Girls had left for various reasons and had been replaced, but none of the remainder could drive. I contacted the Land Army and the lady in charge told me, she had just the girl, I needed, well experienced in all tractor work. Apparently she had been living in the farmhouse where she had worked since the outbreak of war, and she and the farmer's son had fallen in love. The farmer, a Methodist lay preacher who would allow no work on the farm on the Sunday except for the essential care of livestock, caught them in bed together one night, and although they had both declared they wanted to marry, he'd thrown the poor girl, Brenda, out in the middle of the night. I interviewed her and sent her off with Tom to test out her capabilities with a tractor, with which he could find no fault and she started the next day. The drier was at full capacity by the start of the second week in May. I asked the staff involved about working Saturday afternoons and Sundays until we'd completed the first cut on all fields intended for drying. The reply was swift and unanimous and was best answered by Miles, who had a son in the army. When I asked him he gave me a somewhat scornful look and replied, 'Don't reckon my boy an' other lads in forces can stop work at weekends, so I don't see why the hell us should. We're all in this war together and the more us gets stuck in the quicker it'll be over.'

Our agent had no problem selling dried grass; whatever the analysis might be, he couldn't get enough of it. Nevertheless there were times when we had between forty and fifty tons in the store waiting for collection due to the difficulty of transport. The first cut of the lucerne and cocksfoot early in July produced a very high-quality meal and an excellent price. As soon as the field was cleared it received a top dressing of 1 cwt of nitrogen per acre. Just before the first cut was taken, I had an unexpected visit from Sir George Stapledon who happened to be passing through the area. His remarks were most flattering and it was on his advice that I immediately applied the nitrogen. He suggested we do this after every cut, but added the proviso that if we did it would be essential to give it a good dressing of phosphate and potash as well, early in the coming year.

Hay and harvest loomed ominously ahead, both operations in those days being labour intensive. I had been able to reduce labour slightly as, like on many farms, we were able to rick the hay in the field, sweeping it up to the elevator to build the stack with a hay-sweep attached to the front of a tractor, or as at my home and many other places, with an old car converted to run on paraffin. Even having done this, before it was ready for the livestock, many more hours of work were involved. First the rick had to be thatched, then when required, the hay was cut out from the rick and carted loose to wherever it was required, forked off into a barn or empty loose box, from where it was finally fed to the animals. The alternative, which was much more convenient, was to cut the rick out in benches, tying the hay into trusses weighing about half a hundredweight each. Pick-up balers, as one sees flying around fields these days spewing out neatly packaged hay or straw every few seconds were, back in the 1940s, just a dream for the future. I had read that one firm had been developing a stationary baler, but hadn't really followed this through.

A couple of weeks before the first meadow would be ready for mowing, I was just about to leave the office one morning when I received a phone call from our neighbour at The Grove, Ted Clarke, saying he wished to see me urgently. Could he come over right away? Wondering what the problem might be I agreed. Ted was with me within twenty minutes, armed with a pamphlet giving full details of a stationary baler produced by Denings of Chard. It had been thoroughly tested in the field and Ted had been to see one in use the year before and been much impressed. In fact he had been so impressed he had put his name down for one, but was told that it would probably be at least two years before one would be available. The morning he came to see me he'd had a phone call from Denings, saying that someone had reneged on an order and there was a baler available for immediate delivery if he still wanted one. Ted had said yes, but something he hadn't enquired about when he'd gone to see one working and provisionally booked one, was the price. This was so unlike Ted that I found it hard to believe, for he was a very shrewd and businesslike man. However, he assured me that he had been so impressed and as a possible delivery date was so far ahead he hadn't given it much thought until the phone call that morning. When he'd asked the price he'd had one hell of a shock, for it was about £420 delivered. I know this sounds peanuts today, but you could build a pair of three-bedroomed cottages, with all amenities at the end of the 1930s for £600 which made the baler a very expensive piece of equipment. Ted told me that he, like so many others, had to buy quite a lot of machinery to comply with the War Ag requirements and although he was sure he could get what he required from the bank he didn't really want to do this. He reminded me of a conversation we'd had in the men's bar at The Bull's Head, a few weeks earlier, on market day, when I'd been saying what a godsend a baler would be. I remembered it well and asked him what he had in mind. This was whether I thought the Colonel would consider sharing the baler with him. I asked some very pertinent questions, particularly what happened when we both wanted to use it? Ted had done his homework and his ideas seemed both feasible and workable. I could not think of a better agreement and suggested we get this down on paper before we went any further. Ted's reaction was fiery to say the least – was I suggesting he wouldn't keep his word etc, etc? I calmed him down, explaining that I was accountable to the Colonel for what I did and his policy was that I keep a record of any arrangements or deals that I made. Having pacified him, I rang for Megan Pring and she quickly had copies of the memo available. Ted turned to me and said, 'Will you phone the Master now?' (Ted was a great supporter of the hunt and on the committee). I replied 'No'. I could see Ted starting to build up a head of steam again, but before he could say anything, I added, 'If I did, I'd be told I was employed to run the estate, as far as the day-to-day management was concerned, that's what he pays me for and then I'd probably get a right bollocking as well if he was busy, which he always is. No, go ahead Ted, buy it and let me know when you want a cheque for £210 and I'll see you get it immediately.' With that we went into the house to join Ethne, for a chat and a drink.

The purchase of the baler proved to be one of the best investments we made and, rather surprisingly, Ted and I never really had a cross word as to who should have the use of it during haymaking; at times, it was almost like a shuttle service running between Marsh Hill and Chilborough, Ted's farm. The only occasion when we really clashed, was once when the weather had been showery and then turned to a spell of hot sunny June days. We started mowing at the same time, resulting in us both having hay ready to bale after a few days. Ted had the baler and said, weather permitting, he'd only need it for a day and a half, so I told him to carry on. Tom was somewhat concerned over this and wanted to know if I intended ricking our field. My reply was no. We'd turn the swaths, but not row it up until the second day that Ted Clarke was baling, then I wanted the hay swept into rows, leaving the width of the baler between them. My plan was to have four men pitching hay into the baler which would mean moving it every few minutes. I knew Tom thought it was taking a risk and the crop could be spoilt if we had a downpour, but the barometer in my office was high. More importantly the sun was very red as it went down of an evening and the swallows and housemartins were flying high. The latter I put particular store by, for over many decades I have found such old country weather lore frequently to be more reliable than what is predicted in the forecasts given out on both radio and TV. Such old wives' tales, as many would call them, did not let me down and we saved the hay in perfect condition. The amount of work the baler saved more than justified its cost. No sooner was the hay safe than we were into harvest. Once the corn was ripe and the dew had gone in the mornings we could start cutting. The sheaves had to be stooked as quickly as possible and, when the weather was good it was a case of 'all hands to the pumps'. Even Ron Chamberlain, who started his working day at 4.30am, and his helpers would come out after they had had their tea. When we carted to the ricks Ron would pitch sheaves up on to the trailers until dark. When we worked late, which was most evenings, I continued what, for generations, on many farms had become an accepted custom – harvest beer, a pint a man and, during the war, a pint a Land Girl. Sometimes I would collect what was required from The Prince of Wales, having left a small churn with Mrs Leversuch earlier, telling her how many pints to have ready by 8.00pm. If I was working in the field, usually on a trailer loading it, then Ethne or Rose would bring it out to the field. Old Joe Swaine was self-appointed beer dispenser and that pint and ten-minute break paid dividends, for the gang would then keep on happily working until dark.

Harvest over, muck had to be spread before winter ploughing and sowing started. However the next major event was the Shorthorn Society's Show and Sale at Reading, the first week in November. There were two entries from the Roundhill herd, although we had several more young bulls they were not, in my opinion, the quality required to win. Any herd could have up to five entries, but I wasn't interested in taking anything that didn't have a chance of getting in the awards and, if they didn't, they would most likely make a better price at one of the collective sales regularly held at both Reading and Banbury. The two bulls were the first to be shown sired by Diamond Wild Duke, whose progeny looked really promising. Ron and his two charges left around 2.00pm the day before. I had entered a third bull who I never had any intention of sending, it was simply to give Ron space for his show box, as the big wooden chests were called, in which stockmen kept all their necessary equipment for preparing and showing their charges. The extra stall also provided room for Ron to kip down beside his charges, just to ensure they were not interfered with. Sounds unlikely I know, but competition was hot and there was one particular herdsman who would stop at nothing to win, a fact well known to his rivals.

I was at Reading sale yard by 8.00am the next morning. Ron was already busy titivating our entries, both looked magnificent. One, Roundhill Sharon Prince, was a deep red, full of quality and was in the senior class. Our second entry, Roundhill Lord Wildeyes, a roan, was in the yearling class and a special class where the dam had to have an officially recorded lactation with a butterfat percentage in excess of 3.75%. This class was open to all ages.

I joined Harry Hobson, Stanley Chivers and Henry Hamilton, who managed the Duke of Westminster's farms on the Eaton Estate in Cheshire, to watch the judging. There were between twenty-five and thirty in the class and the judge, having gone over all the exhibits, quickly called Ron into the centre of the ring, where he remained alone for several minutes, before he was joined by the other four selected. My friends congratulated me and Harry Hobson said he was sure Prince would sell well. What reserve did I want to put on him? I named a modest 120 guineas, at which Harry laughed and said he'd certainly make double that. I put the same reserve on Lord Wildeyes and went off to join a jubilant Ron. I'd brought one of the other herdsmen with me, who had remained with our second entry. When he saw Ron and I returning and the former carrying the coveted red card, he let out a yell of delight.

For the next hour or so I was on tenterhooks, for Lord Wildeyes was in the yearling class, invariably the largest, and that year was no exception. At last they were all in the ring and Stanley Chivers turned to me, smiled and said, 'I think you'll do it again.' I didn't answer. I thought so too, but I wasn't going to tempt providence. Again Ron was pulled in first and then went on to win the Special Butterfat class. However, we hadn't finished for Sharon Prince won the Emil Casares Perpetual Challenge Cup for the best senior bull and then the pair won the much-coveted Thornton Cup for the best pair or trio of bulls. With the average price for bulls sold being just over 100 guineas, I went home well pleased that our two averaged 320 guineas. In addition I had the names and addresses of four people wanting bull calves by Diamond Wild Duke, out of high-yielding cows. I sent the Colonel a telegram from the sale yard and much to my amazement he was at Round Hill when I returned, complete with a magnum of champagne to celebrate.

The year was coming to a close when I had an enquiry from Harry Hobson & Co for a young Berkshire boar to export to the French Cameroons. I had one, but I didn't want to sell him. However, Billy Wiltshire, the partner in the firm who dealt with export enquiries insisted on coming and seeing the youngster, Roundhill Prince Marjua. The price he offered was such that I dared not refuse it, for I still well remember my father refusing 100 guineas for a gilt Billy had wanted to buy for Japan back in the early 1930s and it being dead within days. I cannot remember how Prince Marjua was transported to his new home, but in spite of the war he arrived safely.

As far as the war was concerned things were certainly looking up and Montgomery's success in North Africa was not only a great victory and a tremendous morale booster, but it was to prove very advantageous to many farmers in the months to come.

20. History Repeated and Made

The end of January 1943 saw the first daytime bombing raid on Berlin, which must have gladdened the hearts of many a Londoner, but in spite of many successes the war was still far from over and shortages continued to increase. Everyday things like soap, toothpaste, quality toilet paper and razor blades became almost impossible to find. I actually saw two middle-aged men come to blows over a packet of Jeyes toilet paper on display in a chemist's shop, one market day, in Aylesbury. There were queues everywhere – it almost became a maxim with many people, if you see a queue join it. What is more one could easily form one. A very dear friend of mine, Bill Graham, a Squadron Leader in Coastal Command, who did three tours of ops, was twice recommended for the VC, but instead received the DFC and bar, frequently stayed at Round Hill when on leave. Before one visit he met a delightful girl who seemed to be taking up all his spare time, but he was most anxious I should join him in London on a day she had to be away and this I did. Around noon we were walking along Oxford Street and Bill suddenly stopped just short of the entrance to a shop and said, 'Stand behind me.' Within seconds a lady fell in behind me, asking what were we queuing for. I said I didn't know, but within five minutes there must have been fifty people lined up behind Bill and I. Laughing, my friend started to walk on, saying, 'Just like sheep. Let's go and find some decent beer.'

One shortage which was seriously worrying me was tyres for the MG. I was down to the canvas on two which had numerous gaiters in them, as had the spare. The two on the front wheels had no tread, but as yet the canvas wasn't actually showing. I had asked Wren to see if he could find any, feeling that with his contacts it would be no problem, but he had no success. I also asked the garage we used, Benyon's in Princes Risborough, on numerous occasions telling them that even partially worn ones would be most welcome but apparently the size I wanted was no longer made and they couldn't locate any secondhand ones. Many other motorists were in a similar predicament, for the army and civil defence had first call on what tyres were available. One morning in desperation I set off yet again for Benyon's, only to get a puncture in one of the front tyres, so when I had changed the wheel I was driving with three tyres down to the canvas. Whilst Joe, the mechanic, was fitting yet another gaiter to my 'good' front tyre and I was asking Joe what on earth I was going to do, a man walked in. He looked a right spiv. Joe greeted him warmly and, turning to me, said, 'Ah, here's a man who might just be able to help you if you're desperate and from what I've seen of late you're desperate.' Having greeted Joe, he turned to me and said, 'I'm 'Arry, what's yer problem guv?' I pointed at the car, 'Tyres.'

'Yerse, I can see that. Tricky things tyres – sizes I mean an' them's very difficult, but I know a chap,' he paused, then continued, 'What yer do guv?'

'Manage a large agricultural estate.'

'Any sheep? Nothin' I luves more than a nice bit o' lamb an' th' ole mint sauce.'

'Yes, we run a small flock of Cheviot ewes and use a Hampshire Down ram. The first lambs are nearly ready to sell.'

'Luvely! Th' very thought makes me mouth water. Haven't 'ad a decent bit o' lamb in years. Well, stands to reason don't it, wit' all this rationing. Tell you what, give me yer phone number guv, an' I'll give yer a bell this evenin'. Nine o'clock orlright with you?' I assured him it was. When he had gone Joe said, 'You'll be all right now 'Arry's taken up your cause. Great finder is our 'Arry, no one calls him Harry. He gets no end of stuff for us. I genuinely believe he doesn't nick it, but we don't ask questions, just count our blessings.' It was bang on 9.00pm when the phone rang and I answered. 'Guv?' I recognised 'Arry's voice. 'Yes.'

'Good, I got five o' what yer want. No names now, phones 'ave ears. Remember what I said I were partial to?' I replied that I did. 'Right! Now how 'bout yer fixing me one o' them, without its wrapping, know what I mean, plus twenty smacker? What yer need are mint an' legit. How does that grab yer?' I assured 'Arry it did, as long as everything was as he said. He swore all was kosher. We arranged he'd be outside where I lived on Friday evening at 9.00pm. He said he knew where, 'as th' man who 'ad introduced us 'ad told 'im'. If I drove out at the given time he, 'Arry, would follow me to a quiet spot and we could deal. I agreed and the phone went dead. No sooner had I put the phone down than it rang. It was the Colonel. He told me he had some very important people indeed visiting him for lunch on Sunday, he thought they'd enjoy lamb. Did I understand what he meant? I assured him I did. Next morning I told Tom I wanted a couple of 'Pollitts' ready by Friday teatime, one skinned complete with offal, which I would pick up Friday around 8.30pm, the other jointed as usual which would be collected by the Colonel on Saturday morning. He could take his usual fee for butchering – a shoulder.

At 9.00pm Friday evening I drove out from Round Hill and saw a van pulled into a gateway to a field, just beyond the cottages where Tom lived. It followed me down the road. I went past the entrance to Manor Farm and drew up on the wide grass verge. The van passed me, it was 'Arry. He turned, came back, drove up on to the grass and reversed in close to the boot of the MG. Little was said, except 'Arry remarked 'Cor, wha' a beaut' as he transferred the dressed carcass into his vehicle and the tyres, after I had examined them and checked the size, into my car. They were, as he had promised, as new. I handed over the cash and 'Arry assured me any time I needed his help tell Joe and he'd contact me and then he was gone. I turned and drove back to Round Hill, bearing a sense of both guilt and elation – the latter prevailed. About three weeks previously I'd had a front tyre go, when doing about 50mph and finished up on the verge, so close to a telegraph pole I couldn't get out. Meeting 'Arry could well have saved me a nasty accident. I subsequently heard, via Joe, that 'Arry had truly enjoyed his lamb, 'bloody luvely' had been his verdict.

Everything seemed to be running smoothly on the farms, except there never seemed to be enough reliable labour available. One could always obtain workers from the War Ag pool, but they needed much supervision. On one occasion I had contacted Evans to give a price for flat hoeing between mangel plants – the crop had already been thinned by Joe and old Harry Montague – but there was an awful infestation of Fat Hen. This had been dealt with by horse hoeing the rows, but there was much that wanted chopping out between the thriving mangel plants. Evans had suggested £3 an acre as a contract price, to which I had agreed. Next morning he arrived with twelve Land Girls – their uniforms looked horribly new, as did their hoes. He told me he was going to the field to show them what had to be done and then he'd put one of the girls in charge. He'd be back to collect them at knocking off time. It was a lovely warm spring morning and when I'd nearly finished in the office I went out to the yard and told Harry Wingfield to saddle up a horse for me. I wanted to go across to The Grove and, on my way, call and see how the girls were getting on hoeing out the Fat Hen. When I reached the field there was little activity – all the girls were stretched out on the grass track that ran down the centre of the field, sunning themselves. As I rode towards them I was not a happy man and when I reached them I asked what the hell was going on and who was in charge. One girl stood up and in the broadest Brummy accent claimed she was the foreman. It was only then that I glanced at what they'd been doing, which thankfully was very little, for they'd chopped out the mangels and left a nice stand of Fat Hen! It would be an understatement to say that I blew my top. However, a tearful May, the girl who had been appointed foreman, said Mr Evans hadn't come down to the field with them, but had said they'd easily know which were mangels and which were weeds. They thought the taller plants must be the crop. I cooled off, got down from my horse and asked if there was anyone who wasn't afraid of horses. One girl stepped forward and told me she loved horses, her dad was in charge of a big stable of dray horses for a Birmingham brewery and she often helped him with them on a Sunday. I gave her my horse to hold and showed the other girls how they should do the job. In a little over two hours they'd chopped the mangels out for less than ten yards on only six rows. This was fortunate, but I asked why they had only done six rows. May replied Mr Evans had said, as they were new to the job, they should take it in turns and there was no rush. It transpired they were raw recruits, for this was their first day. All were born and grew up in Birmingham and for one it was an amazing experience as it was the first time she had ever been out in the country. I was sorry I had given them such a ticking off, but what I said to them was nothing to what I said to Evans when I saw him that evening.

It was some time around the middle of March that the Colonel phoned me one morning. I knew immediately that something was amiss. It transpired he'd been to see his Joint Master, Stanley Barratt who was home on leave, regarding the hunt. It all boiled down to the fact that Dev could take no more of Gloria Barratt and was not prepared to continue paying the lion's share of the bills. The outcome was that the hunt was to split back to what it had been many decades before, namely the Old Berkeley East and the Old Berkeley West. The Colonel was taking over the West, all the hunt's good country in the Vale of Aylesbury, together with part of the Chiltern Hills.

When the hunt was first formed in the eighteenth century it extended from what is now Hyde Park to the Vale of Aylesbury. Pre-war, when the International Horse Show was held at Olympia, if a pack of hounds was invited to parade there, etiquette required the Master of the visiting pack to seek permission from the Master of the OBH to enter his hunt's country. I learned that the East were keeping the Amersham Kennels, but half the pack and Tom Healy were coming to the West. I then showed my naivety by enquiring, 'But where are you going to kennel hounds, sir and house Tom?' There was a somewhat sardonic laugh as he replied, 'I've no idea, but you better have. The ball's in your court now. Buy a smallholding, as close to the estate as possible. We have to be out of Amersham by the end of April. As soon as you've bought a suitable property let me know and …' I interrupted, 'But we can't get building materials sir, you know that.' Dev laughed, 'I can' and hung up.

What I found particularly irksome was the fact that there was no mention of the hunt secretary dealing with this break-up between the Masters. Six weeks to buy what would undoubtedly be a run-down property and turn it into hunt kennels was just plain stupid – it would probably take longer than that to find a place. The man was mad. I had started my breakfast when Ethne came in, having been out exercising a couple of the hunters. She took one look at me, 'Who's been stirring you up?' My reply was terse, 'Your stupid father.' I then told her of the Colonel's plans. Ethne thought it great, adding, 'Dad only lands these jobs in your lap because he knows it'll rile you, then you'll achieve what he wants just so you can figuratively raise two fingers to him.' I got up and went out to my office and opened the mail. Tom arrived, as usual, exactly on 9.00am. Just as he was about to leave he said, 'I nearly forgot. I met Phil Oliver yesterday evening, he asked me to tell you he has a tractor disc harrow in good nick and he was wondering if you'd be interested. We could do with it, because we've a hell of a lot of arable now and one's not really enough.' I nodded, 'All right Tom, I'll think about it.' Phil, in peace time had been a horse dealer-cum-show jumper, but now that few horses were required he dealt in machinery, cattle, hay, in fact anything which would make him a few pounds. He just loved dealing.

Later that morning I drove into the yard at Meadacre and blew the car horn. Phil had an Alsatian dog who would bite you as soon as look at you if Phil wasn't there to stop him. Phil appeared and called across the yard, 'It's ok, he's locked up.' I got out of the car and we went to look at the disc harrow. It was indeed in good nick and after much haggling I bought it for thirty pounds less than the asking price. As we walked towards my car Phil said, 'You seem a bit browned off this morning, what's the problem?' I told him about the splitting of the hunt back into two packs as it had been many years before. He was most enthusiastic, to a degree that revived all my earlier irritation. 'It's all very fine for you, but where the hell am I going to find a suitable property to turn into hunt kennels by the end of April?' Phil grinned from ear to ear, 'Just down the road.' He then mentioned someone who was a bit of a recluse but had a smallholding, Dodds Charity, which was bang opposite the entrance to Manor Farm. Phil had been talking to the owner the evening before and he had said that he wanted to get out. He'd only about twenty acres of land left and, as he said, no one could make a living out of that. I thanked Phil, jumped into the car, drove the couple of hundred yards down the road, parked just inside the gateway leading to Manor Farm and walked across to Dodds Charity. The owner was at home, he looked frail, undernourished and generally miserable. I told him what Phil had said and asked if it was correct. He replied that it was, but he hadn't been to see an estate agent yet about selling it and agreeing a price. I asked him if he'd show me round, which he did with pleasure. There was a brick, tile-roofed cowshed which would convert nicely into two good-sized lodges for hounds, a cart shed could be made into a feedroom and a number of small buildings which would be useful. The land would make a good hound paddock. I was shown over the house. It was a bit of a barrack of a place, but dry, I could find no sign of damp. The major snag was that there was no bathroom, but the roof was sound as, so it seemed, were the windows. I suggested to the owner that there was no point in involving an estate agent and paying his fees if we could do a deal without one. How much was he asking? He thought for a minute, looked at me under lowered eyelids and said £5000. I laughed and said, 'What sort of a sucker do you take me for? You know jolly well it's not worth even half that. If we do deal, how soon can you be out?' There was no hesitation over his reply. 'Two days once I get the money.' I looked at him for a minute. 'There'd be no problem over that providing our solicitor finds the deeds in order, if they are I'll give you £2000.' I knew this was way over its market value, but I was buying time as well as the property. He shook his head and started to walk away, he called after me '£2500.' I turned round and thought, poor old bugger, what was another hundred or two to the Colonel. 'No. I'll make it £2200 if you can have the deeds with me by tomorrow morning.' For the first time he smiled, 'You won't have to wait until then, I've got them in the house.' He disappeared and came back carrying a heavy manila envelope. I examined the papers he offered me, certainly everything seemed in order. I looked at the owner, 'Can I take these? I'd like to show them to our solicitor at Amersham. As you know he'll have to check that everything is in order, but the preliminaries shouldn't take very long and if he's happy, I would think I could let you have a £500 deposit within the next forty-eight hours.' There was a very obvious look of relief and delight on the owner's face, for he knew, as I did, that he was getting about double what he would if the property went up for auction. He happily handed over the deeds and we shook hands on the deal.

I phoned the solicitor as soon as I got back to the office, told him what was afoot, and said I'd be with him at 2.00pm. Our meeting was short. He said he could see nothing wrong, certainly go ahead and pay a deposit and he'd give me a document, before I left, to be signed by the owner which would make the sale legally binding. I asked if I could use his phone. I rang HDA and was put on to Miss Moon. I asked if the Colonel was available. She replied he had someone with him. I replied, 'Never mind, put me through please.' She said she didn't think the Colonel would like being disturbed. I replied I'd take a chance on that and please put me through. Seconds later my eardrum was nearly shattered as my boss roared down the phone, 'What the hell do you want? Miss Moon told you I was busy.' I waited a second and then said, 'I've been busy too. Can your men start work on the new kennels on Monday.' I heard a gasp, 'What the hell are you talking about?' I explained, told him I was with his solicitor, and that if he'd send me a cheque for £500 that evening, once it was cleared through the bank, conversion of the buildings could commence immediately and Dodds Charity house would be vacated forty-eight hours after completion.' There was silence for a moment then a somewhat subdued Dev asked, 'Where the hell's Dodds Charity?' I winked at the solicitor, 'Oh sorry, I didn't realise you didn't know. It's just the other side of the road from the entrance to Manor Farm, so it will come within the compass of the estate as a whole.' There was a chuckle, then, 'Well done. I'll see you at the weekend and arrange for Tom and one of my senior maintenance staff to come along. Work on the new kennels will start next week.' The phone went dead. Tom Healy, his family and the hounds were safely installed at Dodds Charity the first week in April. If one looks in Baily's Hunting Directory one will see it now kennels the Vale of Aylesbury hounds, a combination in May 1970 of the OBH West, the South Oxfordshire and Hertfordshire hunts.

I heard on the grapevine that a POW camp had been set up just outside Aylesbury in the main for Italians captured at Alamein. Further, it was said that it was likely that some would be allowed to live away from the camp to work on farms if accommodation was available. This sounded highly unlikely to me, but on the basis of there being no smoke without fire I phoned Mr Walley, the Chief Executive Officer for the Bucks War Ag. The rumour I had heard was true, providing certain criteria were met. The chief criterion seemed to be suitable toilet facilities, namely a water closet. Yet again I was left wondering how the bureaucratic mind worked, for it obviously had not occurred to them in Whitehall that both sides had to do without such amenities in the North African desert. However, at Round Hill this was no problem as, if I was successful in my application, I proposed turning the loft over the main entrance to the farmyard into their quarters. The washroom was at the bottom of the stairs leading up to this and was complete with wash-basin, electric water heater, which was never used and, of course, the all-essential wc. The Colonel thought it an excellent idea. Once all the formalities had been completed, which I seem to remember were many, he arranged for one of his electricians from HDA to put in a socket for an electric cooker, surplus to requirements at The Meads, which he sent down together with a trestle table, some chairs and bunks. When the accommodation was inspected by an officer and sergeant from the camp, the latter was very scathing about luxury living for the useless buggers, claiming they'd be more comfortable than his men. I was told that amongst the six I had applied for would be one with some knowledge of English and a corporal who would be in charge. Should any of them misbehave and break their trust the minimum punishment if returned to camp would be thirty days solitary on bread and water. Further, they had to be in their quarters by 10.00pm whilst it was light and by dark for the remainder of the year. When they arrived they were a cheerful bunch of lads and all had a smattering of English. Two brothers, Frank and Carmelo Passero, were farmers and another had been a driver in the army, which might prove useful. All six were delighted to be out of the war, out of the prison camp and promised to work hard – they kept their promise.

There was only one slightly embarrassing moment. Just as they were moving in Megan Wood was leaving the farm office to come over to mine. She was very 'easy on the eye' and this caused some very explicit backchat between our Italian prisoners about how they would like to spend time with her and how they would entertain her. She burst into my office scarlet in the face; what neither I nor they knew was that she was reasonably fluent in Italian! This was something I felt had to be nipped in the bud immediately. Reluctantly Megan went back across to the farm with me. All the Italians were in the loft, settling into their new home. I roared up the stairs, 'Corporal, get your men down here immediately.' The corporal was Frank Passero and he was also the one with the best knowledge of English. I told him to fall his men in and then made clear my complaint, which he translated to the others. They all looked very sheepish and I assured them that should there be any recurrence they would all immediately be returned to camp, with a recommendation for the maximum punishment. In turn they came forward and apologised to Megan, who answered them, somewhat hesitantly, in their own language. They proved to be a great addition to the labour force and Frank Passero quickly learned to operate the grass drier and take charge of a shift under George's tutelage. George was leaving to work at ICI's game farm, but he had accepted the job on the understanding that he wouldn't leave the Roundhill Estate until I was able to find a replacement to do his job.

All was running smoothly and at last things were beginning to develop as I had visualised over three years previously. I had even diversified from standard farm crops on the advice of a very experienced market gardener from just outside Marlow. He had a herd of Berkshire pigs and had visited the Roundhill estate to buy a young boar. He asked to see some of the gilts which we ran in outside units. To get to them we had to walk down across Great Ground, which was prepared for sowing spring barley the next day. He examined the soil and declared it ideal for growing onions. I told him I knew nothing about varieties, growing them and even less about marketing them. He assured me that there was going to be a very great shortage in the autumn, they'd nearly be worth their weight in gold and he would advise, collect and sell them at Covent Garden for a commission of 5%. He was a man I had known for many years, for he founded his Berkshire herd from sows and gilts bought from father – I knew him to be absolutely honest. So taking his advice we sowed six acres. Like the lucerne nearly every seed must have sprouted and when thinned, the spring onions alone, which had to be tied in bundles, realised more than double what a good crop of wheat would have made off the same ground. The six acres, after commission had been deducted, came to a little over £2400. I told my market gardening friend that next year we'd grow twenty to thirty acres. He had laughed and said no way. Everyone would be jumping on the bandwagon and one would be lucky to make £100 per acre the following year. I took his advice and time proved him right. The Colonel, who had long since given up as Controller of North American Aircraft and was back running his companies, was staying at Round Hill over the weekend in early June. I took him to see the onions. He seemed to be impressed, as he was when Ron paraded the three young bulls we were running on for the November Show and Sale. Two were again by Wild Duke and one by the bull we'd bought with the Diamond herd, Arden Wildeyes Bellringer. One of Duke's, Telluria Prince, was according to Emerys Parry the best youngster he'd seen in many years of licensing bulls and he covered herds of all standards in a number of counties. He was not alone in his opinion. As we walked back to the house I was enthusing over my pride and joy, when the Colonel stopped. 'I agree, he's magnificent. There should be more bulls like him available to small farmers. It's something

I've given a lot of thought to and that is why I talked to Dr Edwards of Cambridge University who is pioneering work on Artificial Insemination, as you well know, and have arranged for you and Haselden to visit him next Thursday.' My heart missed a beat, surely I wasn't going to be deprived of Telluria Duke for the big event in November. Fortunately the Colonel didn't look at me, if he had he must have seen stark horror in my expression.

Thursday found Clive and I in Cambridge, having travelled there by train. We were met at the station by Dr Joseph Edwards, a delightful man of great charm, and driven out to the University farm. Here he took us through the whole procedure of AI, including taking a collection of semen from a bull, examining it under a microscope, discussing sperm counts and finally storage. He was thrilled that they had kept sperm alive for forty-eight hours, had inseminated a cow with it and she was safely in calf. Clive was full of enthusiasm, but I decided to play devil's advocate. What about all the breeders who relied on the sale of young bulls for a large part of their income? What if a bull widely used through AI did not transmit the genes that had caused – say its dam and grandam to be prolific milkers?

My queries were endless, but Joe Edwards had a cool, coherent and irrefutable answer for each one. Finally he laughed and said, 'Come on, let's go and get some lunch. Michael, I know you were reared in a world of pedigree livestock, there will be a place for such views as you have for many years, because it is people like you who will have to provide the proven sires for AI. You can't put up a logical argument against it and certainly not one on the grounds of economics. The technique works, but there is still much to improve. The physical act of insemination has no detrimental effect on any cow, or any other female for that matter. Economically it is sound and has been accepted as such by farmers in countries who are up to twelve years ahead of us in this sphere. As a measure of livestock improvement I defy you to put up a winning argument against it. You are a devotee of the pedigree system, progeny testing and recording. Artificial Insemination will provide the most important advance in animal husbandry since the practices you so strongly adhere to were introduced.'

As instructed, I reported back to the Colonel on my return from Cambridge. The outcome of this was that I phoned Dr Edwards the next morning and, on behalf of the Colonel, invited him to Round Hill to give a talk on AI. He said he would be delighted and we fixed a date for the first Wednesday in July. I told him that the Colonel apologised for not phoning himself. He was tied up with meetings all day, but he would write on hearing the outcome of our talk. The meeting, which was to take place in the barn converted for such events and parties, was as widely advertised as possible within the OBH country and representatives of the two major weekly farming papers and the *Dairy Farmer* were invited to attend. The Colonel wanted refreshments in the form of sandwiches, beer and soft drinks laid on for the benefit of those who attended. I did feel like asking him if he'd heard there was very stringent rationing, but, probably wisely, refrained. Instead I went to see Daphne Harris, who was running The Bell Inn at Aston Clinton whilst her husband was away in the navy and she gladly undertook the task.

The day came and nearly seventy people attended. Dr Edwards was an excellent speaker and he illustrated his talk with slides. There was one minor disruption when a slide was shown taking a semen collection from a bull. One smallholder got to his feet and loudly said, 'Bloody disgusting showing something like that with a girl present' and stormed out of the barn, slamming the door as he went. The only girl present was Ethne Devereux. The meeting was opened for questions and after a number had been put and answered, I asked, if an AI station was to be started, what sort of age bull would Dr Edwards recommend, as it was unlikely that a proven bull, with adult progeny, would be easily obtainable. His reply was at least two-and-a-half years old and one where some progeny could be seen. This was the cause of much relief to both me and Ron Chamberlain, who was sitting at the back of the room, for Dr Edwards had ruled out Telluria Duke. Questions over, the Colonel got to his feet, thanked Dr Edwards profusely and then, to my horror, went on to say that as Master of the OBH West he was anxious to help farmers within his hunt country in every way possible. Therefore, if Dr Edwards was prepared to help set up a centre together with Mr Haselden and then hold a watching brief, he would put up the money to start a centre immediately if there were ten or more farmers within the hunt country who would like him to do so. He then invited those who would support his offer to hold up their hands. Over thirty hands went up immediately. The Colonel smiled broadly, then looked down at me. 'I have to go to America at the weekend and won't be home for just over three weeks. When I get back, Michael, I will expect the necessary accommodation to be ready and, most importantly, a bull of the highest quality and outstanding milk records behind it.' He came down off the stage and walked straight across to me. 'I meant what I said.' I looked him straight in the eye and replied, 'I know that and what is more I've second guessed you, for I felt this was coming. The top left-hand section of the weaner house at the piggeries can fairly easily be converted into a laboratory and three good-sized loose boxes. Then it just wants the surrounding walls building up to six feet and a service crate, for the teaser cow, set up in the yard. The biggest problem is to find a suitable bull and, of course, somehow get the building done.' The Colonel laughed, 'The bull's your worry, I'll see about the building. How soon can you get the section cleared and clean?' It was my turn to laugh, 'It's already done. Your men from HDA could start tomorrow. Oh yes, if you're off to America you had better leave me an open cheque, with a limit of course, but what is wanted will be pricey and a lot of breeders won't be interested. The majority are still very anti-AI. Once this becomes public knowledge, finding the bull we want will, to say the least, be bloody difficult.' Dev laughed, 'In that case you've got to get your skates on haven't you.' With that he walked off to chat to various farmers.

Next day I sought the help of Billy Wiltshire of Harry Hobson & Co. I told him what the Colonel wanted and that it was very, very urgent. I didn't tell him why. I knew that time was of the essence, for, as I had told the Colonel, once a report of the meeting appeared in the farming papers, which would be in nine days' time, an awful lot of doors would be closed when I went looking for a bull. Billy called me back later in the day to say that he thought he had found the bull I wanted. It was a good deep red and both milk yields and butterfat had been excellent for several generations. I told him the Colonel wished the deal to be done through Hobson's and I'd tell him the whys and wherefores later. The outcome was that I went down to Sussex with Billy the next day to a very famous herd. I saw a number of very promising heifers by the bull we'd come to see and bought him for 600 guineas – I didn't quibble over the price. I also arranged with a local haulier to pick the bull up the next morning as early as possible. Billy Wiltshire paid with one of the firm's cheques, so there was no problem over this. It had been a hair-raising day for me, for I had been at Reading University with the son of the owner, something I did not mention and, fortunately, he was away for the day. I phoned the Colonel that evening. He was delighted and also highly amused because he'd had Hudson, the Minister of Agriculture, on the phone, telling him he could not start an AI Centre. Dev had replied that there was no legislation that gave Hudson the power to stop him and he was going ahead. Presumably Emerys Parry, who was at the meeting, must have mentioned it to one of his seniors, who in turn told the Minister.

When the news broke in the farming press I received a most abusive letter from the breeder of the bull, Iford Lord Lavender 32nd. According to Devereux's solicitor, it was extremely libellous. Furious at what had been written I replied in the most polite manner, quoting Dr Edwards' comments that AI was the most important advance in animal breeding since the introduction of the pedigree system and thanked him for his cooperation. For good measure, I asked Eric Guy, a noted animal photographer, to take Lord Lavender's photo, which I sent to the farming papers and a progress report regarding the Centre.

The Kimble Centre was operating one month before the one at Reading University and, surprisingly three months before Cambridge. By the time the Colonel returned from the

USA I had engaged a graduate from Cirencester Agricultural College, who had been taught the technique by Joe Edwards and Clive Haselden, and over thirty cows had already been inseminated, Ethne had taken over the lab work. On the Colonel's return, he'd sent down one of his top scientists, who, after consultation with Dr Edwards, produced a magnificent cooling/storage cabinet which enabled semen to be kept successfully for ten days. Truly a little acorn from which the vast AI tree grew, but it was 'planted' on the Roundhill estate. Incidentally, Telluria Duke did not win the Championship at Reading but he was Reserve Champion. The champion was sold for 500 guineas, the reserve champion 900 guineas. Roundhill won another class and created what I believe was a record by winning the Thornton Cup for the second year running, the three bulls selling for an average of just under 500 guineas.

21. A Visit from the Minister

On 10 September 1943, the Italian government announced its surrender, following the landing of the allied forces in three areas of southern Italy, but the war was far from over, nor was the toil and sweat that had so rightly been predicted by Winston Churchill.

Holidays were a luxury that never entered the mind of farmers, yet alone going on strike as the miners did at some 150 mines early in 1944, but there had to be moments of relaxation. In my immediate circle horses, and the hunt in particular, fulfilled this need throughout the winter months whilst gymkhanas provided much pleasure and raised money for the Red Cross on many a Sunday, during the summer. Ann Devereux was becoming a very accomplished rider and was soon having more than her share of success, but it was well deserved. Her father had bought her a very nice 12.2hh pony and not only was she nearly always in the cards with this, but she was winning a number of firsts for her riding ability, a fact in which I took great pride. One of her main rivals was Pat Moss, whose brother, Stirling, was a consistent winner in children's showjumping, at which he demonstrated the same competitive spirit that made him one of the greats in the years that followed as a Formula One driver. Another keen competitor, particularly for the riding prize, who Ann frequently came up against, was Princess Alexandria. It was all very informal and a lot of fun.

Every evening for a week in the spring John Robarts, Ted Clarke, Frank Roads, several other farming friends and I met to shoot the young rooks, just as they emerged from their nests, most of which were in the top of high elm trees. This was an essential cull, for the rooks did a vast amount of damage, not only consuming the freshly sown corn, but, what could be even worse, just as the sprouted corn was coming through they would work along the rows pulling it out in their search for wireworm, leather-jackets and other grubs. It seemed that the more one shot the young ones the bigger the rookeries would become. The formula was the same for each evening. We'd meet around 6.30–7.00pm, shoot the rookery, pick up the dead rooks and return to the host's house for supper. This was either rook pie, or home-cured ham, usually with about three to four inches of fat encasing the lean meat. Rook pie can be excellent, but if it is not made to perfection it can carry a taste equivalent to the strong and somewhat noxious smell that emanates from all rooks and in particular young ones that have just left the nest.

In 1943 we were shooting the Roundhill rookeries. There was a big one between Manor Farm and John's Kimblewick Farm and we also used to shoot a rookery at Rogers, a smallholding between Marsh Hill and The Grove. The Colonel had recently sent a Ford V Eight Station Wagon to the farm, which I drove round this particular evening to bring back the dead rooks. We had a great shoot, the bag was something around 400. When we returned to the house I left the vehicle outside with the windows wide open to prevent the stench in the morning being intolerable. Rose McKellar and her family had returned to their home at Richmond, the blitzkrieg by the Luftwaffe having ended and I had taken on a man by the name of Tarrant to, amongst other things, drive Marguerite and Ann to school. There was no public transport except one bus a week that left from The Prince of Wales for Aylesbury at 1.00pm on a Saturday and returned at 5.00pm. When he arrived in the morning I told him to take the Ford and dump its exceedingly smelly cargo. He looked at me in horror. 'You don't want to do that sir, they'd sell well to London hotels for making game pie.' After a little chat I said, 'Right if you are so sure, take the girls to school in my car and I'll make a deal with you. Take the rooks up to London, if you can sell them then the estate pays your wages and the petrol. If you can't, then you lose your wages for the time you're away and pay for the petrol. If you're successful I'll give you a third of what you get for them as well. Do you still think you can sell stinking rooks to London hotels?' His answer was a very emphatic yes. When he returned I was in the office. He came in all smiles and put a wodge of notes on my desk. He'd sold the lot at half a crown each to two well-known hotels, one in Piccadilly and one in Park Lane. Both had said they would be delighted to take more in the near future if available.

As soon as harvest was finished the same party would have a week's partridge shooting, walking up stubble and root crops. Ploughing stubble wasn't achieved in days or weeks as is the practice in agriculture today. Ploughing was an ongoing process throughout the winter, firstly turning over the land for winter-sown corn then for the spring cereals, and finally well dunged for root crops. This resulted in a more natural habitat for our indigenous grey partridges and, indeed, so much of our depleted wildlife. We met around 8.30am and moved off at 9.00am and usually shot through to between 5.00 and 6.00pm, sometimes longer. They were great fun days, the bag usually being between twenty-five to thirty brace. Each gun received a brace and then the host distributed the remainder amongst friends. We also shot hares, which were particularly abundant on The Grove and Chilborough. What you shot you carried. On one occasion at Chilborough, one of our usual party, Roger Grace, a tall very strong man was walking the left flank and when we finished that particular walk he was carrying eight or nine hares hung around his neck attached to a length of cord. The does weigh roughly 7–9lbs, the bucks are a pound or two lighter, so, whatever the sex, Roger was humping around half a hundredweight of hare by the time we reached the end of that particular walk. Roger, a farmer from the other side of Aylesbury, was unique, some might well say mad but this was not so. He simply did not know the meaning of the word fear and lived life to the full. His exploits would fill a book, but two I feel should be mentioned. They were carting hay at his farm one day and Roger was building the rick, if one can call it that, in a Dutch barn in the farmyard. Several children were playing happily around when, somehow, a far from pleasant two-year-old Shorthorn bull broke out of its loose box, came round the corner of the Dutch barn, saw the children, gave one bellow and charged down the side, passing immediately below where Roger was on the hay. Without a second's hesitation he jumped, landing astride the bull. (This story is irrefutable – someone present managed to snap Roger, arms above his head, as he straddled the bull and I saw the photo.) He then apparently brought the bull to the ground, in true Western rodeo style, pulled its head back and held it until some one brought a bull pole, snapped it on to its ring and all was under control. The second feat worthy of note is that he is the only person I have ever met who could have three pints of beer lined up on a bar and with the wireless on, from the first stroke of Big Ben striking nine o'clock, down all three before the last stroke. It was, to use a modern idiom 'a nice little earner' – there were many people, who did not know better, who would bet quite large sums against him. The evening after a day's partridge shooting was much the same as when rook shooting. Hares that were not needed for one's own consumption, or for friends, were readily accepted by Smith, the leading butcher in Aylesbury, who, like all butchers in those days, did his own slaughtering. In return we were able to get a really good joint of beef for the evening's party.

One Monday morning early in February a major disruption occurred. I had just gone into my office after breakfast when Megan rang to say that a Mr Broome was on the phone and wished to speak to me. I knew 'Pirate' Broome well. He was chairman of the hunt committee and long before I went to Roundhill I had schooled horses for him out hunting. Like the Master, he was a bold, but not over brilliant horseman with not the best of hands; this invariably led to his horses starting to refuse. I had also helped him about a year before, when he'd bought a smallish farm of a little over 200 acres. He asked me if I knew anyone who might fill the post of working farm manager. I had put him in touch with Ron Chamberlain's father, George, and 'Pirate' had engaged him. However I had heard things were not going too smoothly. He was very much out of a similar mould as Dev, but with not quite the same ability, but he was still a very rich man. When Megan put him through he greeted me warmly, then said, 'I thought I ought to let you know one of your men applied to me for the job as farm manager and I have engaged him.' I was surprised but, at that stage, not overly concerned. 'I thought

George Chamberlain was doing that job for you?' 'No, he's a cantankerous old so-and-so. I've sacked him.' I couldn't help thinking, talk about the kettle calling the pot black. 'Well, who is it you've poached from here?' It was said half in fun and half in seriousness, for good farmworkers were very thin on the ground. 'His son, Ron.' I literally gasped, 'What? You must be joking. Ron's life is the herd here. He's a brilliant stockman, but he's no farmer.'

'Well that is as it may be, or as you thought, but I felt I ought to tell you he applied for the job last night and I've given it to him.' With that he hung up. I sat at my desk, almost numb with shock. I rang Megan and told her to find Chamberlain and that I wanted to see him in my office immediately. A few minutes later he knocked on the door and walked in. He looked frightful. There were no preliminaries. 'I've just had Mr Broome on the phone to tell me that yesterday evening you applied for the job your father had. He tells me he offered it to you and you've accepted. Is that right?' Ron, who normally never swore, replied, 'Oh shit. When I left I asked him to let me think about it and I'd get back to him.'

'That's not what he's saying. He claims you've definitely accepted the job. True or false?' In almost a whisper Ron replied, 'True.'

'Is that it? You're happy to throw away all you've worked to achieve here? Ron was silent and then said, 'I've taken the job, so I'll go.' He looked so miserable. 'You can always say you've changed your mind, and we can put the whole matter behind us. If you do go I'd have a sizeable bet it won't be a year before you're back with a Shorthorn herd.' Ron shook his head, repeated 'I've said yes' and walked out. I was then the one to swear, for there were herdsmen about, but those with the knowledge of the breed and the ability of Ron Chamberlain could be counted on the fingers of one hand. Tom arrived at the office and I knew at once he'd been talking to Ron, for they were good friends. Little by little I learned that Broome had filled Ron up with whisky and, crafty old devil that he was, had painted a picture of a job where he didn't have to start work until 7.00am, he'd virtually be his own boss etc etc. He had also promised a wage, or so Ron thought, which was more than he was earning at Round Hill, which turned out not to be the case. Having heard what Tom had to say, I went across to the farm to have another talk to Ron, but he was very morose and said he'd made his mind up. When he'd been engaged, the terms were he had to give two weeks' notice, not the customary week. When I told him I would hold him to this he just walked away.

What followed might have led me to think there was a guardian angel watching over me, for when I was faced with the dilemma over a building for the grass drier, I solved the problem in minutes. Similarly, such good fortune came my way over the hunt kennels and I placed the finding of a suitable head herdsman in the same crucial category. I was mulling over in my mind where I might be able to poach a stockman of the calibre of Ron, when a car drove up and I saw Archie Andrews walking towards the office. Archie was working for the War Ag, but desperately missed his Shorthorns and, whenever the opportunity offered, called at Round Hill and Manor Farm to see some of his old friends. He knocked and I called for him to come in. He took one look at me and asked, 'Whatever has happened?' I waved him to a chair and told him of my problem. Archie listened until I'd finished, then shook his head, 'Silly, silly man. He won't last a year with Broome. He'll be back with Dairy Shorthorns before a year is up.' I laughed, I think probably for the first time that morning, 'That's what I told him, but he's just being obstinate.' Purely for the record we were right. He was back with a new herd that was being built up just ten months later and produced the Female and Reserve Female Champion at the first Royal Show after the war. Archie looked thoughtful for a moment, then told me he'd heard that Dick Powley was very unhappy where he was and wanted a change. The Powleys were a well-known family in the Shorthorn world. They were six brothers whose father had for many years been head herdsman for the Duke of Westminster, in charge of his 500-head herd. Dick was the eldest son and had been second in command. One morning Dick and Henry Hamilton, who managed the farms, had had a disagreement, resulting in Dick leaving. Whether he left or Henry sacked him I never quite discovered and it is really totally irrelevant. However, had that not happened Dick would have been head herdsman for the Eaton herd, for, only a few weeks after he left, his father was kicked on the head when milking a heifer and died within forty-eight hours. Dick Powley was certainly one of the herdsmen I would count on the fingers of one hand!

I asked Archie if he was sure about this and he replied he was absolutely certain, further he had Dick's phone number and I should be able to get him at lunchtime, or after six in the evening. I opted for the former. I told Dick who it was that was calling and said I'd heard he was looking for a job. He replied that was correct, but he was looking for a post as head herdsman and, much as he liked and respected Ron Chamberlain he did not wish to play second fiddle to him. I assured him that was not my intention and that I wanted someone to take his place, Ron was leaving. To begin with Dick couldn't believe it, but when the penny had dropped I asked him if he'd be interested. The answer was a very strong affirmative. When would I like him to come for an interview? My reply was as soon as possible. Dick suggested in two days' time, saying he'd let me know what time he'd get to Stoke Mandeville station, his easiest way being up to London and then catch the train for Aylesbury. I met Dick at the station and we arrived back at the farm just after the cows had been brought in for afternoon milking. As we entered the cowshed Ron was at the far end. When he saw who was with me he burst into tears and disappeared out through the far door. Dick moved in two days after Ron moved out and the care of the herd, to the standard I required, continued without so much as a hiccup. My guardian angel had done it again.

The end of April was the moment of truth, for the first calf by AI from the Kimble Centre was born. The owner was thrilled to bits not only with the calf, but also the publicity it received. At the end of May we held an Open Day. I arranged to have about ten calves from various farms on view. Clive Haselden was there, unfortunately Dr Edwards had cancelled at the last minute, but Emerys Parry was present, strongly advocating the use of AI, as was a representative from the Reading Centre, with whom we had an arrangement whereby they supplied us with Guernsey semen and we reciprocated with Jersey. We now had three bulls, a second Shorthorn and a top-quality Jersey, Snailwell Crown Jewel, the latter a proven sire with a number of excellent daughters in-milk. He had outlived his usefulness in the herd where he came from and probably would have gone for slaughter had I not heard of him. The sperm count of his semen was amazingly high and around 79% of cows inseminated to him went in-calf the first time. Both the farming press and several of the national press were present and it was an altogether successful event.

Only a week or two later I had a phone call from Mr Walley of the War Ag: Lord Addison had been asked by the Minister of Agriculture to arrange for him to visit two of the leading farming enterprises in the county. It was something he hoped to do throughout the country. It appeared that the Roundhill estate was both Lord Addison's and Mr Walley's first choice. Would a visit be in order? I said I was sure it would be, but naturally I would have to consult the Colonel and then get back to him as quickly as possible. The Colonel was as pleased as punch and wrote to the Minister inviting him and his party to lunch. Mr Hudson replied almost by return, accepting, but on the understanding that he would not go near the AI Centre. There is no doubt in my mind that Hudson was the best Minister of Agriculture the country has had in my long lifetime. Reason? He farmed several thousand acres at Pewsey in Wiltshire and ran a dairy herd of some 350–400 Friesians. Quietly I thought the whole thing was something of a feather in my cap, but that appeared to be a personal point of view.

The day came, the weather was kind and the party arrived around 11.45am, which gave us time to take a look at the herd, young bulls and the lucerne/cocksfoot mixture. The latter seemed to impress the Minister who asked me quite a lot of questions about it. He told me they made a lot of silage for his dairy herd and the mixture seemed ideal. We were back at the house in time for sherry and an excellent lunch, which I seem to remember was roast 'Pollitt' and mint sauce, followed by strawberries from The Meads and Round Hill cream. Dev had wined us well, which was no doubt what caused me to comment as the Minister was helping himself to cream, 'Be careful sir, that's stronger than the cream you are used to, it's Shorthorn cream.' Friesians at that time were noted for the low butterfat content of their milk. The Minister laughed loudly, 'Young man have no doubt about it, my breed is the breed of the future, your love is the breed of the past.'

After lunch we visited the grass drier which the Minister found most interesting and he asked many questions before moving on. Dev led the way to the piggery and we started to walk towards the farrowing house. Suddenly, I'm not quite sure how he achieved it, the Colonel had Mr Hudson through the big door into the AI Centre. Waiting at the entrance to the lab were Ethne and Clive, both in spotless white coats. I was expecting an explosion, but before anyone could say a word Ethne, who had been with us at lunch, spoke up. 'Ah, Mr Hudson, I'm just about to do a sperm count on a collection we've taken, only minutes ago, from the Jersey bull, I think it might interest you.' With that she turned and walked into the lab. To my utter amazement the Minister followed. No storm, no rebuke, but an awful lot of interest – we must have spent nearly an hour there. There was only time for a very quick look at the pigs before the Minister had to leave. That had been on a Wednesday. The following Monday morning, at around 7.30am, a large black car, flying a small flag on the wing, drove into the piggery yard as I was about to leave. It looked remarkably like the car the Minister of Agriculture had travelled in the previous Wednesday and sure enough it was, for out got Mr Hudson. Our conversation was brief, but very much to the point. He would like Clive and I to visit his farm at Pewsey and set up an AI Centre for his own herd. He gave me three possible dates and a phone number where I could contact him direct at the Ministry. This was done and Clive visited the Centre once a month until he was sure all was well. In due course I received a personal letter from the Minister, expressing his appreciation at what had been achieved on the Roundhill estate and saying how much he'd enjoyed his day.

After some discussion with the Colonel, over a year previously, I had placed an order for a combine harvester. I hadn't really expected that we would be allocated one, but 'if you don't have a fly in the water you can't catch a fish'. The phone call I received early in July therefore came as a something of a surprise, but was greatly welcomed, for it was to tell me that there was a Massey-Harris 21 available if we still required a combine. The answer was yes and how soon could it be delivered? Happily, it arrived in time for Sudden to become well acquainted with it before harvest began. Compared to a modern harvester it was very basic, but then it was a mighty leap forward in farming technology. The cut was $7^1/_2$ feet. The corn, when cut was carried from either side on a canvas, similar to those of a reaper and binder, and then on to a central canvas which fed it into the machine. The corn and weed seed came out into sacks, exactly in the same way as it did from a threshing machine. There was a chute that carried three filled sacks at a time, which could be dropped together for collection by men with a tractor and trailer. The time and labour saved was quite unbelievable and it left me free of an evening as Tom was more than able to supervise the routine work on his own, for from early July onwards most of my evenings were otherwise occupied.

Having the hunt kennels on the estate had added an extra dimension to my workload. There was no phone at Dodds Charity and absolutely no hope of getting one. Not even the Colonel could fiddle that one despite his many contacts. That meant any carcasses that had to be collected from farms for the hounds had to be dealt with by me through either the estate office or house phone. Further, before the hunting season hounds need exercise to get them fit and lots of it. The Master had obtained a number of hounds from various packs, to add to the twelve couple or so he took over from Stanley Barratt, which were certainly past their prime, and the pack had been increased to twenty-two couple. No huntsman could exercise that number without a whipper-in. So after I'd had my tea, most evenings around 6.30–7.00pm, I'd set off with Tom Healy to take the hounds out for a minimum of two hours' road exercise. I'm not saying I didn't enjoy it, I did, for on a fine summer's evening it was very relaxing. However, it could account for the fact that at slightly over six feet and starting my day at 6.00am, eating all that was put before me and regularly downing several pints of beer every day, I had a twenty-six inch waist and my normal weight was around ten-and-a-half stone!

22. All Good Things Must Come to an End

Although Italy had surrendered to the Allies, our Italian POWs had no desire to return to their homeland, even if they could have. On hearing of the country's capitulation, Hitler ordered his forces in Italy to disarm all the country's soldiers and their immediate deportation to Germany for forced labour. Those that fled were to be hunted down and either shot, or, if captured, sent to Germany to join their comrades. It seems the King of Italy knew where to go, for when the Germans entered Rome, he wisely beat a hasty retreat to territory occupied by the Allies. The unfortunate Passero brothers learned, some weeks after the invasion of their country, that their homestead had been totally flattened and their parents both killed, together with a number of relations. Their small farm had been just about the centre point of the Salerno landing.

Phil Oliver came to see me, obviously very concerned. Could I help him? I remarked that the boot was normally on the other foot, but, yes, if I could I most certainly would. I knew Meadacre was not owned by Phil, it belonged to a Mr Payne, a great showjumping enthusiast but I never really knew who owned what as far as the horses were concerned. Phil explained that Payne had decided to give up his jumpers and was going to sell the farm and he, Phil, could not afford to buy it? Did I think the Colonel might buy it and let him stay on as tenant. I thought this was highly probable, for it joined Manor Farm on one side, The Grove on the other and only a lane separated it from Dodds Charity. The lane led to more land, not part of Meadacre, which Mr Payne owned, and which included Kimblewick Covert, one of the best fox covers in the Vale. This I felt would certainly be a major attraction as far as the Colonel was concerned. Phil said he wasn't really interested in keeping on the land that surrounded this, but would if it became a condition of remaining at Meadacre. I told him I could not give a firm answer until I had spoken to the Master, but suggested he should ask Mr Payne to do nothing further until I came back to him. The outcome was that Meadacre became part of the Roundhill estate, the latter taking over the land surrounding Kimblewick Covert.

I have found, in many years of farming, that progress can frequently produce hitherto unforeseen problems and so it was when reseeding grass fields in accordance with the doctrine of Sir George Stapledon. The grass seed mixtures he advocated were vastly more productive than the old permanent pastures which had existed for decades, in some cases probably centuries. In addition to rye grass, cocksfoot and timothy, all of which were far less vigorous than those being produced and nurtured at Aberystwyth, these old pastures contained a wide variety of herbs and grasses such as crested dog's tail, Yorkshire fog, sweet vernal, various varieties of vetch and indigenous clovers. I had ploughed one such field at Manor Farm, first taking a crop of wheat off it, having undersown it with a grass seed mixture recommended by Sir George. The result had been excellent and we took an early and heavy cut for drying, top dressed the field immediately with nitrogen and within a very short time there was some six inches of lush succulent grass. The drier was working to capacity, with more grass available than it could cope with, even working two shifts. So I decided to strip graze the field at Manor Farm with the aid of an electric fence and, after a few days, much to my delight, there was a marked increase in the milk yield of the herd. Regrettably my delight was short-lived. About ten days later I was standing in the yard, watching the cows coming in for afternoon milking, when Whinnow Duchess 2nd, a prolific milker and the dam of Diamond Wild Duke, came through the gate. As she did so she seemed to stagger, but continued until about halfway to the cowshed, when she gave a muted, choking sort of bellow and dropped to the ground – dead.

I was utterly shattered, for she was a superb high-yielding specimen of the breed. I raced back to the office, phoned Clive Haselden, who fortunately was at home and came at once. Clive, on arrival, diagnosed grass tetany, or, to give it its scientific name – hypomagnesaemia, brought about by a shortage of magnesium and calcium. Had it been spotted earlier an intravenous injection would have saved her life. Clive said he had met several cases on farms that had ploughed old pastures and re-seeded with a modern mixture. The treatment was comparatively simple to administer and so I kept several bottles available should they be required, as they were on several occasions. The effect could be quite miraculous. I remember one cow that seemed as near dead as made no difference as she lay stretched out on the ground. I got a needle into the vein, gave her the prescribed dose and within minutes she was on her feet and walking away.

By May there seemed little doubt that slowly but surely the Allies were getting on top, but the war was far from over for those who had dear ones in the forces and there were few who did not come within this category. For them the dread of seeing a uniformed telegram boy approaching their door remained a stark reality. A vast number today barely know what a telegram was, but, at the time of the war, it provided the quickest means of communication to the general public. Messages were sent by telegraph to a post office where they were written out on an official form and delivered at speed by a lad on a bike. It was through this medium that notice of the death or the missing in action of a member of the armed forces was made known to the next of kin. Nanny Hurst had married during the 1914–18 war and had a son, but like so many women of the time her marriage had been cut short. She was so proud of her son when she heard he had received his red beret, making him a full-blown member of the Paras.

On the whole the estate was now running like a well-oiled machine; inevitably there were problems, but not on a scale comparable with those of the past. The workforce was experienced, hard working and proud of the fact that the estate had been chosen for a visit by the Minister of Agriculture. I was a stickler for routine, punctuality and insisted on the rule of a place for everything and everything in its place. Quite simply if a tool was used then, when finished with, it should be returned from whence it came – if it wasn't all hell was let loose. It was probably to my advantage that, in my very early days in charge of the estate, I had gained a certain reputation through the somewhat unceremonious eviction of Mr Prouse.

It was in 1944 that the Roundhill herd became Attested, after an agonising period of bi-monthly tests when twice on what should have been the penultimate test we had one reactor. Much to my annoyance the Roundhill herd was the second one within the county to achieve this, I had hoped it would be the first. It would have been if Clive Haselden had not put back the test for two days.

On 6 June I was visiting a Colonel Ashton's farm near Thame. He had a Shorthorn herd and had applied for four non-pedigree Dairy Shorthorn cows to be examined for inclusion in section A of the Breed Society's Grading Register. In those days it was possible, in four generations, by using a registered pedigree bull, to upgrade a line so that the fourth generation was eligible for Coate's Herd Book and classified as pedigree. I had been asked by the Shorthorn Society to carry out the initial inspection. I was chatting to the owner, when his wife came running out to the yard to say we had invaded France. Col Ashton was jubilant and insisted I come into the house for a glass of champagne.

About a year previously Harry Wingfield had been offered the chance of joining a well-known horse dealer in Leicestershire, taking charge of one of his yards and, if he proved successful, there was the carrot of a possible partnership. I asn't really surprised as Harry was exceptionally good at his job and an above-average horseman. Somewhat unexpectedly it did not take long to find a replacement. An experienced studgroom, Ernest Gamble, who I knew from the Whaddon Chase country telephoned, said he had heard Wingfield was leaving and would like to apply for the job. There was no question about his ability, but his manner, whilst polite, was abrasive; however it was pretty much a case of beggars can't be choosers and so I engaged him.

Whilst the odds seemed to be almost money on that the Allies would now win the war, there were still some horrendous moments ahead. By no means least, with hindsight, was the ill-fated drop by the Paras at Arnhem, the event recreated in the classic film *A Bridge Too Far*. Like thousands of others throughout the country it was a nail-biting time for those who had friends and relations involved. Nanny Hurst was remarkably buoyant and would say that lightning never struck twice in the same place. I was leaving my office one afternoon when I saw a telegram boy turn in through the main gate. I stopped him. He said he had a telegram for a Mrs Gertrude Hurst. I took it and walked towards the house. I saw nanny looking out of the nursery window, she must have seen the boy. I took it in to her. Nanny held out her hand, 'Give it to me please, I've been expecting it all day.' I handed the wretched thing to her, 'It may not be as bad as you think.' She was still dry eyed. 'Oh yes it is. Do you think Michael, there is a God?' She paused and then continued, 'If there is, what have I done to have to suffer such pain twice in my lifetime?' Then the tears came, I went to comfort her, but she gently pushed me away and whispered, 'Leave me please with my memories – they're all I have now.' I did as she asked. It was the only time she ever used my Christian name. She was a quite remarkable woman. She had joined the Devereux family in 1931 and remained with them for sixty-three of her ninety-seven years, dying in the Round Hill farmhouse on 6 February 1995. It is often said that sorrow comes in twos, for not long after nanny's son was killed, we learned of Jack Devereux's tragic and unnecessary death. He had done well in the RAF and had returned to base from a mission and, according to his father, was in a hurry to get to a party. He jumped down from the cockpit of his twin-engined plane and, in his rush, ducked under the wing before the propellers had stopped. The Colonel was heartbroken, but he had more grief to come. Ethne, whom he idolised, announced that she was going to marry Gamble. She didn't duck the issue, she faced her father with it at a horse show and gymkhana at High Wycombe, where she was showing a young horse she had recently bought and, at the same time supervising Ann, who was continuing on her winning way and was rapidly heading towards needing a bigger size in hats. Dev went berserk and speechless with fury, leapt into his car and raced back to Round Hill. Fortunately, Ernest Gamble, knowing that Ethne was going to tell her father of their intention had very wisely made himself scarce; had he not done so I hate to think what might have happened. To everyone's surprise the marriage lasted. Many years later I met them at the Cheshire County Show and they appeared to be very happy. Ethne and her father were eventually reconciled and the couple had a son, born four years after their marriage.

Although the Allies were making progress Hitler was not yet finished and on 13 June he unleashed the first V1 rocket, the infamous and frightening doodlebugs, which landed on London. Indiscriminate as far as a target was concerned, it was a weapon simply designed to terrify and kill and it has to be admitted, whilst it lasted, it was pretty successful. When the engine cut out it might glide on several hundred yards, nosedive, or even turn back on its track. It was very scary and made bombs seem almost like old friends. By July the V1s had caused many to again be evacuated from London, but the doodlebugs did not confine their activities to the capital – they seemed to have roving commission! It was sometime early in the month, on a very hot night, that I first made their acquaintance. The heat was such that I had the door to my room open, as well as the window and was asleep on top of the bedding, when suddenly there was a very loud explosion around 3.00am and I found myself virtually blasted on to the floor. I got to my feet and ran out into the stable yard, but all seemed well there, as it did with the house. I heard the phone ringing in my office and hurried to answer it to find it was Phil Oliver – were we all right? I said as far as I could ascertain no serious damage had been done, but we'd see as soon as it was light. He commented that it had been one hell of a bang and hung up. I went across to the house and entered the hall, nanny was there, she told me the children were still asleep, but she was just checking to see everything was OK. I reassured her that, as far as I could tell, there was no serious damage and returned to my room. I did not attempt to go back to sleep for soon it would be dawn, so I shaved and dressed. As soon as the sun started to rise I had a good walk round, there were a few windows cracked, one at the back of the stables shattered, but no major damage. I was returning to the house, when I heard my phone ringing again. It was a very shaken Phil, asking if I would come to Meadacre at once. When I arrived about five minutes later, Phil was waiting in the yard. Without a word he led me round the end of the house, where there was a small paddock of about an acre and a half. In the middle was a massive great crater and, not more than twenty-five yards from it two horses were grazing. The blast had gone roughly north east and south west, had it gone due east and west there is little doubt that Phil and his family would have been killed, as would the horses. Later in the day, it took three strong men to lift what appeared to be the exhaust on to a trailer from where it had landed in a field about 300 yards from the hole. The V1 had damaged a number of windows in the piggery, but on the whole we had been extremely fortunate.

The following Sunday I went home for lunch and to spend a few quiet hours with my parents, whom I had not seen for about three months, although I only lived about twenty-five minutes drive away. I hadn't been in the house ten minutes when the air-raid siren went off. Father commented, 'More bloody doodlebugs. They've been coming over this morning like coveys of partridges.' We went ahead with lunch, mother said it would spoil if we waited for the all clear. We heard the distinctive engine sound of a V1 on several occasions during our meal, but far enough away to cause no real concern. Having helped with the washing up, I went to a room at the back of the house which had first been my brother's and my nursery, eventually becoming our den as we grew older. Mother and father departed to the drawing room, I suspect for forty winks. The den had French windows and as it was a very warm day I opened them and looked down the path that led to the end of the garden, beyond which seven of the estate workers had allotments. The nearest one was Harry Jaycock's, the estate lorry driver, whom I'd known as long as I could remember and I could see he was busy gardening. I made a mental note that I must have a quick word with him before I left to go back to Round Hill in about half an hour, but our meeting was sooner than I expected. Again I heard the rapidly approaching sound of a doodlebug, but this time it was much louder than the ones we had heard whilst having lunch and was getting louder by the second. I looked out across the allotments and I could see a V1, flying very low and heading straight for us. I rushed through to the hall, yelled to my parents, 'Doodlebug, get out, quick,' then doubled back and out through the French windows and raced down the path to the fence. Harry joined me. We stood as though mesmerised, gawping as it thundered overhead, belching flame from the exhaust; it was so close that even the rivets, in what I suppose could be termed the fuselage, were visible. It cleared the house with only feet to spare, passing between the two remaining forks of the poplar that had once looked like a massive trident and from which the centre prong had been sliced off by shrapnel earlier in the war. One, two seconds later, it might have been more, it might have been less, the engine cut out, but from then to the explosion seemed like eternity. Thankfully the doodlebug had come to rest in the middle of a field about 150 to 200 yards away, doing only minor damage. After a cup of tea, laced with a liberal shot from father's precious stock of whisky, I headed back to Round Hill. Fortunately, the RAF was eventually able to locate and destroy the point from which the V1s and even bigger V2s were being launched. Had they not the outcome of the war might well have been different.

Doodlebugs or no, preparations had gone ahead for the Royal Windsor Horse Show, which was being staged in Home Park. The Colonel decided we should support it fully, which meant that Ann would show her pony. According to the schedule there was a cup for the best child rider from the three pony classes. Even Ann's mother was beginning to come round to the general opinion that her youngest daughter was getting just a wee bit too big for her breeches, as far as her riding ability was concerned. It was time she was taken down a peg or two and realised she was not the only girl who could show a pony. I totally agreed, but was quietly inordinately proud of her achievements, for I had spent many hours trying to achieve the first thing she'd ever said to me,

'Daddy says you're going to teach me to ride.' In addition the Colonel was entering an outstanding heavyweight hunter, Gold Dust, on whom I had whipped in for a number of seasons. He was a superb jumper, but sadly he would not go for the Master who was a bit hard on his mouth. In addition we were entering Dorothy Devereux's Topper, a very showy hard-going 14.2hh cob in one of the driving classes. I cannot remember why he was known as hers, for I never saw her drive him. With Topper had come a governess car and a phaeton. The resurrection of all kinds of horse- and pony-drawn conveyances had been very much to the fore throughout the war, resulting in, I seem to remember, eight well-filled classes. These classes were to be judged by Horace Smith who owned the Hollyport Riding Academy, between Windsor and Maidenhead – one of first covered riding schools in the country. It was he who taught both Princess Elizabeth and Princess Margaret to ride. In addition he had a stable in London and his always immaculately turned out horses were to be seen daily being ridden in The Row in Hyde Park. Horace Smith was also a noted whip and the way he could handle a coach and four would have made Prince Philip green with envy.

The day of the show dawned bright and sunny and it remained so throughout the day. The entries were huge, as was the ring, so there was masses of room to really gallop on and show the horses paces to full advantage. Hunters were first in the main ring, to be judged by 'Tiddley' Lucas, a brilliant horseman whose knowledge of horseflesh was second to none. I was first to enter the ring on Gold Dust. As I walked the parameter, waiting for the order to trot on, I came level with a small marquee surrounded by an enclosure. In front of the marquee were a number of deckchairs, some already occupied. I glanced down to see Their Majesties King George and Queen Elizabeth smiling up at me. I had no time to doff my bowler, I could only bow and ride on, but I did have time to notice that both the Princesses and Princess Alexandria were with them. In due course I left the ring with the champion hunter rosette attached to Gold Dust's bridle and bearing a silver cup.

After handing Gold Dust over to a groom I crossed quickly to the collecting ring where Ann was waiting with the rest of the 12.2hh ponies, who were next in the ring. I didn't have time to count them, it was a bit like being in the middle of an army of ants! Ann was all smiles and confidence. I didn't try to give her any advice, except to tell her to take care when galloping on, something her pony excelled at. I added that I had been told the top four ponies out of each class would return to the ring when the judging of the ponies was completed, to compete for the cup for the best child rider. I saw that Pat Moss and Princess Alexandria were amongst those in the class. I just had time to see Ann pulled in first and receive her cup (so much for taking her down a peg or two!), with a rather disconsolate Pat Moss second. I hadn't time to congratulate her for nanny came rushing up to say Topper's class was about to go into the driving ring, resulting in my having to sprint back to the horse boxes. Topper, lived up to his name and of course the general quality of the turn-out was also taken into account. It was with considerable joy and pride that I shook hands with the great Horace Smith as he handed me the red rosette. What a day!

I was back at the main ring just as the ribbons were being handed out in the 14.2hh class. I learned from the collecting ring steward that the judge had said she only wanted the three first prize winners to come in for the riding cup. That was good. By then I'd forgotten we'd brought Ann to Windsor chiefly because, as her mother had put it, she was getting too big for her breeches. Ann was waiting to go into the main ring again. I went across to her and gave her a hug, congratulated her and told her about Topper. Then I explained that the largest pony, the 14.2hh winner would lead, then the 13.2hh and finally she would be 'tail-end Charlie' as, in theory, she would be the slowest. I went on to say, 'When you're told to gallop on, go for it, but for goodness sake take care on the corners.' Ten minutes later the judge called out 'gallop on' just as they were turning into the straight down past the royal enclosure. Ann did just that, passing the other two before they were told to pull up. She was able to do that in seconds, before either of the others could. The judge did not hesitate and called my protégée, at least she was partially mine, into the centre. Another rosette and a vast cup. Proceedings were then halted for a short lunch break, during which there was a parade of the Garth Foxhounds, which met with great acclaim. I joined the Colonel and Mrs Devereux at their car. Dev had already popped a champagne cork. He turned to me and said, 'What a day, Michael, what a day. How I wish Ethne, Jack and Dean were here.' I agreed, then laughed, 'True, but it's not over yet. There's still the driving championship to come.'

'Oh that's a foregone conclusion, has to be. The Princesses have both won a class. I don't think even Horace Smith would dare to put either of them down.' I said nothing, time would tell. Three quarters of an hour later the winners entered the main ring, in class order, headed by Princess Elizabeth. We were told to trot on. Topper was going beautifully and he comfortably passed most of the turnouts except Princess Elizabeth's. I noticed that the judge kept turning to look at Topper. At last we were signalled to walk and, on the judge's instructions, the steward called Her Royal Highness into first place and, greatly to my delight, I was called in next – Reserve Champion. Princess Margaret was next to come into line. To use a modern phrase, she was not a happy bunny. Mr Smith handed the Champion rosette to Princess Elizabeth, came round to my right and handed the Reserve Champion one to me. He then turned to Princess Margaret and, to my amazement, said, 'You can take that look off your face young lady, you're in the right place.' Who said Horace Smith wouldn't dare put either of the young Princesses down? As I was congratulating Her Royal Highness the steward came up and asked that we do a lap of honour. The Princess laughed happily, then turned to me and said, 'Don't you dare pass me.' It was my turn to laugh, 'I wouldn't dream of doing such a thing ma'am. I don't want to spend the night in one of the castle's dungeons.' Laughing merrily she set off around the ring at a cracking pace, the applause was terrific and, having done one circuit, as we came to the exit into the collecting ring I pulled out, leaving a worthy winner to do a second lap. It had been a truly wonderful family day – a brotherhood of the highest to the humblest totally relaxed in the enjoyment of a common interest that so many would now destroy.

The war in Europe was slowly but very surely heading towards victory for the Allies. However, during the latter part of 1944, when lives were still being lost on all fronts, there was a feeling of great animosity towards the wave of strikes in both the coal mines and vital engineering businesses which caused three times the number of days lost in 1944 as 1939. As old Joe Swaine so ably put it, 'Don't know why us wasted sweat feeding bouggers like t'em. Reckon a spell up in front line 'ould edicate th' bastards.'

Food was still in desperately short supply and would remain so for a number of years to come and so there was no let-up on the farming front. I became chairman of the Princes Risborough branch of the National Farmers Union, at the age of twenty-five and the youngest in the country, resulting in my becoming a member of the County Executive Committee. I was a keen supporter of the NFU and felt it should have a much greater say in the national agriculture policy.

The estate continued to run smoothly and all seemed to be going well until early 1947, when there was a hell of a bust-up on the board of High Duty Alloys. Dev resigned as chairman and according to him, took over £4 million out of the business in order to set up his own major operation. Very much involved in this were the Jakobis, particularly Leo, eldest of the three brothers. His farming efforts had not been going well and somehow he had become involved with a farmer on the Hereford/Wales border whom he employed as a consultant. It seems Leo 'sold' the idea of using this man to the Colonel, who put it to me. In view of what I had achieved I was not very receptive to the idea, to a degree that I and Emerys Parry, who knew where the man's farm was and quite a lot about him, motored across to Herefordshire together with Archie Andrews to take a look at it. We knew he was to be at the Jakobis the day we went, so we took a good look. We were not impressed. An impasse developed over this between the Colonel and I, which came to a head in June 1947. I was given an ultimatum, one evening in my office, by the Colonel. I would either fully cooperate with this man or

I could get out. I remember I smiled and started to say, 'In that case I'll get ...' I never finished the sentence, for the Colonel barked, 'You're fired.' I held his gaze, 'Not quite, I was quitting when you interrupted me. When would you like me to finish?' He looked at me for several seconds, then said, 'You mean it?' I nodded and he said, 'Right, the end of July. Let's go and have a drink.' I wasn't worried over a job, I had had two offers within the last month. One was to join Horlicks and organise and run the new AI Centre they wished to open. The other was from the newly appointed general manager of the Meat Marketing Board, who had been agent for an estate in Berkshire and against whom we had competed many times at Reading. Neither appealed. The following weekend Dick Powley was going up to spend a couple of days with his brother at the Duke of Westminster's farms in Cheshire – the news was already out that I was leaving. Towards the end of the next week I received a letter from Henry Hamilton, who managed the Duke's farms, which started off, 'I hear there are to be big changes at Roundhill ...' I read no further, but thought, oh yes, he wants Dick to go to Southern Ireland to look after a section of the Duke's famous Dairy Shorthorn herd, which I knew he intended moving over there. I was extremely busy and put Henry's letter in my desk and did not read it for several days. When I did I found it was not about Dick, but wanting to know if I would be interested in going to Ireland to manage the farm the Duke had bought in Co Kildare, a mere 167 acres. My reply was thanks for thinking of me, but having been responsible for some 1500 acres, the grass drier, the AI Centre, an ever-increasing stable of hunters plus the hunt kennels, I felt that such a move would be a somewhat retrograde step. However, if his Grace wanted an agent-cum-farm manager to run his other farming interests in Ireland, plus his stud farm, then I might be interested. I left Roundhill at the end of July with no real regrets, for having built something up out of chaos I had no desire to see history repeat itself. I did, however, regret leaving the staff and, even more so, Ann, Marguerite and Nanny who had to all intents and purposes become part of my family.

After a week at home I departed to Mousehole in

Cornwall, to stay with my good friend Jack Wallace and his wife. I had helped Jack, an experienced and most able longshore fisherman to buy a thirty-five foot, twin-engined boat, his having been sunk whilst he was away in the navy during the war. For the first two weeks I hired the boat to go out fishing, or whatever I wished. I just wanted to relax and completely unwind, for I had not had a holiday, of any kind, for over seven-and-a-half years. At the end of the two weeks I stayed on as unpaid crew and if we hadn't a party to go fishing, then we were longlining or working a small trawl. The weather was fantastic, life was bliss. I had asked father to open any post that might look important. One Friday evening we came in from sea around 6.30pm and there was a telegram for me. A letter had arrived from the Duke of Westminster's chief agent, requesting I meet him at the Duke's London house at 12.30pm the next day, to discuss my going to Ireland as the Duke's land agent. As I looked out at the peace of Mount's Bay I reluctantly accepted that all good things have to come to an end.

About Farming Books and Videos Ltd

Farming Books and Videos Ltd is a small family run business
that offers a wide range of publications for the farmer,
smallholder and country dweller.

For further information or to request an up to date
catalogue please write to:-

Farming Books and Videos
Po Box 536
Preston
PR2 9ZY
Tel 01772 652693
info@farmingbooksandvideos.com

www.farmingbooksandvideos.com

By the Same author

The Spacious Days
ISBN 0-9542555-8-5

This account of growing up on an estate at Burnham in Buckinghamshire in the 1920s and '30s recalls an agriculture in which there was a large labour force, time to do a job well and time to talk, chaff and enjoy country sports. This, Michael Twist's first book, is a tale about real people and real places providing an insight into days long gone when a caring relationship and natural balance still existed between man and nature.

Hallowed Acres
ISBN 1-904871-00-3

In tandem with The Spacious Days, this second volume of Michael Twist's reminiscences is full of humour in its depiction of the characters on the estate and the experiences of a young lad growing into manhood. It tells of the wildlife that abounded throughout the country, of his friendship with a family of true Romany gypsies, of country pastimes and of agricultural shows and competitions.

Ireland—The Ducal Days
ISBN 1-904871-02-X

In 1947 Michael Twist moved to Southern Ireland as Land Agent to the 2nd Duke of Westminster, confident in his ability to deal with any eventuality—but then he hadn't met the Duke!

In addition to building up the Duke's fine herd of Dairy Shorthorns the author must dig deep into his diplomatic reserves when he is caught in the crossfire between two dukes and a lord in a dispute over a Chippendale mirror, smuggling whisky on His Grace's behalf and instructed to buy a bank.

Michael became one of the senior members of the Duke's staff involved in 'Operation Death Duties', instigated by the chief agent, George Ridley, to protect the Grosvenor fortune from heavy death duties. This led to a whirlwind redistribution and investment of capital - proving so successful that by 1953 one of the richest men in Britain was literally 'too rich to tax'.

This fourth volume of Michael Twist's fascinating autobiography draws us, with humour and disarming honesty, into the near feudal, post-war world of estate management.

You've Done What, My Lord?
By R Clark
ISBN 0-9542555-1-8

When James Aden applies for the position of Deputy Agent at Rumshott, one of the finest landed estates in England, he little realises what he has let himself in for. Negotiating with royalty, tenant farmers, lost parrots, escaping sheep and the imperious Lady Leghorn all appear to be part of the job description. This is a highly acclaimed first novel by former land agent based on his real experiences working for some of the largest estates in Britain.

An English Country Manner
By R Clark
ISBN 0-9542555-0-X

When tragic circumstances force James Aden to leave Scotland he eventually finds a new job as the agent on Sir Charles Buckley's vast Suffolk estate. Once again he has to deal with an unusual list of problems. Rogue chimney pots, unsavoury tenants and delinquent sheep are just some of his responsibilities. Much awaited sequel to Rory Clark's popular novel, 'You've Done What, My Lord?'

All in a Day's Work
By Patricia Warren
ISBN 0-9542555-9-3

Borrowing £50 from the farm accounts farmer's wife Patricia Warren set up the very first lonely hearts introduction agency for farmers. Her aim was to introduce couples with the hope that their friendships would develop into long term relationships or marriage.

Some twenty years and countless couples later Patricia has written a book charting the rise of the Farmers and Country Bureau and some of the characters and stories she has encountered along the way in a highly entertaining book.